EVERYDAY EVALUATION ON THE RUN

2ND EDITION

Yoland Wadsworth

ALLEN & UNWIN

DEDICATION

This book is dedicated to

the Minister for Community Services
the Honourable Kaye Setches;

the former Minister for Education, and later Premier of Victoria
the Honourable Joan Kirner;

the Minister for Health,
the Honourable Caroline Hogg;

and

the late Pauline Toner
former Honourable Minister for Community Services;

for supporting this cross-portfolio work,
and for believing in the importance
of giving a voice to those
for whom social justice
has not yet been achieved.

First edition published in 1991 by the Action Research Issues Association (Incorporated)
Reprinted 1993

Second edition published in 1997 by
Allen & Unwin
9 Atchison Street
St Leonards NSW 2065
Australia
Phone: (61 2) 9901 4088
Fax: (61 2) 9906 2218
E-mail: frontdesk@allen-unwin.com.au
URL: http://www.allen-unwin.com.au

National Library of Australia
Cataloguing-in-Publication entry:

Wadsworth, Yoland.
Everyday evaluation on the run.

2nd ed.
ISBN 1 86448 416 0.

1. Evaluation. 2. Evaluation research (Social action programs). I. Title.

001.4

Set in 10/12 pt Garamond by DOCUPRO, Sydney
Cartoonist: Simon Kneebone (08) 8370 9152
Computer artwork: David Alderson
Cover design: Toni Hope-Caten
Printed by Alken Press, Sydney

10 9 8 7 6 5 4 3 2 1

FOREWORD

FOREWORD TO THE FIRST EDITION

'Evaluation' has become something of a popular incantation, regularly invoked to ensure that the bad spirits of inefficiency, ineffectiveness, and inappropriateness do not characterise our human service efforts!

Yet, like 'research' and 'science', it has become a technical speciality with its own language and high priests. This often makes it difficult for those who use or provide the services to feel confident evaluating their own services. We want this guide not only to make evaluation understandable, but also to give readers a sense of the satisfaction that can come from this kind of activity. There can be a real feeling of achievement and purpose from a self-directed learning effort that leads to services which are more spot-on and responsive to users.

Evaluation continues to be used as a reporting and accountability strategy by funders and other authorities. Yet their purposes of providing value for money are not served well if the evaluation does not 'get at' either the qualitative nature of people's experience, or if it counts the wrong things, does so at the wrong times, or if it is done for the wrong reasons. This book attempts to outline ways of evaluating that provide meaningful and useful accounts of situations.

As with *Do It Yourself Social Research* (Wadsworth, 2nd edn, Allen & Unwin, 1997), to which this book is a sequel, the assumption is that readers are best served, not so much by a 'cookbook', but rather by describing some of the underlying concepts and principles. Given an understanding of 'why', we have found that people are able to apply the 'how' in flexible ways to their own varied situations.

We would like to thank all those who have contributed to the various reference groups in which the ideas in this book were developed, debated and tested. We look forward to your feedback for our own further evaluation!!

We would like to thank Yoland Wadsworth for her inspiration, rigour and untiring efforts to articulate new and better ways of grasping the business of evaluation and research. We know she considers this book to represent 'work in progress'. However we are aware that its ideas represent new ways of thinking about and dealing with problems that have already been seized on enthusiastically by those in the field. We hope these ideas will be widely discussed over the coming years.

Finally, the vision and funding provided by the Victorian State Government Social Justice Strategy has allowed this project to be undertaken. The abiding 'achievement indicator' for the long-term evaluation of the project's success will be whether people find (or are assisted to find) a 'voice' with which they can speak more clearly and loudly about the conditions that are problematic to them, and about the human services which are intended to meet their needs. Under conditions of financial stringency it is all the more critical that we have evaluation approaches which enable us to focus clearly on the ultimate purpose of all our effort.

Sue Kenny
Action Research Issues Association (Incorporated)

1ST
PREFACE

PREFACE TO THE FIRST EDITION

While 'research' and 'evaluation' are commonly thought to be separate activities, this book describes evaluation as a process of assessing the value of things around us, or things we do, using the same logic and sequence of steps as does the kind of research process described in *Do It Yourself Social Research* (2nd edn, Allen & Unwin, 1997).

What this book does as a sequel to *Do It Yourself Social Research* is to examine in far greater detail the *evaluative* elements of research which become uppermost in our minds when we call our research 'evaluation'. Matters dealt with more fully in the previous book—such as descriptions of techniques, questionnaires and interviews, other resources available, and so on—are touched on only lightly here.

To focus separately on research and evaluation is to focus on different elements of an integrated process. If the previous book looked through the windows of a house, then this book provides some ideas for looking up the front path, in the front and back doors, and down the chimney!

It has been interesting to find that the subject of evaluation has seemed even harder to tackle than that of research in general. It seems that as soon as we move closer to talking explicitly about 'values', there is both more at stake and less that is certain. Many people feel uncomfortable about the loss of certainty and apparent objectivity. In an attempt to reduce this discomfort, there has been a tendency to reach immediately for formal written statements of objectives and specific targets against which activities or practices can then be measured. However, this does not necessarily provide us with the fullest way of evaluating, for reasons that are made clearer in the book. Some of this is difficult terrain; however, while this book is more dense than its precursor, it carries three simple overall messages:

- Evaluation is a more or less easily accomplished facet of our daily life. Grasping how we do this equips us with exactly the conceptual framework for larger and more conscious efforts.
- The more we engage in regular, simple, small-scale, theory-building evaluations, the more we will stay 'on track' and the less we will need to resort to large formal and sometimes crisis-provoked theory-testing evaluations.
- The key to keeping all parties to an evaluation focused on the relevant criteria for judging value (merit, worth or significance) lies in increasing our capacity to hear and voice consumer (or other end-beneficiary) issues and concerns.

YW
December 1990
Melbourne

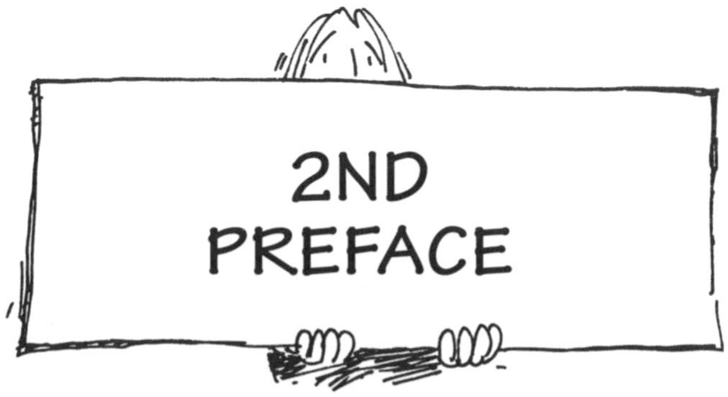
2ND
PREFACE

PREFACE TO THE SECOND EDITION

There continues to be a gap—even a chasm—between the elaborate and sophisticated activities of evaluation professionals and the small-scale but essential everyday evaluative activity of all those others engaged in human activities, efforts and services.

Yet the need to build on the capacity for thoughtful, reflective, evaluative practice of the latter group, and to decrease their loss of confidence in their abilities to do this, has never been more urgent.

When professional evaluators share 'war stories' of the wastage of their efforts, what I suspect is really at issue is the dearth of built-in ways for people throughout the social systems that have engaged their services to stop and think about what they are doing, to inquire into the effects, to discuss this among themselves, and then narrow the distance between the desired and the actual. I hope this book makes a modest contribution towards building a broader culture of evaluation throughout human systems.

Yoland Wadsworth
February 1997
Melbourne

THANK YOU TO . . .

ACKNOWLEDGEMENTS

Many people contributed to this project over its initial eighteen months of gestation, either directly or by participating in a more general evaluation culture. Special thanks go to:

- The Social Justice Partnership Project Steering Committee members, for their support and for their intellectual contribution
- Lynton Brown, Nominee of the Minister of Education
- Sue Kenny, Action Research Issues Association
- Des Lavery, Nominee of the Minister for Community Services
- Helen Lee, Brunswick resident—co-opted member
- David Legge, Nominee of the Minister of Health, and Manager of the Partnership Project, Health Department Victoria—until January 1990
- Onella Stagoll, Deputee of the Manager of the Partnership Project, Health Department Victoria, February–March 1990
- George Preston, Deputee of the Manager of the Partnership Project, Health Department Victoria—from April 1990
- Veronica Spillane, Social Justice Strategy Unit, Department of Premier and Cabinet—until December 1989
- Ros Johnson, as above—from January 1990–April 1990
- Mary Baker, as above—from May 1990
- Gai Wilson, seconded project worker from Melbourne District Health Council until September 1990
- Jane Wexler, Project worker from October 1990
- Ros Wood, Nominee of the Collective of Self-Help Groups

The Readers Sounding Board, including Ann Barry (Low Income People's Network), Jacques Boulet (Phillip Institute), Bob Connell (Macquarie University), Joan Chan (Broadmeadows Community Health Centre), Linette Hawkins (ARIA), Stephen Kemmis (Deakin University), Fiona McDermott (University of Melbourne), Rick Mohr (evaluation consultant, Sydney), Barbara Potter (Alzheimer Society), Stuart Rees (Sydney University), Gavan Thomson (Friends Of The Earth), Jenny Trethewey (Brotherhood of St Laurence), the late Robyn Walker (Springvale Community Health Centre) and members of the Steering Committee.

Those associated with the Alzheimer Society 'Carers as Researchers' and 'Professional Carers' Seminars' evaluation project—Barbara Potter, Margaret McLaren, and the carers who met at Kerang; those associated with the Royal Women's Hospital midwifery consumer study, including Margaret Mabbit, Lynne Maggs; those associated with the Community Development in Health/District Health Councils 'Deep Thought' project, and later, the Researchers in Community Health (RICH) Network including Fiona Gardner, Janice Jessen, Catriona Knothe, Demos Krouskos, Erica Moulang, Marjorie Oke, Gavan Thomson and the late Robyn Walker; Joan Byrne of the Women's Arthritic Task Force; the 1989 3rd year PIT Social Work research course students; those associated with the North Richmond Community Health Centre and its 'Positive Visions' project, including Colleen Pearce, Ian Sharpe, Julie Shiels and Annie Sprague; Kate Sommerville and those who attended the Richmond Fellowship Service Agreement Workshop; those who took part in the Consumers' Health Forum Grants Program Group Self-Evaluation; Gaylene Kyrgiou, Mary Furman and Lou Iaquinto of the Colanda deinstitutionalisation research project; Susanne Baxandall and Pat Dodson from the self-help/support groups evaluation project, Anti-Cancer Council of Victoria; Lyndal Grimshaw, Di Otto, Joan Roberts, Maggie McGuiness and Terry Melbourne, involved in two projects of the Victorian Mental Illness Awareness Council designed to introduce the direct participation of psychiatric service-users in evaluating, influencing and making decisions about these services.

Members of the Melbourne Evaluation and Research Group etc. (MERGe), especially those participating in the discussions on standards manuals, service agreements, performance indicators, and internal and external evaluations, also in particular Inez Dussuyer, Jerry Winston, Mary Crooks, and Marie Brennan; Lucinda Aberdeen, David Green, Meg Montague, and Wendy Weeks of the Action Research Issues Association; members of tenant groups at Ross House, in particular Robyn Tumelty (VICRAID), Lesley Holton (Caravan Parks) and Lyn Romeo (formerly of Shelter Intellectual Disability Linkages project); those involved in the development of the Notes on Running An Introductory Workshop on Evaluation, in particular Rhona Miller and the ten trial workshops' participants.

Simon Kneebone, cartoonist, for his wonderful illustrations.

For permission to use other material and illustrations: Marcia Plummer; Ian Sharpe; Michael Quinn Patton and Sage Publications and the Public Health Association of Australia (for themes of qualitative inquiry); Denise Fry and the Australian Community Health Association (for CHASP example); Combined Pensioners Association of NSW Inc. (for *Consumers' Fair Go! Kit* Feedback sheet and cartoon); Robin McTaggart (17 characteristics of action research); Margaret McLaren and the Alzheimer Society of Victoria (seminar evaluation form); Hugh Guthrie, TAFE National Centre for R&D (cartoon from *Making Changes*); Victorian Association of Citizens Advice Bureaus (self-evaluation kit cartoon); Patricia Morrigan (Neuro Linguistic Programming definition); Southern Community Health Services Research Unit, South Australia cartoon; Ministry of Education (*Group Self-Evaluation Reader* and *Destination: Decisions* illustrations); Stephen Kemmis (Barry McDonald commentary); Egon Guba ('forms of inquiry' table); Consumers Health Forum (program evaluation material); Susanne Baxandall and Pat Dodson, Anti-Cancer Council of Victoria (self-help groups' evaluation); Victorian Council of Social Service (cartoon from cover of *Do It Yourself Social Research*, 2nd edn, 1997). The *Tumbleweeds* cartoon by Tom Ryan is reproduced with the kind permission of King Features Syndicate, USA.

GUIDE TO CONTENTS

WARNING!!

THIS BOOK CONTAINS SOME UNFAMILIAR AND THEORETICAL IDEAS THAT MAY SOMETIMES SEEM LIKE HARD WORK. PERSEVERANCE WILL BE REWARDED! PLEASE READ THIS PAGE.

CHAPTER ONE: INTRODUCTION

This chapter explains why built-in 'naturalistic' everyday evaluation is so valuable and introduces the familiarity of its process. It sketches the ideas contained throughout the rest of the book by the example of an evaluation of a humble coffee mug.

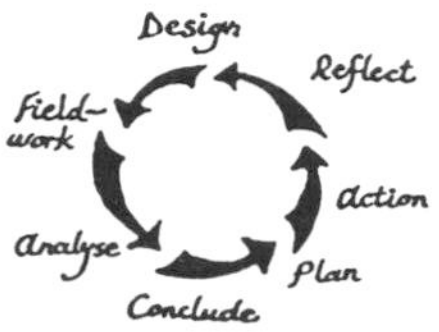
Design
Reflect
action
Plan
Conclude
analyse
Field-work

CHAPTER TWO: A CONCEPTUAL FRAMEWORK

This chapter tracks around one cycle of the evaluation research process—from reflection, to design, to fieldwork, to conclusions and assessing of future options for new practices, and finally to their enactment. It includes a lengthy discussion of the matter of who the evaluation is for, and also a discussion of the pros and cons of 'insider' and 'outsider' evaluation.

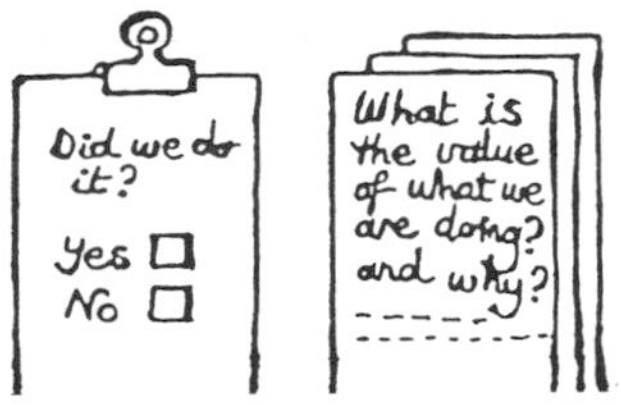
Did we do it?
Yes
No
What is the value of what we are doing? and why?

CHAPTER THREE: TWO APPROACHES TO EVALUATION

This chapter commences by asking whether we need to do more evaluating or whether we already know enough to report to those who might have a need to know. When we need new evaluation, two different approaches to evaluation are then contrasted: an 'open inquiry' approach that asks 'Is it working?' and 'Why?', and an audit review approach that asks 'Did we do what we set out to do?'. This is fairly heavy going, but attempts to dispel the myth that evaluation can only start from formal written objectives. Evaluation should also proceed from tapping our large mental store of intuitively held experiences, intentions and purposes.

CHAPTER FOUR: DOING EVALUATION

Phew! Now with all that theory behind us it is hoped that we can see how to actually build in evaluation as part of our everyday lives. This chapter proposes the idea of a 'culture of evaluation', ranging from the most micro and short-term to the more macro and long-term—reflecting the different levels of our activities and purposes, from overarching philosophy right down to whether we should, for example, change the phone answering machine message this morning!

TOOL BOX
PTY LTD

CHAPTER FIVE: THE EVALUATION INDUSTRY'S TOOLBOX

Do not sit down and read this chapter from start to finish! Instead we suggest skimming its index and picking and choosing. The Further Useful Reading at the end is also for the enthusiast. Everyday evaluators can almost certainly get by without knowing all this (however bits of it might be very useful!).

WHAT'S IN
THIS BOOK

CONTENTS

LIST OF GUIDES AND DIAGRAMS

GUIDES

DIAGRAMS

PREAMBLE

WHO AND WHAT THIS BOOK IS FOR

THE VALUE OF DOING EVERYDAY EVALUATION—AND WHY WE DON'T DO IT

You're already flat out just getting through the day. And then—on top of it all—an evaluation?!! Perhaps you *want* to do it, but it keeps getting put off. Or maybe *They* want it, and now at last it *has* to be done. Maybe committee and staff meetings always seem too full of other items. Maybe it's been delegated to the one more or less enthusiastic 'volunteer'. Maybe that 'volunteer' is you! Or maybe last time it got cobbled together rather unsatisfactorily, or got farmed out to an external consultant who came and went and left behind a report that didn't seem to

... WHAT DOES THE EVALUATION REPORT SAY?
... WE'D BE TOO BUSY TO USE IT...

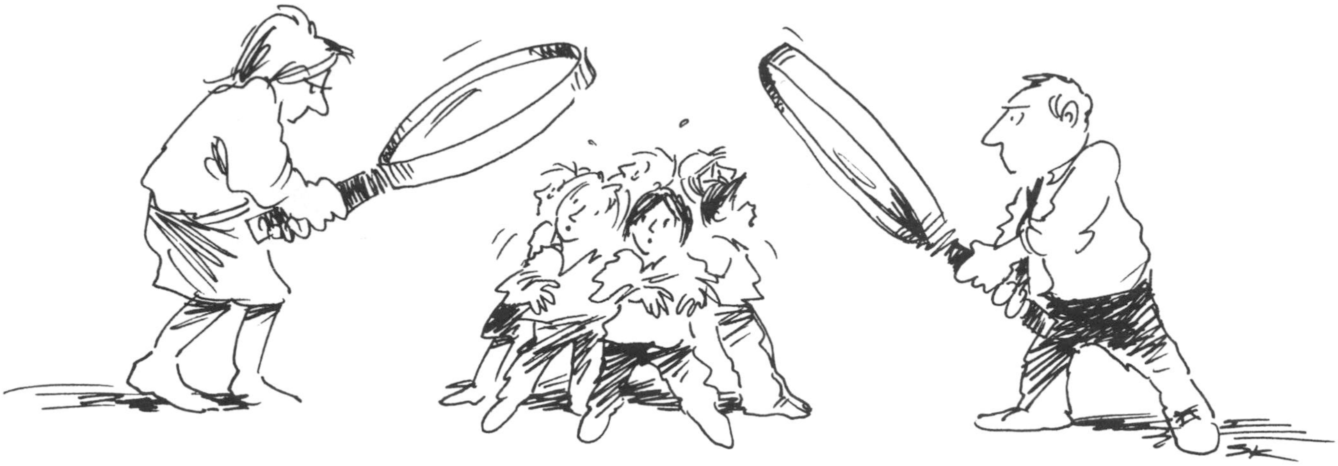

change things much, or changed things in ways you didn't specially like!

These kinds of experiences suggest to us that one of the most pressing needs is for evaluation to be practised as an *ordinary everyday part* of what we do—rather than saved up till later when things have settled down, or when there is more to show for what we've done, or when we can afford the time, or when it seems easier. But when do things ever settle down?! When is it ever easier? When is there ever time? And meanwhile, can we risk going on not getting it right?

There is a lot of talk about needing to build in evaluation but we still seem stumped as to how to go about this, apart, perhaps, from having a computerised statistical database or an annual 'evaluation day'. Yet it is also obvious that people *must* be able to do their own ongoing evaluation. The idea of bringing in an external evaluator to every one of thousands upon thousands of human services presents a financial nightmare when we think about the sheer volume of such services.

Not only is it impractical and costly for people not to do their own evaluation, but it is also wasteful of insiders' vast store of practical wisdom and experience on which we all act daily anyway. In a later discussion about the pros and cons of internal and external evaluation it will be seen that the insider's evaluation stands a better chance of being more practically fruitful. The outsider can however, among other things, contribute a perspective that can assist insiders to be more self-critical or see things in a fresh and different way. But, rather than insiders being assistants to outsiders, it would seem to be less costly and more effective for outsiders to be the occasional assistants to insiders.

In moving towards a situation where every user and provider of a service can confidently self-evaluate, there are a number of hurdles to be leaped—not least of which are the ideas that evaluation is difficult, uncomfortable, time-consuming, and requires specialist expertise. It is hoped that Chapter 1 of this book will show that evaluation *is* easy and *very* do-able (actually we do it all the time without even being asked!) and should more often be experienced as a great relief. The view of evaluation as a hard, disempowering and unwelcome torment relates to an important set of very ingrained assumptions that lead us to think evaluation has to be done in a particularly unnatural way.

First of all evaluation is commonly experienced as something done 'to', 'at' or 'on' us. This is often justified by saying we are too biased and value-laden to do it ourselves (and expert specialist Others somehow aren't). When we have it *done to, at,* or *on* us, it can make us feel very powerless. This can also be very threatening—especially if we are trying to do things we are not sure everyone likes (whether fellow group members, managers or service-users), or if we would like to have something exposed that Some Other People don't want exposed. There is no point in anyone just insisting that evaluation won't hurt us. The way round this is for evaluation to be self-directed for our own learning—for all of us involved (service-users, providers, administrators, funders, etc.).

WHOSE VALUES?

Ultimately it is for *us* to examine our own practices and act to improve them. Then we will have trust and confidence in and feel empowered by the process. This goes for both service providers and service users. However, while service providers must be able to do their own evaluation, they are not, in the final analysis, doing it directly for themselves. The crucial point of logic relating to all the possible stakeholders or audiences for evaluation is that, in the final analysis, evaluation is for those whose unmet needs provide the benchmark and driving values for checking whether a service, campaign or activity works. Thus we must effectively point evaluation in the direction of always seeking to identify 'who' or 'what' it is all for.

This also indicates to us who must be most importantly involved *in* evaluation. Conventionally, in relation to human services funded by Western governments, the direction of evaluation might be illustrated as a pyramid whereby the Westminster

MINISTER
BUREAUCRATS
SERVICE PROVIDERS
CONSUMERS

system of government ensures that the Minister, elected by those who the government services are all for, directs from above what will be done for citizens.

However, this may be better conceptualised as the users, or those who have the needs to be met, being surrounded by various networks of supporting arrangements, some close and providing daily support, and others, including those of the government-funded services, generally at more of a distance.

In evaluation it is critical to retain this perspective throughout as it is the decisions about the user's or consumer's needs—expressed as values—that provide the ultimate benchmarks for all evaluative judgements about whether a service or other effort is working or not. Even when we are part of the pyramidal bureaucracy or professional service provision, and have our own needs and values, or views about what users and consumers' needs and values are or should be, clarity of purpose and effort lie in keeping the direction of one's gaze firmly on the ultimate purpose of all our effort. This book is designed essentially for anyone who wants to evaluate an activity or human service from the perspective of who it is *for*, that is, the user, consumer, participant, resident, client, patient, taxpayer, claimant, customer, citizen, self-help group, community, etc. There are complexities involved in identifying these groups, but the effort must continuously be undertaken. In Chapter 2 there is a full discussion of this matter and an exploration of how best to assist the consumers or users (or critical reference groups)—as well as all other parties to evaluation—to raise their questions, explore them, reach conclusions and then go on to improve their activities or services.

Administrators and managers who are remote from the ground have a huge stake in this kind of evaluation being done, as their ultimate reason for being stems from and back to those same critical reference groups.

BUT HOW ON EARTH CAN WE MAKE TIME FOR IT?

Even if we see ourselves as able to do our own evaluation, why do we never seem to have time to devote to it? Why is it that thinking about what we do and why we do it so easily gets swamped by the doing itself? Why do we quickly pick up the ringing phone, feel compelled to open the mail, meet that deadline, feel driven to take on that extra task, squeeze in another appointment or meeting or just find ourselves doing the same-as-usual, even though we might have growing feelings of unease? Why do we prioritise these other things—but *not* prioritise reflecting on whether they are worth doing? Why do we go on doing all sorts of things when we may not have thought consciously about their value? Perhaps because it feels easier to do what we've always done. Perhaps because it seems to work well enough. Perhaps stopping to think doesn't feel legitimate. Perhaps it doesn't seem that doing so will make enough of a difference anyway. Perhaps we feel uncomfortable at the thought of checking what we are doing with our end-user populations.

For most of us, everyday evaluation won't be

FEDERAL, STATE AND LOCAL POLITICIANS
SELF-HELP GROUPS
FRIENDS
HOUSEHOLDS
BUREAUCRATS AND PROGRAMS
LABOR ORGANISATIONS
CRITICAL REFERENCE GROUP
SERVICE PROVIDERS
WORKMATES
NEIGHBOURS

done regularly 'on the run' unless we are able to change the initial value we place on spending all our time *doing* rather than setting aside time for *thinking* about the value of what we are doing. To successfully blend evaluation into our everyday lives requires us to deliberately set aside time—a minute at the start of that activity or end of that discussion, a few moments at the end of each meeting, an hour a week, a day during a month's campaign, or a week each year to reflect on the value of what we are doing or planning to do. This time needs to be collectively agreed upon as valuable, labelled legitimate and treated as precious. Only in this way will we gradually get the evidence we need that will guide and strengthen our practice and reduce any fears and anxieties about what we are doing.

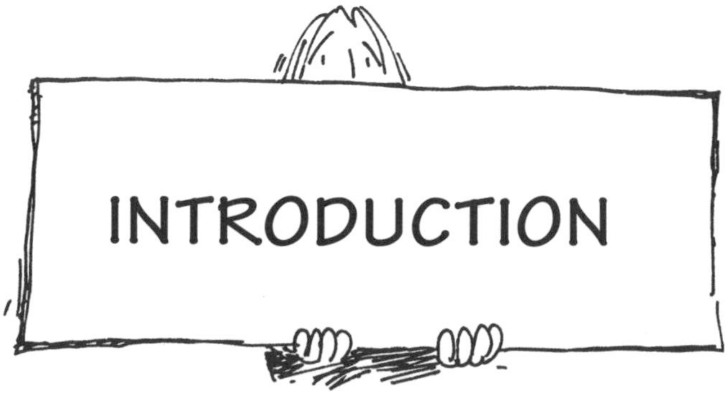
INTRODUCTION

chapter 1

WHAT IS EVALUATION?

A FAMILIAR EVERYDAY PROCESS

When did you last conduct an evaluation? Last year? Never? This is evaluation with a capital 'E'. However, in practice we are evaluating all of the time.

Consider last night's community committee of management meeting:

Leanda: *'I quite like going to our Centre committee meetings—I get to feel more in touch with what's going on.'*

Carolyn: 'Heavens, how can you tell?!! I'd rather be home watching "Pride and Prejudice".'

Leanda: *'Well, yes, I know what you mean—they can be a bit tedious: all that stuff about the funding service agreement and that. But at least you and I and some of the old crowd get to catch up!'*

Carolyn: 'Yep, that's great!'

This is evaluative talk! It is talk which reflects upon the value, merit, worth or significance of the thing in question—in this case, committee meetings (*and* funding and service agreements, telemovies and friendship!). We could easily extract from this exchange at least four 'performance criteria' for committee meetings—including two which might be breaking new ground in relation to currently more familiar formal indicators. (Answers are at the end of this chapter!)

Actually you may have done half a dozen evaluations since you got up this morning. Perhaps even before getting out of bed! Firstly a judgement about the weather conditions followed quickly by an evaluation of the clockface; then a brief review of the previous day's events; yet again noticing those irritating cobwebs in the corner of the ceiling; then an evaluation of what the baby did to the cat's fur yesterday; an anticipatory assessment of tonight's school reunion; and finally a groan about the house loan payment due on Wednesday. Later you might have made a series of deft judgements about the best route to your first destination for the day, the state of a friend's or partner's mind, the lunch you bought from a new shop and so on.

We evaluate all the time. From the minute we meet someone new, or sift through the day's mail, or walk into a shop or office, or decide on the week's activities, we are evaluating. We decide whether things are valuable or unimportant, worthwhile, or not 'worth it'; whether things are good or bad, right or wrong, are going OK or 'off the rails'; are attractive, difficult, exciting, offputting, useful, undesirable, important, functional, effective, boring, expensive, too much, too little, just right, interesting, too simple, much too complex, or a disaster! Every time we choose, decide, accept, or reject we have made an evaluation.

You have evaluated the possibility of buying or reading this book. You have evaluated, even if only in a preliminary fashion, what you have read so far!

Let's look a little more closely at what is involved in the act of evaluation.

WHAT ARE WE DOING WHEN WE EVALUATE?

We find we are suddenly evaluating when we are busy going about our everyday business, and then, for some reason, we *notice* something.

We notice a discrepancy or a split between what we expected (or didn't expect, or wanted, or didn't want), and what actually has occurred. A difference between an 'is' and an 'ought' (or an 'ought not'). Or more accurately, the difference between a valued (or it might be an unvalued) 'is' and a valued (or unvalued) 'ought' or expectation. The reason why we notice is because we have *already* stored in our heads descriptions of the world on which we have placed a value—descriptions we sometimes shorthand term our 'values' or 'interests'. When these 'fail to compute' with what we are seeing or experiencing in front of us, the sense of discrepancy is felt by us to be problematic.

Essentially, we are taking a piece of the world and comparing and contrasting it by holding it up against something that we *already* think and know and have decided the value of—whether good or bad, useful or not, high, medium or worthwhile, right or wrong. This existing 'descriptions of the world', against which we compare and contrast the piece of the world we are evaluating, is our benchmark, criterion or standard, or a kind of template. (This is a bit like those little plastic maps some of us traced around at primary school and made a shape we knew was our country.) We carry these around in our heads and pull them out when we want to check new things. And then, when we decide on the value of something new, we store that away for future reference as well.

Thus the examples given: we wake up and glance at the clock, and evaluate it in relation to a mental picture of the time. This mental picture might be of the time at which we had already decided we wanted to get up, or perhaps of the time we hoped it would be, or perhaps of the time we feared it would be! Or the weather strikes us as pleasant or unpleasant depending on how discrepant it is with the picture of the weather we had expected or wanted. Our previous day went well or not, depending on what we had anticipated. The cobwebs are irritating because they are not valued in relation to a mental image of a clean (cared for) house minus cobwebs. And so on.

We evaluate like this constantly, effortlessly, as a natural built-in part of our everyday lives. But when we examine a little more closely what we actually *do* every time we accomplish such an everyday evaluation, we find we are doing *in microcosm* exactly what we need to do on a larger scale when we 'do' a Proper evaluation. Let's take an example.

AN EXAMPLE—YOUR TEA OR COFFEE MUG

Let's magnify one of these little microcosm evaluations and see what it consists of. Take something close to hand. It doesn't matter much what it is, because the technique will reveal pretty much all the basics about evaluation in a nutshell! For example, take your tea or coffee mug. Bring it closer and examine it carefully. You will need a context. Say you are at your community service, in the kitchen. You open the cupboard door to take out a mug to have a cup of tea or coffee or whatever. Now evaluate it.

You might say: 'Um, well, I like it. I like it a lot. I chose it myself. (Q. *Why?*) Well, because it's lightweight, fine bone china. And it's nice and white, and there are those pretty little yellow flowers round the top, and I like this fluting, and there's a really thin lip with a gold rim. It's nice to drink from. I use it all the time.'

Or, if it was a work mug, and somebody else had made you a drink and brought it to you, you might have said:

'Well, this one is OK. It's functional. But it's a bit "clunky" and not quite big enough. The colours are nice but the pattern is yukky. The handle doesn't feel quite right either. I wouldn't fight anyone for it!'

In each case:

- You have questioned yourself more closely; 'Well what *do* I think of it—and why?'
- You immediately *noticed* the things that are most noticeable or problematic, whether positively or negatively valued, in relation to a general guiding purpose for the mug.
- You either resorted to 'historical' (memorised!) *records* of 'fieldwork' of having used it and drunk from it before or, if it was a new mug to you, you did some new 'fieldwork': picked it up, felt its weight and shape, etc. Other memories were then examined. If asked about them, you might be able to explain that the gold rim and flowers remind you of your grandmother's pleasant afternoon teas or your mother's teacups for special occasions, and so on.
- You had 'analysed the data' and drawn a *conclusion* about its value.
- If I asked you to, you could tell me your *recommendations* regarding whether you'd choose it again, or prefer something else—and why. You might by now have so raised your consciousness about mug selection that you become very discriminating!
- We could then see what you next did in practice and either confirm your conclusions or raise new questions if you didn't do as predicted!

DESIGN
TECHNIQUES
ACTION!
GROUP MEETING

In tiny microcosm, you would have just done a little piece of evaluation research; or rather, one more cycle in an ongoing process of acting and evaluating, acting and evaluating.

This cycle is explored in much greater detail in Chapter 2 and is illustrated also in the foldout wall chart at the back of the book.

Just before we leave our mug-evaluation-in-microcosm, let's make some further observations of what we did (and didn't do) in order to throw some more light on the process of evaluation, and on some of its paradoxes explored further in later chapters of this book:

- You may never have actually stopped and evaluated your mug in this very conscious way—yet it turns out that you had already repeatedly evaluated numerous previous mugs, and stored away the valued and un-valued images and memories for later use. The finely detailed descriptions of the world that we carry about in our heads may literally *only* be in our heads! Some of the most fruitful, rich, extensive, imaginative, creative, and valuable 'evaluation criteria' that we have may not be written down, much less formalised as measurable service objectives. Maybe they never will be. Maybe if they were, we would find ourselves using such a tightly constricted and over-elaborated set of objectives, translated into standards, that we may set our expectations rigidly in concrete so thick that change becomes difficult.

  If we had, for example, drawn out from practice what the implied specific or targeted characteristics would be for our mug evaluation (to be lightweight, to be made of fine bone china, to be white, fluted, have a traditional delicate flower design, thin lip with gold rim), and then evaluated all other mugs against such a tight specification, we may have found ourselves wanting to say 'Oh, but this one's nice too. I don't mind it being a bit clumsier because the design is such fun', or 'Well, I'd prefer that melamine one today because it's for a picnic', or whatever. Often we find ourselves resorting to more abstract generalities—'To be appropriately designed', 'To be functional', 'To be visually attractive', 'To be an appropriate cost'. These are helpful because they give broad guidelines, and are grounded in the pooled insights which can be accrued from many efforts at 'evaluating' mugs. They leave out, nevertheless, the deeply refined qualitative detail that operationalises the abstract generalities in actual practice, and we can also spend a lot of time discussing what 'appropriate' or 'relevant' mean!
- Evaluation against formalised, written down, clearly articulated, passed on and inherited criteria will generally be extraordinarily helpful, but may never be the full answer. It may *always* need to be complemented by evaluation against as-yet unnamed, unarticulated and even unthought of criteria. Broad criteria must always be put into actual practice in highly specific ways. It is often best to keep these highly specified targets as provisional or flexible. The

art of both these kinds of evaluation is discussed in Chapter 3.

- If the mug was well-known to you, you may have found the exercise more difficult or more tedious—or literally pointless. It is hard to problematise and notice (and thus evaluate) the taken-for-granted. The drive to evaluate lies essentially in values that express interests that give us a purpose and our guiding frame of reference. In the coffee mug example, everything about our evaluation changes if the purposes shift from 'drinking coffee at work', to 'drinking coffee at a friend's' to 'drinking beer in a pub' or 'going on a picnic'. We might not trouble too much about the differing purposes that attach a slightly different set of values to a mug for work compared to a mug at a friend's, but seeking a mug to drink beer from at the pub or to take on a picnic might suddenly illuminate a problem if we only had bone china in our cupboard!

  Thus, depending on how much a discrepancy relates to our already stored 'descriptions', 'templates' or 'values', we will either return to our taken-for-granted existence (if the discrepancy is insignificant), or we will be propelled to a sense of unease (or elation!) or find it a downright problem, particularly if the discrepancy is significant.

  Sometimes it is helpful to actually try to see if there is a problem you hadn't been aware of. Some people find that kind of review exercise more enjoyable while others find it tedious. For example, you might ask 'Is this mug really good enough for my purposes?' 'Could there be a better alternative?'—even though it doesn't *seem* to be a problem. Sometimes this alerts us to situations we tolerate without realising they are less than ideal.
- You found the fieldwork to evaluate the mug more or less effortless because you had no trouble doing the 'interviewing' and knowing what to ask—because the whole exercise was for *your* tea- or coffee-drinking pleasure! You naturally made observations which were directly relevant to the intended purposes and desired outcomes: an efficient and effective tea- or coffee-drinking experience for *yourself*! If, however, you were evaluating a mug to be used by someone else, you might immediately have needed to plan some other fieldwork. In Chapter 2 there is an extended discussion of how to orient evaluation to those who it is all for: what we will call the critical reference group. When there are so many well-meaning and highly qualified people around who are there to help you with your tea- or coffee-drinking experience and advise on (and make policy about) optimal tea-and-coffee-drinking apparatus, you may well find that the seeking of your own opinion sometimes gets forgotten!
- The best data will be that which makes it clear what your evaluation of the mug is—for you. For example, if you say 'It is durable', this *looks like* a positive evaluative statement, but further exploration may reveal you saying, 'My mother would always have wanted me to ask if it is durable, but to be honest, that always conjures up hotel-standard thickware, and I'd rather buy a supply of fragile flowered bone china.' The most important clarifying question you can ask in evaluation is '*Why*—'*Why* is that?', '*Why* did you choose that?', *Why* did you say that?'. The 'Why' questions (or associated questions like 'Can you say a bit more about that?') will get at the all-important *context*. Context gives *meaning*. And *meaning* is essential. 'I like the colours' becomes less trivial if it turns out that the colours are the purple, green and white of the women's movement. The meaning of the colours is 'constructed' by those who give them that meaning. It is literally not the same coloured mug for different observers *with different purposes*.
- As noted at the outset, we could become more conscious of the reasons and purposes that lay behind our evaluation of the mug, and more consciously draw on these next time we go to choose a mug to drink from. Provided we do that sensibly, in proportion to the task, and with openness to the possibility that our conscious inventory of 'objectives', 'standards', 'performance indicators' and 'targets' might need to change, then we may find that a valuable exercise. We may find it speeds up our discriminating powers ('Ah! Now I know why I feel dissatisfied every time I look in this kitchen cupboard—all the mugs are too clunky! I'll go out and buy a more delicate one!').
- Say you now go out and buy a satisfying-feeling fine bone china mug. Everybody promptly chooses it and you can never lay your hands on it! You have another discrepancy to resolve! You embark on another piece of action evaluation! Or, you go out and buy a satisfying-feeling fine bone china mug and you use it constantly. For a while, you lovingly evaluate it against its objectives. After a while, you cease to bother, life goes on, taken for granted! . . . until something leads you to 'problematise' it again.

There are several final points that can usefully be made while we are thinking of the coffee mug evaluation. Firstly, this has been a straightforward self-evaluation exercise:

- Say that, instead of it being in the context of going to a cupboard and choosing a mug for your own personal use, it was a group of staff volunteering their evaluations with a view to one of them going out and buying a set of mugs for the other staff. This may seem a little presumptuous—why not let the group choose their own mugs?—but it is a common scenario in the human services area. It becomes clear that the group doing the buying (or making the policy about the buying) must primarily not merely consult the mug-using group, but provide the conditions for that group to clarify and build their own consensus about what are their evaluations and what they want in the way of mugs.

- Say that part of the group is going to buy the mugs for others in the group. Now it becomes clear that we would be in a consensus-building exercise around what criteria or characteristics would be the basis for their selection. People would need to start with clarity about each others' likes and dislikes. Indeed the bulk of the 'evaluation' will comprise a free exchange of perceptions, and the reaching of increasingly refined and possibly imaginative conclusions about what action to take. As Robin McTaggart has said:

> Action research [or evaluation] is the way groups of people can organise the conditions under which they can learn from their own experience . . . (Nicaragua, 1989)

Secondly, as with most everyday evaluation, the kinds of discrepancies perceived are generally of a 'Yes' or 'No' nature. That is, things are either OK or not OK, better or worse, acceptable or not good enough. Questions of extent (How OK?, How much worse?) are frequently of less concern to everyday evaluators. But when finer amounts of discrimination *are* called for, then some kind of measurement may become necessary. This is one way in which 'quantification' may enter the area of evaluation. It can generally be kept very simple and straightforward by using everyday ways of comparing and contrasting, such as along a simple scale (a lot, some, not much, none) or by ranking (most, less, least).

The major need for exactitude in quantifying and measuring is often nothing to do with evaluation *per se*—but about convincing others who do not share the same views or values.

The other main way 'quantification' may enter evaluation is if the question is one of 'how many' think that such and such is of a particular value, merit or worth or 'how often' does such and such happen. Again, and as with all survey research, the questions and interests of the research or evaluation should drive whether the questions call for answers that are 'how many' or 'how much', or whether they are questions of 'who, which, what, when, whether, where, why or how'.

There is a further discussion of numbers and quantification in Chapter 3. Evaluation and research do not equal surveys, questionnaires and statistical and mathematical computation. These latter are merely tools, and often ones which are over-used and quite often badly used. They are techniques for particular purposes, and their use is not automatically warranted.

CONCLUDING REMARKS

This chapter has used the simple everyday-type evaluation we might do of our tea or coffee mug as a microcosmic example of the full evaluation research process explored in Chapter 2. It has also shown the simple process of inquiry ('What do we think of this mug?') that characterises the kind of evaluation most effective in drawing out an understanding of what is problematic, with a view to developing or improving a situation, service or practice. It has illustrated, in a very rudimentary form, how this kind of theory-building exercise can result in an account of *implicit* values, intentions and purposes ('What are we looking for in a mug?'). When these are consciously written down as a formal statement of goals and objectives, they can then be used to 'audit' or review any *subsequent* situation or future service or practice ('Does *this* mug accord with our objectives for mugs?'). These two approaches to evaluation are explored in Chapter 3.

Finally, this introductory chapter has tried to show that evaluation is a process that happens naturally on a very tiny scale throughout everyday life. I hope to show in Chapter 4 how this process can be 'scaled up' through a range of different levels, and, in this way, can become a more truly built-in and naturalistic element of any situation or service.

ANSWERS TO EVALUATION OF COMMITTEE MEETINGS QUIZ

1. The first comment reveals a traditional criterion—that of information-dissemination.
2. The response to the first comment suggests a new criterion—either capacity to entertain or give pleasure or (if this is a community health centre committee or hospital board) a qualitative study of whether 'Pride and Prejudice' presents further ideals of what constitutes good service practice!
3. The second comment suggests that funding body issues may be of secondary concern to committee members and that 'tedium' could be either a useful indicator of when these interests are prevailing over those of service users (and hence spark a search for creative solutions) *or* of where staff need to convey things differently *or* of where funding bodies need to tailor their demands more to the needs of service users.
4. The second part of the second comment suggests another possible new criterion—that of conviviality.

A CONCEPTUAL FRAMEWORK

chapter 2

THE EVALUATIVE RESEARCH CYCLE

INTRODUCTION

This chapter explores in more detail the elements or steps that make up a cycle of evaluative research. It is illustrated by the wall chart at the back of the book. If you lose your place, just check the heading for the section you are reading and relocate it on the wall chart.

To 'do an evaluation' is actually to do a piece of research or inquiry—but with the focus or emphasis on finding out what *value* people place on things. Doing an evaluation is actually doing a piece of research regarding people's evaluations of things. There is value in knowing what people think of things, but even more value in knowing *why*, and thus what they would *prefer*. People's preferences or possible future options can then also be evaluated by them and the agreed 'best way to go' subsequently enacted. (As new enacting will rely on those very same people, all the more reason for their participation in the evaluation.)

Thus, while any evaluation will follow the steps described below, it is also essentially setting in place processes which enable *others* (who are making value judgements) to effectively follow the same steps for their own evaluations:

- Reflecting on *their* discrepancies.
- Seeking more answers to their questions.
- Thinking it through.
- Reaching conclusions about what they and others think about things and *why* they value things or not, and what they would prefer.
- Considering future actions.
- Then acting on them.

This is the meaning of action research or action evaluation. It is not research or evaluation done by some people and (it is hoped) followed by action by some other people—it is action which is evaluated and researched with a view to identifying both where it has 'worked' and what to do if it can be improved *by those who are parties to that action.*

This kind of evaluative research therefore starts with action and *reflects* on it.

Now if you take the foldout wall chart at the back of the book, you may in practice be at any point—perhaps in the middle of theorising why you are seeing what you are seeing; perhaps weighing options for future action; or perhaps at the point of implementing a new action. However, in order to begin the discussion in this chapter, the middle right of the diagram marks a 'natural' point of a narrative—both an end and simultaneously a beginning when we stop, and metaphorically look back over our shoulder at what we are doing . . .

REFLECTION

Noticing discrepancy

We have seen that any piece of evaluative research commences with observing (or questioning whether there is) a discrepancy between an 'is' and an 'expectation'—a 'problematising' of experience, where you hold an image of the world about which you have already decided the value, up against a description of the world-as-it-is-here-and-now.

ACTION
MEETING

We find ourselves doing this either whenever our taken-for-granted world strikes us as being too different from what we expected, or when we consciously pause for a moment and ask ourselves, 'How are we going?' or 'What do I think of this?'. Sometimes we've already been stopped in our tracks and we can't proceed until we deal with it. At other times we may feel surprised, confused, uncertain, puzzled, troubled or just feel an uneasy sense that all is not well. At yet other times everything may seem routine.

'Problematising' here does not, however, always mean noticing 'a problem'. It is more about questioning. It can also happen when things are going *so* well we notice them! Most of our experience of noticing discrepancies or problematising is where we have descriptions or images of a desirable or valued world in our heads, against which we determine that what is happening in the world is *not* valued and is indeed undesirable—propelling us to want to fix things and change them for the better. However, it is possible also to have expected the worst and done better—or expected a good outcome and noticed an even better one!

This approach is described briefly in Chapter 5 as the technique of 'positive evaluation', which may not necessarily be about everyone finding that they

are doing a good job—but is instead about identifying the conditions under which things went well for a change!

Now if we raise our problematisation to the level of consciousness and notice what the discrepancy is, then this drives us towards generating an answer to the question, 'How are we going?'. The sharper and clearer we experience the differences between the two sets of descriptions or valuations of the world, the easier will be the evaluation and the faster the impetus to resolve the split.

The importance of the driving nature of the discrepancies we experience—and our awareness of them—is fundamental to evaluation and illuminated by the following story. It concerns the possibly apocryphal science experiment in which a frog that is thrown into boiling water will promptly jump out, but a frog that is put into a pot of tepid water which is slowly heated to the boil will not 'notice' the small increases in the temperature of the water, and will eventually boil to death!! (Senge, Peter *The Fifth Discipline* Doubleday, Currency, New York:1990)

The moral of the story might be: when we feel ourselves in 'merely' tepid water—we should evaluate!!

This is not to say that we don't attach a value to those matters that remain taken-for-granted. It means only that until we examine or review these matters consciously, we can't really say what value we have or haven't attached. We might guess—and guess at others' values—but it remains guesswork until we self-reflect or ask more explicitly, and in ways that effectively allow us to examine what we or others really do think and feel.

DESIGN

Planning to evaluate

No matter how small or how elaborate the evaluation, the 'design' involves deciding what is to be evaluated, for what purposes and by whom. These in turn will determine what questions need answers, and of whom these questions should be asked.

DESIGN
ION!

This planning phase of working out exactly what the evaluation is *of* (and *for*) is probably the most important 'moment' of the whole process. Get this right and the rest will flow. Get it wrong and you may end up with the wrong answers to the wrong questions. Here's what typically can go wrong in planning of evaluations!

When we pose ourselves the question (or have it posed to us), 'How is it going?' or 'Is it working?'—there can be a number of responses:

- We think it's going really well but have to pretend we don't know (or They'll say we're biased) so we have to set out to try to prove what we already know. We spend a lot of time rediscovering many wheels (but perhaps failing to address some really sticky questions that had never occurred to us). The report gets called biased anyway.
- We're not absolutely sure how it's going, but we know what They expect, or we fear They want to change us or close us down, so we propose to frantically collect all the positive material we can, and we put our genuine questions on the back-burner. They change our program guidelines regardless.
- We think some things are going really badly *or will look that way* and we do a whitewash job in case They find out and knock off our funds without giving us a chance to fix them. The report gets called biased and they cut our funds anyway.
- Some of us think others are Not Doing A Good Job so we want to try to work out ways for this to become obvious without us ever having to say so out loud. It either works—and those others get very angry and never change, or it doesn't work—because those others sabotaged the evaluation! Nothing changes.
- Some of us think others are Not Doing A Good Job and we plan to tell them (or announce it to the local papers). All hell breaks loose and a lot of people get their backs up. Nothing changes for years until they've all moved on.
- Some of us are afraid we are not doing a good job and this will be found out or it will be made to look worse than it is and nobody really understood us—so we need to sabotage it. Our good work is never given credit.

We need a way through all this, especially when it comes to all the different interpretations of 'value' or 'worth' of an effort, and it is at the planning stage we can find it. The primary task is to focus on the ultimate purposes of the evaluation, and to sort out how all the different parties to an evaluation relate (or don't) to these ultimate purposes.

Who is the evaluation for?

I'M DOING AN EVALUATION
WHOSE VALUES?
SK

The best practical solution lies with orienting the evaluation towards common ground about 'what we're all here for'. And the 'what we're all here for' is essentially those who the effort, activity or service is all *for*—in the sense of being to help or assist overcome their problematic situation, resolve problems, overcome disadvantage or meet the group's needs.

The term 'critical reference group' will be used throughout this book as a general term referring to all these kinds of groups that human services and self-help group effort are *for*. If the term critical reference group sounds clumsy, please suggest an alternative!!* Otherwise we would have to say every time: 'who-it's-all-for', that is, users, consumers, participants, residents, clients, citizens, patients, constituents, taxpayers, claimants, self-help groups, identifiable communities, the humans that human services serve, etc.!

The words 'critical reference group' try to capture the ideas that:

- This is the group whose members' values and practices stem from their shared interests and who are thus the source of the most decisive or critical questions.
- This is the group to which services and providers (as well as the group itself) *refer* if they are to identify accurately what the group's needs are, and what are the best solutions.
- This is the group who finally judge and decide ('critical' comes from the Greek 'to judge' or 'decide') whether the services or actions 'got it right' and their needs are met or their problems overcome, etc.

Because those whose needs are unmet are those who are often getting the rough end of the pineapple,** words like 'powerless', 'disadvantaged' 'discriminated against', and 'oppressed' might also be terms useful for identifying critical reference groups. Additional descriptions might be ones implying disempowerment such as age (for example, very young, elderly); gender (for example, women); ethnicity (for example, Turkish, Egyptian) or Aboriginality (for example, Koori, Murri). Other descriptors may refer to the nature of the injustice (for example, violence, poverty, structural unemployment or discriminated sexuality); or the kind of group being hurt (for example, abused children, battered women); or the kind of disabling condition (for example, physical, learning, height or weight).

The questions driving evaluative research are meant to be self-consciously value-driven (although some evaluation pretends to proceed as if it isn't). This makes it both easier and also more difficult to sort out *whose* values are predominating. On the one hand it is easier because it is clear—even just from the term 'evaluation'—that values are being used to judge practices. On the other hand, it can be more difficult because evaluation can try to appear objective in the sense of neutral or value-free (for purposes of legitimacy, certainty, agreement, etc.). This may make it more difficult to realise that value is not inherent in what is being evaluated, but is ascribed by all those observing it (including by those whose actions, practices and beliefs are being evaluated!). Sometimes this situation makes it more difficult for the critical reference group (who it's all ultimately for) to have a say.

In the final analysis it doesn't work for anyone else to decide *for* critical reference groups, as there is no way of knowing if they 'got it right' for them except by reference to at least some kind of expression by the critical reference groups of their experiences and will. Sometimes this expression can be very clear and direct (such as where a well-organised and articulate self-help group analyses their experiences and makes a request for what they require), or the signs of expression can be subtle and require great interpretive sensitivity by others (such as where someone with an intellectual disability or Alzheimer's disease is unwilling or unable to communicate their will except by non-verbal body language).

Nevertheless, the effort must be made to seek out the expression of critical reference groups' will—and all possible barriers to this continuously dismantled.

Nor can we rest with the idea that a few representatives of critical reference groups can make everything go right by sitting on a Committee of Management for a couple of hours once a month filling in a customer satisfaction survey, or contributing to a consultation once every few years. These are necessary but insufficient ways of hearing the voice of the critical reference group. We must look to constant *everyday* ways of doing this. Every time there is contact, for example, between service users and providers, users must have channels for 'voicing' their experiences and needs, and providers must have—and show they have—'ears' and 'eyes' to hear and see. Then there need to be ways for providers and users together to discuss the feedback and jointly plan consequent changes in practice.

MY VOICE IS NOT VERY STRONG...
...IT IS WHEN PEOPLE ARE LISTENING TO IT!
SK

* Some of the language used in this book is a bit heavy and clumsy! This is largely because we don't talk about these things a lot, and haven't yet invented words for many 'problems without names'. As we become more familiar with the ideas, we might 'happen upon' better ways of naming things. Suggestions are welcome!

** Australianism for not only not getting what you need but being dealt a painful lot as well.

Where there are multiple views among critical reference groups then this variety must also be able to be expressed and heard, and if lack of consensus is a problem then ways must be found for communities-of-interest to work this out among themselves.

There may be an effect of glossing over this matter of ultimate orientation by including parties to the evaluation in a kind of pluralist partnership between service providers, managers, users and other community members. There is a sense in which a plural partnership captures nicely how a piece of collaborative evaluation must proceed in the practical social sense, but this ought not to be at the expense of obscuring that the partnership is still *primarily for one of the partners only*: the critical reference group.

In the next section there is a discussion of the other parties to evaluation which points out that the same conditions that apply to critical reference groups must also apply to them, namely, respect for their ideas, and time and safe space in which these ideas can be expressed and taken into account. As well, other parties to the evaluation may identify with the interests of the critical reference group. However, they are not the critical reference group *per se*, and many evaluations founder because they lack the guiding compass of a critical reference group perspective that can navigate a path through all the views and ideas and eventually evaluate the evaluations, and drive the effort to new and better ways of doing things.

It is important—if starting from a critical reference group's concerns—to identify the sorts of services that might be relevant to them, or—if starting from a service—to identify their critical reference groups. Some examples are shown in Guide 1 below.

Of course these services may serve other interests besides those of the critical reference groups listed. For example, Citizens Advice Bureaus might also be meaningful places for voluntary work by local women; general practices may also serve as training places for medical students or as small business ventures; women's refuges, Community Health Centres, labour schemes, residential institutions and legal aid offices may provide valuable work opportunities for a range of non-professional and professional workers who are keen to make a contribution to creating a better society and also have paid jobs; a Poverty Action Program may also promote a government's image as supporting social justice; academic research may provide publications that are essential to an academic's job chances; psychiatric hospitals may indirectly provide respite care for family members suffering exhaustion or even physical injuries received from the distressed person who is hospitalised; and schools may serve the business community's and industry's need for a trained labour force and parents' needs for day care for their dependent children.

Some of these other interests may be able to be related to critical reference groups, and some may be only remotely related, and some may even conflict with their needs. For example, human services may also serve to provide data to reassure central managers, or they may provide well-paid jobs or professional social status, or they may provide a service in such a way as to perpetuate a person's loss of dignity or subordinate status.

The now-folkloric episode of the British comedy television series 'Yes Minister', in which a Hygiene Award-winning hospital functions without patients touches nicely on our understanding that such a travesty is funny because it is both 'impossible' in terms of what a hospital is for (treating sick and injured people) and possible in terms of what else a hospital is 'for' (providing work opportunities; being kept clean, administered, maintained and managed; legitimation of a government keen to be seen to be doing Good Things; keeping down the bed–day statistics, and so on).

It is terribly important that these other interests (both benign and not so benign) are understood and effectively incorporated as part of the evaluation effort, however, it is critical that they be recognised

GUIDE 1
SOME EXAMPLES OF SERVICES TO BE EVALUATED AND THEIR POSSIBLE CRITICAL REFERENCE GROUPS

Service	**Critical reference group**
Citizens Advice Bureaus	Local residents
Doctors	Patients
Women's Refuge	Women experiencing violence
Poverty Action Program	Low income people
Academic research into Aboriginal health	Aboriginal people
Community Health Centres	Local populations
SkillShare	Unemployed young people
Residential institutions	People with disabilities
Psychiatric hospitals	Inpatients and outpatients
Schools	Students

as secondary to and dependent on the existence of the needs of the primary or critical reference groups.

Even where individuals or groups have the best interests of critical reference groups at heart, it is important to distinguish between primary and secondary (and even tertiary) interest groups. This is especially so in ambivalent cases where, for example, a 'secondary' interest group may become a primary reference group in its own right—for example, where a group of carers-of-people-with-Alzheimer's disease form a self-help group to deal with their *own* physical and emotional health issues; or where a group of prison warders or police officers form an association to create a death benefits scheme to insure their families against their loss while on active duty; or where a group of violent men from a 'Violence Anonymous' group meet to understand the why and how of their situation. Another example would be students doing vocational welfare courses. They would be the reference group of staff in relation to *learning* from the course, but staff would have their own industrial and emotional interests and form another reference group of their own. The critical reference groups for both students and staff in terms of the course *content* would, however, be the students' future clientele.

While it is important that secondary and tertiary groups organise around their own interests where it is relevant, the conceptual link with the primary reference groups (and logical distinction from them) should *never* be lost for two crucial reasons:

- Firstly, the secondary and tertiary groups' own actions or difficulties may not make full sense except by reference to the kind of problem suffered by the primary reference group. A full understanding of one may throw important light on the other. However, it is the primary or critical reference group's experiences which provide the necessary compass point.
- Secondly, if this conceptual link is not retained, the resolution of the interests of the secondary or tertiary groups may be at the expense of those of the primary group—hence risking compounding the long-term resolution of all groups' interests anyway.

In either case, the situation for both groups may remain problematic.

This is easier to see if it is the professional interests of workers which are beginning to take precedence over those of clients, however, there can be very-fine-line cases where, for example, the needs of family members for tranquillity and the preservation of their own health (and workers assisting them) can lead to the involuntary committal of their relatives experiencing schizophrenia.

Here we enter an arena in which *both* reference groups need their own advocacy and bases of strength from which negotiation and dialogue can take place and alternative solutions can be worked on which have the best outcome for *both* groups—while not forgetting that as a class of people, those with schizophrenia in this case remain the primary disadvantaged or critical reference group (the problems of the secondary group stemming from and depending on those of the primary group).

The other parties to the evaluation, in relation to the critical reference group

There is a discussion of all the various parties to research in *Do It Yourself Social Research*, (Wadsworth, 2nd edn, Allen & Unwin, 1997, Chapter 2) that is worth reading or re-reading. It notes that there are conceptually four kinds of potential parties to any evaluative research effort:

1. The evaluator or evaluators.
2. The evaluated (also called 'the evaluand').
3. Those the evaluation is for (to help meet their interests, solve their problems, etc.—the critical reference group).
4. Those the evaluation is also for (in the sense of informing, inspiring, empowering, influencing or convincing them to act for the critical reference group or not to act against it, or to provide a service differently, or to fund it or not de-fund it, etc.).

It is tremendously important that these four conceptual groups (and who belongs to which) are identified at the planning stage of evaluative research. Even when evaluation is for an 'us' of the paid staff, or even an 'us' of the service administrators or funders, it remains *ultimately* and *primarily* for the relevant critical reference groups.

Conceptually, all four groups overlap completely if it is, for example, an evaluation of, by and for a self-help disability group, and potentially not at all if it is, for example, an evaluation by an external consultant for a funding body, and of a funded institution representing the interests of (but not run by) people with disabilities.

The different constellations of these four parties represent varying opportunities for enhancing or limiting the chances of successfully ensuring that the critical reference group perspective drives both the evaluation and consequential change. The greater the overlap the better the chances, while the least overlap presents the greatest risk of lack of common ground, not hearing clearly the voice of the critical reference group, and also not communicating effectively with the other parties.

Of course an evaluation *can* be conducted entirely by and for parties other than the critical reference group—such as an external consultant employed by a government department to evaluate a service program on the basis of statistical returns and annual reports with neither the knowledge nor the participation of the service providers or users. The chances of such an evaluation 'getting it right' for consumers may be slim however—especially if neither the consultant nor the Department have much familiarity with the service or its local context. However, it is possible that such a 'remote control' study might get it right. (Perhaps the evaluator did have such familiarity and was able to use a consumer perspective and the Department was implementing a consumer rights policy and evaluating against this.) Perhaps, ironically, this may have been the best way of bypassing one or two local 'gatekeeping' service providers who were themselves unable to adopt a user perspective.

However, such an outcome—while 'successful' in the short term—must be considered a long-term risk on both methodological and practical grounds. That is, a non-participatory, non-democratic process of evaluation cannot *ensure* a user-appropriate outcome. A participatory and democratic evaluation process is a better way of increasing the chances that critical reference groups—through their participation in the evaluation—both determine the 'descriptions of the world' which are used as the basis for evaluation, and also are able to judge the value of these images or descriptions if the evaluation is intended to contribute to the improvement, change, and development of services for them. These ways of participating go far beyond conventional notions of representation on evaluation committees, and penetrate deep into the everyday fabric of service provision; but more of this later. Furthermore, by involving the other parties in such a democratic or collaborative evaluation, the chances are increased of their contribution, understanding and enthusiasm.

Differences of interests must be part of the contextual material of the evaluation. Nevertheless, when an evaluation comes down to a practical collaborative effort, it is only the ways in which interests *overlap* with those of the critical reference group that can form a practical basis for proceeding.

Target group terminology

In the light of this discussion, we might pause briefly to evaluate critically the common use of the term 'target group' by professionals and managers as a description of the critical reference group. The strong implications are that the professional or managerial group are planning to do something *to* or *at* the critical reference group, when the more appropriate approach would be partnership actions *with* and *for* the critical reference group. This latter approach would imply taking seriously the matter of involving the critical reference group in the planning and implementation of services or measures intended to benefit them. 'Target group' terminology may imply an almost militaristic paternalism towards a passive 'sitting duck' group, and an absence of that group actively determining what is to be done.

It might be more understandable if the critical reference group used the term target group to refer to groups of professionals or managers or identified sources of their problems!

However, instead of either group targeting each other, it is the *issues* which compound critical reference groups' problems—such as the unhelpful prevailing ideas, organisational structures, cultural expectations, and material conditions that hold the problems in place—that need to be targeted. These issues can then be addressed by all parties from each of their differing perspectives—within a full discussion of the different perspectives and their rationales or contexts, and using the guiding criteria of 'Is this good for the critical reference group?' or 'Is this best for the critical reference group?'. These are important tasks of the fieldwork that should be planned for at the design stage.

Taking a critical reference group perspective

In relation to the above, service providers, policy makers and managers must carefully search their own values for those which are congruent with working *for* and *with* their critical reference groups. Services that meet the needs of consumers cannot be designed and implemented without insightful understanding by providers of the needs and interests of consumers. And such understanding cannot be gained without

DON'T SHOOT THE TARGET GROUP!
-LET'S TALK!!

service providers grasping, through acts of empathetic and active understanding, the nature of critical reference groups' interests, values, situations, ideas and perceptions. More than this, however, such empathetic understanding must continue to be driven by these values and interests if the service provider is to 'get right' the design and implementation of a service. In its deepest sense, collaboration by providers with consumers is the methodological route to both more effective service provision and more valid and trustworthy service evaluation.

This adoption of a critical reference group perspective involves a number of criteria being possessed or adopted by anyone who works to meet the needs of critical reference groups. These criteria are listed in Guide 2 below.

People whose purposes or job or role means they are not primarily there as a member of a critical reference group can have such a perspective and indeed must have this if their work is to benefit the groups it is intended to benefit. As well, if the paid service staff are part of a self-help group, or if the service administration includes user representatives on a management committee, then these people occupy dual (or multiple) positions in both the critical reference group and in the advocacy group which acts for the critical reference group. However, if they are service providers, they are neither consumers nor consumer representatives *per se*. They *advocate* a consumer perspective. A strong test of identification with a consumer perspective is if this advocacy is at the expense of their other interests, for example, furthering their status or career interests, or if they are prepared to concede that their own profession's or service's or sector's activities might be disadvantaging or damaging consumers.

Many service providers who advocate for a consumer perspective have been made aware in the past of how organisational pressures seem to work in favour of being silent about consumer needs. However, there is currently a new wave of organisational interest in 'customer satisfaction' and 'client-driven

GUIDE 2
WHAT IS A CRITICAL REFERENCE GROUP PERSPECTIVE IN EVALUATION RESEARCH?

- A capacity to identify the interests of those who are meant to be served by the services or actions being planned, provided, evaluated or otherwise researched, and who may currently be suffering disadvantage, discrimination, deprivation or injustice or otherwise identifiably unmet needs (the primary or critical reference group).
- A capacity to identify *with* these interests—either because you are part of the critical reference group, or because you can see that there is a relationship between your own situation and that of the critical reference group:

> If you've come to help me, you're wasting your time.
> But if you've come because your liberation is bound up with mine,
> then let us work together.
>
> —Lilla Watson, Aboriginal educator and activist

- A profound respect for those who belong to the critical reference group, and a deep recognition of the legitimacy of their/our viewpoint—feelings, beliefs, ideas, opinions, attitudes, and ways of living.
- Such respect is borne of direct personal and continuing experience of the critical reference group's situation. Hence such a perspective rests on being in touch with (or knowing how to be in touch with) this experience—knowing how profoundly to *see* and to *feel* the lives of critical reference groups and to *hear* their/our voices.
- A sharply felt dissatisfaction with any conditions impinging on the critical reference group which are identifiably detrimental to the meeting of their/our growth or development (physical, social, emotional, learning, creative, spiritual) needs or interests, or are overtly damaging (unfair, humiliating, hurtful, injurious, abusive, oppressive, unjust or repressive).
- A consequent commitment and determination to work in relation to the critical reference group towards the best way of overcoming these conditions, and corresponding adoption of the appropriate value-driven evaluative research questions.
- The adoption of a collaborative question-raising problem-solving style involving working in or with the critical reference group. Individual actions stem from, and refer back to, the collectivity.
- The adoption of effective theory and thoughtful practice which focuses also on those groups who benefit (even if unintentionally, and including ourselves) from existing conditions which may hurt critical reference groups; and a preparedness to 'study up'; to be sceptical of current dogma and to have the courage of our convictions to advocate and retain a critical reference group perspective even in the face of any pressures to abandon it.

services'—stemming in part from new management practices in the commercial sector—which connects with longer-standing human services traditions of community involvement, compassion and empowering the disadvantaged.

For critical reference groups who are evaluating services that they are receiving (or assessing other situations that they are experiencing), the conditions for collaboration in an evaluation will include:

- A capacity to identify accurately the ways in which, and extent to which, providers or others are prepared to be with them and for them (without either overestimating this and risking disappointment, or underestimating this and risking a fear-determined 'backs to the wall' stand-off).
- An ability to identify accurately whether there are real opportunities to participate, and what these are.

Just as providers don't 'need' users to participate—but risk getting it wrong; users don't 'need' providers to collaborate—but risk inaction through lack of the conditions for understanding, or obstruction (even if unintended), and thus slowing of desired change.

How does this affect the evaluation?

The use of a critical reference group perspective will effectively shape the evaluation by:

- Focusing the evaluation around the values, interests and purposes that should be paramount in applying judgement and reaching final agreement.
- Ensuring a minimum of extraneous effort, particularly fieldwork.
- Focusing the selection of options for recommendations and maximising the relevance and applicability of future actions.
- Ensuring future objectives and standards will be appropriate.

In asking about critical reference groups' evaluations of things—and what they would prefer—we are implicitly asking about their own formulations of both their needs and values, and also the images that supply their own standards or criteria. This gives a clue as to why splitting 'needs assessment' off from 'evaluation' is an artificial exercise that can risk severing theory from practice. There are two kinds of needs at issue here. Firstly, there are the guiding values or interests (principles and philosophy) about what is valued, wanted and needed. And secondly, there are the more specific valued forms in which people are able to concretely imagine their interests being met.

When it is said that 'People don't know what they need' often what is meant is 'I (or somebody else might) have a better specific image than they have of how the need could be met'. This misses tapping people's wisdom about their own values and interests, and simultaneously risks the 'better' image not being tested with the critical reference group. Conventional evaluation often does not pursue clarification of critical reference groups' views by supplying or otherwise ensuring there is a range of specific options for them to consider. This is due to a misconception that this would 'bias' or 'contaminate' the results.

What of the place of the external evaluator?

Before we leave this matter of the 'parties to the evaluation', it is worth assessing the possible place

—YOU ARE LISTENING!!

...I DON'T KNOW MUCH ABOUT IT - BUT I KNOW WHAT I LIKE!!
THE BASIC INSIDER

AN OUTSIDER WHO MISSED THE INSIDERS' VIEWPOINT
I KNOW A LOT ABOUT IT - BUT I DON'T KNOW WHAT THEY LIKE...

NOW WE KNOW A LOT ABOUT EACH OTHER, WE WORKED OUT WHAT WE LIKED!
THE END RESULT OF USEFUL OUTSIDER/INSIDER COLLABORATION

of 'outsider' evaluators or facilitators of evaluation. While this book is written on the assumption that people do, and should be able to do, their own 'everyday evaluation on the run', there is value to be had from the strategic input of certain kinds of 'outsiders'.

Many people have expressed disappointment at the past use of outsiders—particularly of private consultants who might tender for an evaluation, come in, quickly interview a range of people, rush off, write up a report and exit. Let's look at what criticisms have been expressed from both sides about the pros and cons of external and internal evaluation as shown in Guide 3 on the following page.

It is regrettable that insiders' detailed knowledge and everyday practice wisdom have been systematically undermined by the rhetoric of 'independent expert objectivity'. This has often led to a false credibility for outsiders which is not based on their real value as a source of different or specialised ways of seeing things (the value of which can be judged by reference to a critical reference group perspective).

The fundamental situation in human and community services is that outsiders can come and go, but insiders are the ones who are there to stay. Ultimately, an outsider can only effect useful change *through* and *with* insiders. Indeed, where an outsider is used because no staff have the time to spend on a particular evaluation exercise, it may well be cost-effective in the long run to pay to release the insider and get a locum to carry out that person's job and pay an experienced consultant for a few hours back-up to the on-site insider, rather than handing the crucial evaluation task over entirely to someone from outside.

The basic strength of insiders is their store of

IN HOUSE
OUT HOUSE

GUIDE 3
PROS AND CONS OF EXTERNAL AND INTERNAL EVALUATION

	Insiders	Outsiders
Pros	Insiders may have: • long-held deep understandings of the world they work in, • deep tacit knowledge of what works and what doesn't, • accrued considerable 'practice wisdom' based on sometimes documented but often extensive undocumented 'evidence', • already been practising more or less successful evaluation of their work over many years without ever formalising it as such.	Some outsiders may have been able to: • ask questions that hadn't been asked before, • notice things and 'hear' things in the fieldwork phase that insiders hadn't noticed or heard as clearly, • come up with novel ways of explaining things, or show things in a new light, • break new ground with solutions, • act as a catalyst for change, for example, loosen established patterns.
Cons	Outsiders may have been brought in because it was feared insiders were: • too biased to recognise the truth of matters, • too stuck to see ways of getting out of ruts, • too invested to give up favoured ways of seeing things, • so caught in busy daily practice as to be unable to get reflective distance in order to see new discrepancies, or the contexts generating them.	Some outsiders may be reported as having: • asked questions that were considered wide of the mark, • reported on things that insiders had long known, or that were not very central to the practical task or critical question at hand, • explained things in ways that annoyed insiders or made them feel misunderstood, under-represented or wronged, • recommended precisely what insiders had been unsuccessfully suggesting for ages or missed recommending what insiders had been unsuccessfully suggesting for ages, • not been listened to either!

knowledge—and the major countermeasure they need to take is, therefore, to be sceptical of their current assumptions, beliefs and understandings, and creative about new ideas. The basic strength of outsiders is their fresh perception—and the major countermeasure they need to take, therefore, is to 'get grounded'. We can see, thus, what is required of each.

Requirements for outsiders and insiders

Useful outsiders (in relation to insiders) need:

- Strong respect for insiders' knowledge combined with a capacity to critically question (to be a 'critical friend'—raise a critique, not give criticism!).
- A strong critical reference group perspective (see Guide 2), and ability to retain it.
- Access to a range of past and current experiences, some of which are in similar areas, and some of which are in completely different areas.
- Experience in doing other evaluations and knowledge of the logic of evaluative inquiry as well as of methods.
- Skills in facilitating group discussions and clarifying complex issues, and in promoting a climate of self-illumination and development.
- Flexible abilities to theorise and conceptualise (for example, good use of analogy and metaphor).

And insiders need (in relation to outsiders):

- An appreciation of a different perception.
- Preparedness to suspend existing wisdom to consider the value of new ideas (including being keen to examine long-held beliefs about how to do things).
- Capacity to bring experience to bear on different theoretical ideas.
- Ability to exchange old practices for potentially more fruitful new ones, while retaining a strong

handle on philosophical principles or guiding missions (derived from a strong critical reference group perspective).

The best spots for outsider input are often:

- Right at the beginning—to help insiders clarify their purposes and questions.
- At the point where a list of questions to be explored in the fieldwork is drawn up.
- To assist fieldwork discussions where a facilitator might be helpful.
- When material is being analysed and conclusions are being drawn out and recommendations for future action are being considered.
- To read a draft report.

(For more detail on use of experienced researchers see *Do It Yourself Social Research*, Chapter 6.)

Outsiders can, of course, be used to actually do some of the work; however, every time this happens it reduces insiders' chances of contributing and learning by doing it themselves. If the effort is so big as to require someone else to do it, and no insiders can be released, then we must anticipate it migrating out of the bounds of everyday practice, and risking being separated from that everyday practice. It also delays users, practitioners and group members getting feedback on what they are doing.

Insiders as outsiders—and vice versa

In a way, the outsider and insider positions are not intrinsic to people but are a function of where one is placed. Under certain conditions insiders could act as outsiders, or outsiders could 'come on board'. An insider can become something of an outsider by using such a simple mechanism as working from home one day a week in order to get a bit of distance and have a think about things in a way not possible on the job with phones ringing constantly and everything happening. A whole group of insiders are trying to be their own outsiders when they go away for a residential weekend. The Australian Taxation Commissioner recently tried to become an insider in his own organisation when he became 'Trevor the Trainee' on an inquiry counter, answering public inquiries. Indeed, the whole new wave of managerialism devoted to getting down onto the shop floor and making direct contact with customers is in this same vein.

There are other ways of outsiders being more of insiders by dint of where they place themselves and for how long. The best traditions of critical anthropology saw, for example, anthropologists carefully 'going native' in order to mitigate the mistakes of previous anthropologists who imposed white, male, colonial or European interpretations on what they were seeing.

For everyday evaluators who have already usefully 'gone native', there are a range of different concrete and practical ways of both becoming outsider-insiders and also of drawing on outsiders (to act like insiders). Each of the methods listed below tries to overcome the drawbacks of outsiders' lack of familiarity and lack of 'connectedness' with insiders' worlds, while utilising outsiders' sceptical distance and reflective, question-posing capacities. For example:

- People belonging to similar groups or working in similar services might form peer group networks and meet or assist each other or ask each other to visit them on site.
- Large service organisations or groups of services or clusters of community groups may be able to designate one full-time or part-time person as having research and evaluative catalyst responsibilities (that is, not to *do* the research and evaluation, but to work with other members or staff to assist *them*). Alternatively, they might engage an evaluation consultant to facilitate evaluative thinking at various times over a number of years.
- Central funding or administering bodies might have (or fund) units dedicated to providing this kind of support to particular groups or organisations. This kind of ongoing support, provided over a long period of time, would also build up (and build on) already-acquired knowledge.

Returning to the evaluation question

Thus, the answer you would give to our original question—'How are we going?', or 'How is this service going?' or 'Is it working?'—should now be examined in the light of *whose* perspective the questions are asked from. Are you a service user, one of the critical reference group? Or are you a staff person—in which case do you think your answer would be shared by the critical reference group? Now think about your hunches as to why your answer to the previous questions is so. Whose ideas are these? Who do you need to share them with or check them out with to know whether you might be on the right track? And if you are right with your answer and hunches, how will you convince others?

All the parties to an evaluation will eventually need to be asked these same questions which are asked by the people initially proposing an evaluation of themselves. That is, whatever discrepancies have triggered the initial resolution to evaluate need to be checked against the other parties' perceptions—in particular, those of the critical reference group.

Most people can give an immediate answer to the question 'How are we going?'. This answer—somewhere between 'Great' and 'Terrible'—can then be further drawn out or explicated. Great or terrible for whom? How great? Or how terrible? Great or terrible compared to what? In what ways? How did

IT'S FINE!
BUT

we know? Now as we tentatively offer an explanation for our beginning answer to this tantalising question (why 'great'?, or why 'dreadful'?), we find ourselves describing the way the service or situation is now, but in relation to the way it *isn't*. Here we find ourselves saying things like:

> 'We are all doing . . . instead of . . .'
> 'It has come to be more like . . . but we were meant to . . .'
> 'I've noticed they . . . when I expected them to . . .'
> 'We say we are . . . but we are really . . .'
> 'Well it is a bit . . . and I think it should be more . . .'
> 'I thought it would be . . . but was surprised it was actually . . .'
> 'It was very, very . . . and I'd hoped it would be more . . .'
> 'It was kind of OK, but . . .'

No evaluation can proceed without these kinds of comparative statements (and if you find you only have one of the parts, then use this to generate the other part). You will need both an 'It is like this', and also a 'But it could or should have been like that'. They embed two essential things: firstly, a description of the world as observed; and secondly, a description of a world that had either been planned or expected, or a world that has subsequently been realised to be ideal, desired or hoped for. This latter set of 'descriptions of the world' comprise the beginnings of our 'evaluation criteria'—the standards for critique, or the templates and benchmarks against which we compare the 'is' to the 'expected'.

If we lay on the table at this initial planning stage everything we already think and know, then we can examine our conclusions to-date (from previous cycles of everyday 'research'). Do we really know enough? Have we asked all the people who might know the answers (or enough of them to feel

OH-OH. SIGN-PAINTER GOOF.
NO, THE LATEST MEDIA BLITZ OF THE AJAX LINOLEUM CO.
SAY NO TO RUGS!

Tumbleweeds by Tom Ryan is reproduced with the kind permission of King Features Syndicate, USA quite confident)? Can we refer to any records we might have? Where else could we go for more insight and understanding? We might then go on to generate a further question, 'Why is it so?'. Again, people can generally at least have a shot at an answer (often several interrelated answers) to this, and this leads to a hunch or hunches or 'working theories'. These theories begin to give a context for the evaluative comments.

When hunches are turned into sceptical questions, they can become the research questions to be answered. (An hypothesis is a glorified hunch. But it's important that you can imagine what evidence would look like to both confirm *and negate* your hunches.)

Now our hunches will generally be based on a lot of indirect evidence or 'gut' feelings, which may well turn out to be convincing. However, in the absence of records to which we can point, we will almost certainly need to touch base with our sources and various reference groups to check more directly whether they see things as we think they do. The value of something is not intrinsic to it, but is ultimately determined by those who the 'something' is by and for. This leads into the essential task of the fieldwork.

FIELDWORK

TECHNIQUES

Essentially the fieldwork task involves answering two fundamental questions:

Q. *What are our experiences and what is their value?*

This involves being able to get a picture of each element of what is being evaluated (who, does what, to whom, when, where, why and how), and getting a sense of why these elements have come to be as they are (history, context, rationale, purposes).

At the same time, it involves being able to get a picture of what everyone thinks of or feels about each of these elements (the value of who does what, to whom, when, where, why and how and with what effects—intended or unintended, desired or undesired), making sure that the views of the critical reference group are fully recorded, as well as those of all others with an interest in the evaluation or that which is being evaluated. This involves getting people to identify and describe the discrepancies they experience between the 'existing' and what they 'wanted' (or expected)—to the extent needed to satisfy the audience.

Q. *What are valued experiences and how can we experience them in future?*

This involves getting a set of ideas, images and descriptions of what people would have preferred—and why. That is, it involves ways of working out how to get from the actual 'here' to the desired 'there' that are practicable, realistic, and about which people are enthusiastic.

The planning of the fieldwork involves choosing ways of getting this two-part picture ('What is the value of current practice?' and 'What future practice would be valuable?'), and hence deciding what would count as answers, who is to meet and speak to whom, about what, and in what ways; reading or observing what, with what questions in mind, etc.

The fieldwork task is to get as accurately as possible a picture of what people themselves think or how things appear to them.

Think of the ways in which you normally inform your own everyday judgement and perceptions.

How did you know whether you enjoyed last night's Committee meeting? How would you know if others enjoyed it? How would you judge its value, worth, merit or significance? What do you base your ideas on? Chances are you not only didn't use Multi Attribute Utility Measurement, but that you didn't even resort to a questionnaire! Chances are:

- You *observed* things—you listened, watched, heard and maybe read some things. You watched people's faces and 'body language'; you listened to what was being said, the tone in people's voices; you noticed how many had come and whether they stayed for the whole meeting.
- You *talked* to people—you *listened* to their comments and then their responses to what you said; maybe you then *asked* some questions and got further insights.
- You *interpreted* what you saw and heard in the light of past experience. Maybe you went home and thought about it all. Perhaps you talked to a few people about it—maybe an outsider such as a partner at home, as well as some who were there and some who were not.
- You *compared* all these 'descriptions of the

world' with what you had expected or wanted (whether consciously or unconsciously), and drew some *conclusions*. You may also have changed both your criteria and your observations.
- You may have drawn on all these conclusions to *decide* whether to go to the meeting next month or not.

What you 'expected or wanted' was to get some needs met—perhaps needs to make a contribution, needs for information or convivial company and, in the longer term, to ensure you get access to a service in the shape and form you want. You carried a lot of images of how these needs might be met. You were observing and talking to people in order to supply you with signs of whether or not your needs—as 'evaluation criteria'—were being met. It is essential that these signs are meaningful if the evaluation is to be valid. For example, there may have been a lot of people there so it *looked* convivial, but none of your friends were there so it wasn't actually experienced by you as such. Or, a lot of reports might have been handed out, but they didn't mean much to you, so you went home feeling there were still things you don't know about. If we were to take 'numbers of people' at the meeting, and 'numbers of reports' handed out as signs or indicators of the meeting having been successful, we may not know why community members like you stop coming to meetings.

A 'grounded' or 'naturalistic' approach

Therefore, we go about finding out about the meanings that are real to people the same way we do in ordinary life—by getting to know people well enough to know how they see the world. We 'engage' with life, more like an anthropologist than a laboratory scientist looking down a microscope. We get out and about among people, with people, where people are, where they live their lives in their own natural settings. When we are self-evaluating, we ask ourselves grounded (not abstract hypothetical) questions: 'Why am I doing this particular activity?', 'What does that mean?'; and we ask others grounded questions: 'What made you choose to do that?', 'What made you laugh just now?', and 'What do you think of this?'. We ask the same grounded questions of written materials or documents as we would of the people who wrote them. We read the material ourselves—we get as close to the experience of them as we can. We immerse ourselves in the qualities of the people or situation we are seeking to understand. 'Do they like this?', 'Are they getting anything out of that program?', 'Does this service provide anything of value?'—and 'How can I tell?', 'What signs am I "reading"?'.

We check carefully for what we are hearing—not assuming too quickly that we understand. We probe a bit more, being sceptical of our assumptions and conclusions. Is there another explanation? What do people who disagree with us think? Why do they think like this? Has it anything to tell us?

And we may make (or draw on) written records—records we hope to make (or hope we made!) systematically, carefully, rigorously and as fully as is warranted by the situation. As Lynton Brown has said:

> What turns the flow of life into data is the fact that it is recorded. Special attention needs to be given to keeping effective records on topics of concern. (*Group Self Evaluation Reader*, 1990)

Lynton has also suggested that people's wealth of experience might be thought of as 'data on the hoof'! At some point in time these 'live' recollections may need to be turned into written records in order both to convince yourself that something is indeed happening (or isn't), and perhaps to convince others as well. There might, however, be a tension between those for whom minimal and informal records will suffice (because they are carrying their own wealth of 'hoof data' as background), and those who want masses of formal documentation, often because they have too little personal knowledge of the situation.

Some Community Health Centre staff were asked what they would take to be the signs of success in meeting an objective of 'participation'. There was some baulking at having to come up with the kind of numerical indicator expected by their funding body (a mathematical equation of number of subscriber-members of the Centre multiplied by 1000 and divided by the total local population). Finally, one said he would take to be a sign 'How many people have keys to our community minibus'. Others volunteered, 'If they come into a meeting room and arrange the chairs or close the blinds'. These are more grounded signs of 'ownership' of and responsibility for the Centre. If many signs like these are pooled, better understandings may be developed. Some signs may be recurrent and could be used for standard comparative purposes between services. But for everyday purposes, idiosyncratic but maximally valid signs will be more important for local purposes than standardised but possibly less meaningful signs that central bodies may collect.

Spoof indicators of success suggested by another Community Health Centre were the number of cabbages grown by the community garden group, and number of stitches sewn by the Turkish women's group! But these may speak more loudly for the tendency to choose possibly less meaningful things-that-can-easily-be-counted rather than possibly more meaningful things that can't! (for example, it might be pretty silly to require all community health centres to try to systematically quantify how many people rearrange how many chairs at how many meetings, or how many people have keys to community buses, etc.). It may be that, for managerial and accountability purposes, it would be more useful to know that local people have generated banks of their own meaningful but idiosyncratic indicators, rather than centrally seek the Holy Grail of indicators that mean the same thing to many different services across the board—apart from a few minimal but sensible and abstracted signs of service provision. In Chapter 3 there are some brief suggestions on how else central agencies might satisfy their 'need to know' about local services or activities without having either to distort the data or impose too heavily on people's precious time.

Where users can go elsewhere for the services they need, then providers will be furnished with a profound indicator for their success. But where providers have a monopoly, and users have no other choices, then indicators may range from passive compliance, disinterest, and non-attendance, through to resistance, conflict and what professionals might call 'behavioural issues'. Where users have no choice, indicators of positive valuing will be more complex. Neither more attendance nor verbal gratefulness will be necessarily signs of value to critical reference groups. All such signs require careful interrogation.

There is a chronic problem in evaluation which is known as the '*yea factor*', where people reply in the overwhelming affirmative when asked to evaluate services, particularly by more formal techniques such as interviews and customer satisfaction questionnaires. People find it difficult to volunteer dissatisfaction (particularly if they will have to use the service again) even if confidentiality is promised. The task is to establish conditions for trust and communication where the subtleties of views can be safely and effectively expressed and heard—exactly as in everyday life when you ask someone's opinion and they say what they think will make you feel good! Often it's better to say you intend making changes and then ask, 'How can I improve it?'. This gives people more 'permission' and leaves the negative judgement implicit rather than explicit.

All techniques used should therefore attempt to get as close to people's own realities as possible. Observations should be checked for context, questions should be easily 'askable' and 'answerable', and answers explored to fully grasp their meaning. Remain sceptical for as long as possible—both about your own understandings of people's meanings (keep asking: 'What do you mean by that?' or 'Can I just check I have understood what you mean?') and also about your own conclusions (run them past others, including sceptical others). Accrue much more evidence than you would ordinarily—you need to both convince and challenge yourself and maybe others too.

In this way your evaluation fieldwork efforts also follow all the ordinary rules of social research, and you can use any or as many of the ordinary techniques of social research as seem fruitful. Guide 4 (on the following page) is a list of techniques and sources—some more naturalistic and amenable to everyday evaluation use than others.

The importance of context

From much of the foregoing discussion it will have become clear that answers to questions about 'value' can only be fully comprehended by reference to their context—how other people live their lives; what else they have done in the past, or they hope to do in the future; who and what else impinges on, shapes and affects them. We need to go on asking 'Why', 'Why', 'Why' until contextual meanings are revealed. An example: The new mother from a rural ethnic background who is asked about the hospital service and, despite surgically ruptured membranes, a still-unhealed episiotomy, doors left open so all passers could view her labour, no interpreter and post partum haemorrhage, ticks 'good' on the satisfaction survey—but why? Well, because she came out alive and with a live baby. But will we conclude it was a good service she received? So many questions regarding what is of value (or merit, worth or significance) invoke the response 'it all depends'.

Or the elderly woman with Alzheimer's disease who keeps insisting she wants to go 'up the yard', but is 'evaluated' as having 'behavioural difficulties' by the young nurse who is meant to be giving her a wash but finds she then wets her bed. If the nurse could have inquired into the context of the woman's words, she may have found that the toilet was always 'up the yard' for a woman who has mainly known an era of houses with non-sewered outside toilets. Or the man with Alzheimer's disease who, referring to his new beard, said 'I'm drawing one on', and who was correctly interpreted by a staff member who was aware of his former career as an illustrator.

Contexts for *all* responses should be sought. Not only should we seek the contexts of users' views and suggestions, but also of providers' actions and

(*continues page 28*)

GUIDE 4
USEFUL WAYS OF FINDING OUT

INTRODUCTORY COMMENTS

Different techniques allow us to capture different kinds of records of the discrepancy between how things are and how we wanted or expected them to be—whether we are conducting an open inquiry or an audit review-type evaluation.

For example, collecting a file of all your old 'Tasks To do Today' sheets or of logs of incoming and outgoing phone calls allows you to examine on a daily basis whether you are getting through what you wanted or expected to, and also results in records which allow you to look back over a longer time span to see whether all your daily activities are adding up to a balance of work that expresses your broader intentions or goals. Or, a brainstorming session might provide a way of tabling how things could be in order to evaluate these options for the future. Or, use of a whiteboard in a kitchen or staffroom might give instant feedback on a particular issue, and if items are written down and kept in a file they might give an interesting overview for later examination from another perspective (such as whether people are able to participate in decision-making about the service or organisation).

Records may be routine and deeply built-in—such as case records or project records, or they may be *new* records that are slightly more built-on—such as records of what people thought of an activity or event that are appended to a routine project file, or they may be new records that are one offs—such as a survey or a time series 'snapshot' set of data (where, say, for three months, everyone is asked to describe or give their views about something). Or it may be a single taped and transcribed meeting to enable some more detailed reflection.

The important thing is that records are collected so that, as far as possible:

- They are fairly natural, non-intrusive, enjoyable and immediately useful both to those making the records and contributing the information (for example, both service providers *and* users).
- They can serve as many different purposes as you can imagine. (For example, use the same form to both enrol or register the attendance of someone for something *and* ask for some information about something such as why they want to come. Or use the same form to ask what people thought about something and also inform or give them a chance to make further contact for networking. A renewal of subscription form could also be used to seek feedback. Use information already collected to analyse, for example, gender or geographic residence—rather than ask these again in a questionnaire. Or use an Annual Report writing process as a chance for group self-evaluation.)
- They don't unnecessarily distort the ordinary interactions between people or waste people's time.
- They are systematic, comprehensive and rigorous (for example, if you are going to keep some records of something, keep them properly, don't skip or miss some examples or forget to keep them). If they're too tedious or intrusive or unenjoyable or not useful, then you should consider not doing it, or doing it for only a sample of time rather than forever, or reducing the volume of items or questions, or asking some other questions or whatever.
- Written records are not always necessary. If you habitually verbally ask questions and store the feedback in your memory, then your brain is working as your computer and 'management information system' (and the most powerful yet known!). However, if you are losing track because of information overload, or need to remember over longish periods of time, or if your word is not enough for 'others' and they want tangible evidence, then you will need to be collecting written and accessible records.

With all methods, you can then ask both open inquiry and audit review-style questions.

WAYS OF FINDING OUT

Group discussions and meetings

These might be routine group discussions and meetings (such as committee or staff meetings),

or special purpose ones (sometimes called 'group interviews' if there is a set of questions, or 'focus groups' if there is a single topic). They may be formal or very informal (such as wherever people naturally gather). They might be to collect descriptions of what has happened, or views about these events, or to decide on future actions and the reasons for these (planning or goal setting).
Examples: Search conferences,* group memory work, fishbowls,* stories (narratives and chronologies), brainstorming,* nominal group technique,* teleconferences, public meetings, committee or staff monthly meetings, self-help group meetings, Think Days, group consultation, kitchen table and coffee break meetings, group self-evaluation,* judicial model,* etc.

One-to-one discussions

Again, one-to-one discussions might be routine encounters or special ones (where one person is the questioner and the other answers, or where both discuss a shared list of topics or questions, or where you question yourself!). They might be face to face or over the phone, formal or informal.
Examples: Conversation, kitchen table/office desk/back fence discussions, phone surveys, phone-ins, anecdotes, reflection, recollections and story-telling, point of delivery customer/consumer feedback, 'key persons' interviews ('influentials'), consultations.

Written questions-and-answers

While written questions and answers are often the first way that people think of getting information, they probably should be the last! (Alternatively you might have two or three in a sequence from tentative to more formal.) They can be unpredictably difficult, often artificial, and frequently result in an exchange of misunderstood meanings! They should be as grounded as possible (naturalistic, well-'trialled', etc.). Sometimes called 'questionnaires' or 'one-pagers', they differ from the sheets of questions that might be used for individual or group discussions or interviews (more often called the 'interview schedule'), mainly because you are unable to clarify or explore things. 'Open' questions are useful ('Why did you like it?') unless you already pretty much know what people say and only want to know how many think what, in which case 'closed' questions might be adequate ('Did you like it because it was: Familiar, Understandable, Multi-faceted, Short, or Other . . . ?' Tick one of the above).
Examples: Questionnaires, one-pagers, satisfaction surveys, suggestion boxes, 'ideas' noticeboards, graffiti boards, checklists, cut-off feedback slips, sentence-completion ('I liked it because . . .'), return postcards technique, correspondence, voting, Delphi technique.

Observation

Observation is possibly one of the most valuable and least valued techniques for collecting information for further discussion and clarification of meaning. Observation can take place anywhere and at any time—in offices, shops, on the streets, in schools, kindergartens, workplaces, kitchens, refuges, on trains, trams, and buses, at shopping centres, in hospitals, at home, the movies, cafes, at reception desks and in waiting rooms, churches, railway stations, pubs, in lifts and out windows! Watch, look, listen get a 'feel' and a 'taste' for what you are observing. Look at people's faces; look at what they do, how and when and where they do it; look at who is doing what and under what circumstances. Look at body language, hear the tones in voices, listen to noise levels *and* silences. Examine rooms; how the chairs are placed, what are the signs of care, or of activity, or of wear and tear, or of creativity? Intuit and then examine what you are sensing. Develop your sixth sense! Observation can be active or passive, the observer can be a participant, or the participant can be an observer. Careful notes or records or video or photographs, etc., may need to be made as you will need records in order to talk about what you are observing and what it means. Remember, meaning is not self-evident—it is constructed by you, by those you are observing and by any others who you might ask!
Examples: 'Hanging around', on-site study, field visits, exchange visits, sociometric charts, photo essays, videos, interpretive drawing, tape recordings, ethnographies,

** Asterisked items are described in detail in Chapter 5. (See the index at the beginning of Chapter 5.)*

community studies, case studies, physical traces (for example, contents of rubbish bins!), head-counts, 'walking about' technique.

Existing recorded documents

Sometimes called 'historical analysis' or 'documentary evidence', existing recorded documents are examined by 'interrogating' them with the same questions just as if they were 'live'! What do they 'say' about what are their *implicit* values, purposes, etc.? What insight do they give you to your current situation? How would you want to do things differently or the same in the light of them? What do they 'tell' you about contexts and conditions that cast more light on things? Besides these open questions, you can test your hunches too. Some examples of existing recorded documents follow:

- Files
- Pamphlets
- Memos
- Diaries
- Phone logs
- Books
- Reports
- Rosters
- Photos
- Maps
- Television
- Radio
- Films
- Noticeboards
- Meeting times
- Room bookings
- Referrals
- Newsletters
- Field notes
- Case records
- Rulebooks
- Posters
- Statistics
- Newspapers
- Articles/papers
- Annual reports
- Glossy brochures
- Research reports
- Demographics
- Budgets/costings
- Magazines
- Bibliographies
- Schedules
- Cartoons
- Mileage records
- Appointment books
- Records of requests
- Oral histories
- Archives/histories
- Minutes/agenda
- Circulars
- Notes of lectures/talks
- Journals, articles
- Constitutions
- Timetables
- Correspondence
- Legislation, regulations
- Computerised databases
- Work portfolios
- Daily contact sheets
- Letters of support/complaint
- Longitudinal or time series data
- Resource allocations
- Attendance records
- Visitors books
- Appointments diaries
- Lists of filing cabinet contents

New records

You may wish to purposefully commence *new* record-keeping. Any of the above techniques could be used—either to 'capture' current practice or describe purposes and intentions. To provide a full evaluation you will need both—in relation to each other so you can compare. Thus if you begin to keep a diary, you will need to say what happened *plus* your reflection on its value relative to your philosophical purposes or your objectives. Or if you log your daily activities, you will need a commentary that judges the value of these relative to either your general purposes or specific objectives. Or if you produce a poster or pamphlet about your service or activity you will need to reflect on its value relative to your overall purposes (or specific objectives).

Examples: All of the above.

the rationales and histories of activities, services and programs. In turn, these sit in still-broader cultural, economic and societal contexts. The current phase of your inquiry is coming after numerous past cycles of action and research and action. Knowing where things have come from (and how they got there) provides powerful theoretical handles to enable you to shift things to where you want them to go to.

Because you went into your evaluation with a value-driven purpose with recourse to the values of the critical reference group, this now helps you assess where to go next.

FEEDBACK, ANALYSIS AND DRAWING CONCLUSIONS

GROUP MEETING

You are now in a position to begin to draw conclusions about answers to your two fundamental field questions.

Assessing current actions

Q. *What are our experiences and what is their value?*

You should now have a picture of each element of what is being evaluated (who, does what, to whom, when, where, why and how) and have a sense of why these elements have come to be as they are (history, context, rationale, purposes).

You and those involved in the evaluation also have a picture of what everyone (and especially the critical reference group) thinks of or feels about each of these elements (the value of who does what, to whom, when, where, why and how and with what effects—intended or unintended, desired or undesired).

Planning new actions

Q. *What are valued experiences and how can we act to experience them in future?*

Because 'clues' are actually descriptions or images of the world to which a value has been attached, eliciting these—which has been an important part of the fieldwork—now supplies you or your group with a range of options for future action. This fieldwork involved getting a set of ideas, images and descriptions of what people thought would be better and why, and these were worked through in a dialogue with critical reference groups.

This supplies a kind of second stage evaluative task: 'What is the best way to proceed?', 'Should we try doing this?' or 'Should we give that a go?'. If the fieldwork has been done thoroughly enough it will also be clear how now to value the different options in the light of what people have said, and in the contexts that are now better understood. The findings and material from the fieldwork must, however, be fully shared and agreement reached that things are clear. No further step should be taken until this is the case. If the fieldwork has been fully participatory then this should be a more or less simple task. There should be few surprises by this stage.

Because people's evaluative comments involve them in comparing the world-in-front-of-them with an imagined world-in-their-mind's-eye, it is often very easy to ask about these visions at the same time; that is, when you are deeply immersed in the fieldwork. A fatal mistake is to get a whole lot of evaluations and return 'home' and then have to imagine what on earth to do next. Action research is *not* research followed by hoped-for action! Action research, or action evaluation, is an active set of consecutive cycles of action, reflection, consideration of better ways of proceeding followed by putting them into action followed by reflection on them and so on. Thus when you asked 'What did you think of x?', you should ask also 'What might you have preferred instead?' or 'What could be done to improve it?'. (If the first round of questions did make the mistake of only exploring people's evaluations of current situations, there is now a need for another round of fieldwork to ask what possible ways could be imagined for the future.)

Given this sort of understanding, the presentation of an 'options paper' may be more a sign of still unresolved bewilderment or conflict about perceptions, or a too-early stage of ending the initial fieldwork. It should be possible to have had a stage of the fieldwork in which there could have been argument for or against each of the options, drawing on evidence, and showing which of the options looked like the best shot.

This phase involving evaluating possible future practice—assessing the options—also calls for vision, creativity and imagination.

Here we are trying to break old moulds of thinking, unfreeze old ways of doing, and come up with ways forward that are different from current or past ways. We are trying to shift from one cycle into a new 'gear' to start the next cycle.

But how can we imagine viable ways of doing things we've never done before? How can we imagine the as-yet unimagined? Sometimes it's very easy. We know what we should do next, even as we've barely asked the question of ourselves. Sometimes however, despite our best attempts at self-scepticism, we cannot come up with any better alternatives. In this case we can do no better than keep trying—perhaps having another internal brainstorm or external scout-around for ideas. There is no magical way available to us here. In trying to imagine the unimagined or even the unimaginable all we can do is draw on the best possible sources of ideas we can. These may include:

- *Ourselves and our critical reference groups!* We usually have among us a tremendous resource of fresh ideas, particularly if we talk or brainstorm in a group. Doing this kind of work in groups seems to work better than relying only on seeking separate individual ideas. People trigger each other's creative thinking. As well, there are always some people in every group who have especially good imaginations, or who can think laterally, or who have seen relevant or interesting things happening elsewhere, or who have had experiences we haven't had, or who can put two old ideas together into a new arrangement. Other methods, besides brainstorming, that can be of use are the verbalising or writing of 'future visions', 'scenarios', the use of Delphi-type surveys, and forcefield analysis.
- *Metaphors* are sometimes short cuts to associating known things elsewhere with as-yet unknown things here—indicating a rich source of implications and enabling illumination and new insight. For example, describing our service for the elderly as a bit like a kindergarten may suddenly help us conceptualise the loss of dignity, etc., and suggest alternative, more desirable images. Or asking people to describe their service as a breed of dog; or as a family, and to allocate roles! Or, as Michael Patton has done, take the contents of a kitchen drawer and get people to select an implement and describe how the service is like it!
- *Other people.* Good sources of inspiration and comparative experience are other groups, or other services, or other areas—whether these are directly observed, or heard about, or read about, or discussions are held with them.

Imagination alone can only generate possibilities. A further act of evaluation, or valuation, is required to discriminate among them—and to identify and be critical of the grounds for doing this.

As noted, group discussions are often the best way of both pooling options for future action and weighing their pros and cons. As well, when action decisions are made, the last part of the cycle can then be put in place by the same people who have worked on the ideas chosen.

PUTTING IT INTO PRACTICE

Recommendations for change or improvement can then be framed—and the current cycle of evaluative research 'ends' with their enactment. Because the evaluation process has involved all those who are to carry out the actions and those who are to benefit, there should be fewer problems here. Agreement will have been reached and mutual commitment secured. Conventionally, evaluations are presented in written report form, but the more effective the evaluation has been in its internal process of involving all

ACTION!

relevant people—no matter how simple or elaborate the evaluation—the less there will be a need for or reliance on a written report. A written report may serve as a report to those not involved, or as a written record of the process and understandings reached, but the primary forms of (mutual) presentation will have already taken place, along with mutual learning and lesson-drawing.

There should be a more or less imperceptible movement from the evaluation process to the evaluation outcomes—that is, from the process in which people discuss their ideas and reach agreement about the value of past and proposed actions, to the outcomes of people then adopting those new understandings and taking the new actions.

Thus this end of one cycle is simultaneously the start of the next! (Just as the start of this cycle was the end of a previous one.)

The new actions or enacted recommendations are then checked to see if they were put into practice (the audit or monitoring task—see Chapter 3). And then further evaluated to see if they hold up (the inquiry task). If they work well, everyone can return to taken-for-granted life! But if things are still not quite right, or contexts or purposes have changed, and further unease or discrepancy is apparent, you start the process again!!!

But is it science?

There are some important conclusions to be drawn from seeing evaluation in the ways described above. Firstly, all the tenets of 'good science' *do* apply to evaluation:

- It must be a well-designed effort that effectively inquires into and draws valid conclusions about the value of things for those who the things are for.
- It must be rigorous, systematic and comprehensive in its scope.

- It must be (and it must show it has been) self-sceptical.

Secondly, it turns our view of values round, from seeing them as contaminating little biases to seeing them as the essential driving force of any inquiry. That is, far from evaluative research being value-laden (much less value-free) it is, in practice, *value-driven*. Indeed, just as there are no 'value-free facts' there are also no 'fact-free values'. 'Values' are the conclusions of previous cycles of research that, in turn, shape and drive the next cycle by providing the comparative frame of reference.

It is not 'values' we have to be careful of in evaluation, since we must have them in order to proceed in the first place. What we *do* have to be careful about is whether or not our hunches and conclusions are 'right' for our purposes. That is, did our previous cycle of research get right its conclusions? No-one is well-served by fiddling the findings or by findings that are unconvincing, incomplete, or do not address alternative or competing hunches or theories.

They may even *look* convincing, *seem* complete, and *appear* to address all possible criticism, and we may *still* have got them wrong: although nothing can ever be proven—all propositions always stand open to refutation. It is essential that we always remain open to new and alternative 'ways of seeing' and thinking about things. It is this openness and scepticism about existing certainties that is everyday evaluation's best guarantee of validity. As Einstein has said:

> The whole of science is nothing more than the refinement of everyday thinking.

However, while the comparative method remains fundamental to both science and everyday evaluation, a particular comparative technique—the controlled experiment—may have limitations on grounds of validity and ethics when applied in the area of people. Attempts to replicate laboratory settings may actually distort the things being studied. Naturalistic grounded inquiry in real-life settings may be more appropriate, even if more complex, and measurement may often not be able (or need) to be of such extreme precision.

As Einstein also observed:

> Where there is truth, there is no certainty.
> Where there is certainty, no truth.

SIGNS OF GOOD EVALUATION

This chapter's discussion yields some guidelines for accomplishing effective everyday evaluation. When you think about the best piece of evaluation you have known, or when you think of your own best

...EVER GET THE FEELING LIFE IS A PERPETUAL EVALUATION RESEARCH PROCESS?!!

evaluation of a situation, you may find that the following factors were present.

It did not get out of touch with the situation

Evaluation *can* become totally over-the-top rationalistic-systematic and sophisticated. Not everyone is into this kind of intellectual gymnastics, but pretty much everyone can make simple judgements and have some idea of why they have reached them. If plenty of simple evaluations are done regularly, then services will grow and develop in healthy directions. Most change is incremental—even the best of revolutions are relatively bloodless because almost everyone has already gradually come to see their value. Regular and effective touching base with critical reference groups ensures that things never get out of hand in the first place.

It did justice to everyone's views and ideas

Everyone who needed to had a say, and everyone's say was listened to. To do this, people need to feel their contribution will be respected, and trust that they will be understood. This doesn't mean that everyone agrees with everything others think or think should happen, or approves of everything that is being described—but that viewpoints are asked for, respected, listened to, and understood. Even the person or group we think is most doing The Wrong Thing has a story to tell. And these stories must be heard and understood if we are to understand why and how their situation came to be as it is. If any person's practices need to change (if critical reference groups are to be better assisted), then it is mandatory that eventually that person's story be told and heard. Not only this, but that person must also participate in reflecting on how alternate practices might be better, and identifying how he, she or they might be able to move to such new practices. The direct telling by critical reference groups of their stories can sometimes assist this process by presenting the legitimate demands of the group without mediation by secondary groups. Where critical reference groups' needs are already captured in statements of purpose or objectives, then these need to be used to raise questions about how practices reflect them.

This kind of participatory or interpretive research isn't advocated just because it is a nice democratic idea, but because it makes for good science. People's perceptions or 'stories' (where their particular perceptions or ideas are given a social and historical context) are the stuff of our understanding about what is going on in a service or a situation we are evaluating. People generally do the best they can think of under the circumstances they find themselves in. However, it is good to remember that, even when people are acting from choice, they do not always do so under conditions of their own choosing. Finally, people's different biographies mean they may take a wide range of actions for similar reasons or similar actions for different reasons.

In evaluation we are trying to illuminate *all* these circumstances, conditions, contexts, purposes and actions so we can see where we are all coming from. Later we can reach a consensus—guided by the values, interests and experiences of the critical reference group—about what are the better ways of doing things. But at the first stage of evaluation we must really grasp well the full nature of the current way of doing things. There is a range of techniques for ensuring everyone freely gets to have a say. These include a modified Delphi where everyone writes down their own views and they are then pooled; or groups where everyone agrees to let each person speak uninterrupted—or each person has a supply of matchsticks and uses one each time they speak and when the matchsticks are all used up, everyone will have had the same number of chances to speak; or people are individually interviewed and then the material is aggregated and fed back for a group discussion; or small homogeneous subgroups are used where everyone feels more free to speak up, prior to reconvening in heterogeneous full groups for dialogue.

A confounding element to this is if one or more people or a group of people (and particularly those who are not members of the critical reference group) want to short-circuit the effort by getting their way regardless of the views of others. This is the all-too-familiar territory of power relations. Some people have lower capacities to tolerate other people's points of view and to sit with a process of consensus-building (and not run ahead of it), and they may also have greater capacity to intimidate and exert either authority, influence or control. Either way, the disempowered (often the critical reference group) lose out. Evaluation facilitators need to work carefully with the currents of power relations and associated emotions to avoid continued protection of poor quality or even hurtful practices at the same time as ensuring justice for all participants.

We learned things from it—it broke new ground

Good evaluation does more than tell us what we already know. It also shouldn't miss the mark or misrepresent us or suggest the impossible. It may have validated some of our private thoughts and conclusions and left us feeling less alone, or it may have given us a stronger sense of what everyone else thought. We may now feel a greater sense of shared purpose—or we may simply have a clearer idea of where we differ in our ideas from others; or we may have come away with some 'aha' feelings, as in: 'Aha—that's why we've been doing such and such!' or 'That's fixed my uneasy feelings about whether such and such would be the right way to go!'.

The generation of Good Ideas that come out of Good Understandings is a sign that the evaluation has generated Good Practical Theory. We often feel

REPORT
LONG TORTUOUS PATH

uncomfortable with the idea of theory. This may be largely because the main source is an esoteric and sometimes impenetrable academic literature we usually don't read because it doesn't seem like work at work, but it seems too much like work when we're at home! Yet the stronger our theory, the more focused will be our activities, because we will be understanding more deeply *why* we are doing or valuing (or not valuing) this rather than that, and what the effect has been.

The best way to develop theory and understanding is to follow the inquiry mode (asking: Why or what is going on here? then: Why that or what is going on behind that?, then: Why that? again and again), leading to wider and wider *contexts* of history, social, community, economic and political elements being admitted for examination and consideration. Where did the service or situation come from? Who first was involved? What were they trying to achieve? What was in their interests, and what wasn't? Even asking 'Why evaluate?' often gets us thinking about the hunches or observations we've been building up—possibly over years and years—or it can reveal important matters about the political context in which we are working.

What it came up with was useful

The best evaluation not only develops good illuminating theory, but also gives us leads on where to go next: whether it's to do something we had intended to, but had 'forgotten', or to do something we've only just worked out looks like a valued solution to a problem. We will have been initially satisfied with evaluation if its conclusions merely *look* useful! But then the evaluation that really does a good job will be that which led to new ways of doing things that really work *in practice*. Of course, this implies that we turn these into plans or objectives—and someone else will look back over their shoulder in the future to see if *they* worked!

'Useful' is primarily determined in relation to some identifiable ways by which the needs of the critical reference group are being met. In all successful evaluations, the closer the evaluation gets to the worlds of critical reference groups, the greater the chances are of being able to get this right—and to judge when it's been got right.

'Usefulness' also implies it wasn't actually useless or, worse, hurtful. Evaluation should never hurt the critical reference group or secondary reference groups who identify with primary reference groups, but should always be illuminative. It should not damage other reference groups either, although some may be discomforted or feel damaged by loss of powers or changes in routines which may have been at the expense of others. If evaluation material reflects badly on some groups whose practices have turned out to be hurtful of critical reference g, then these too should be discussed with some grac, for example, explaining the context or story that surrounds the practices, and treating the individual people with respect and understanding. There is no doubt that there are powerful class and gender and other differences (like able bodiedness) that result in conflicts of interest and values between critical reference groups and those who might otherwise want to assist them. Nevertheless, change is best served not only by some faith in there always being at least some shared interests, but also by a wise sense of purpose that justice should prevail. This sometimes may involve the simple insistence that critical reference groups' interests will be looked after, when more powerful groups can't see their way to this.

It took time

Another thing that characterises good evaluation is that, not only does it draw on a history of previous practices and events and activities and intentions *and* take time to listen to everyone's point of view, *and* spend time reflecting, explaining and theorising about what to do next, but it also then puts its ideas into action and then later re-evaluates to see if the ideas worked. It does not take ten minutes or even three weeks; it takes all the time over which a service or situation develops and exists!

'Oh no!' you say. 'But we've only got three weeks to do it!!!' Don't panic. You can do *some* kind of an evaluation in three weeks, or even in ten minutes or ten seconds. But it will be a smaller-scale cycle. It will still have to have some or all of the above elements for it to be worthwhile, but will be correspondingly *modest*!!! In three weeks you might hope to evaluate something like a relatively unproblematic application form used by about 50 people a year. In ten minutes you might be able to evaluate an hour-long interview you just had, or sit in your waiting room and think about its effects on clients (reading matter, colour, smells, voices overheard, languages spoken). But even these apparent 'bits' of evaluation rest on histories backwards and future actions forwards. Large 'quickie' evaluations, even in experienced hands, generally fail to fulfil their promise, apart from keeping up appearances.

The developmental approach to evaluation is the familiar action research cycle of action–research–action–research (or, in this case, action–evaluation–action–evaluation, etc.). Starting with simple open questions ('What do you think of this?'), then analysing the responses and returning to ask about particular themes that arose, and so on, until theory has developed to a point where clearer and more effective future actions have been identified. Then this action is, in turn, evaluated, and so on.

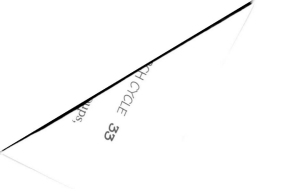

TWO APPROACHES
TO EVALUATION

chapter 3

OPEN INQUIRY AND AUDIT REVIEW

LOCAL AND CENTRAL AUDIENCES FOR EVALUATION

We all know the litany recited to encourage us to do evaluation! It is to help us meet our aims and objectives efficiently and effectively, assist us with planning and accountability, identify both what we've achieved and what we haven't, improve our activities, or support our next funding application!

However, some of the worst confusion that arises in evaluation stems from this common conflation of the needs of two different audiences. One of these audiences typically may be the 'local' audience of on-the-ground providers and users of a service or activity. This audience needs to know the value of what they are doing in order to know how to improve or maintain it in their daily practices. The other of these two audiences typically may be the 'central' audience of those who are responsible for receiving and spending public monies on services and activities that are deemed appropriate and necessary by the elected or appointed representatives of the public interest.* This audience needs to know what is being done primarily in order to monitor for publicly approved appropriateness and value. The local audience are the direct *doers* or participants. The central audience are primarily *auditors* and *transmitters* and *processors* of information about the 'doing' *up* the hierarchy and also of policy directions that come *down* the hierarchy from the elected representatives' assessment of public needs and wishes for new 'doing'.

However, how you go about handling the requirements of central audiences (such as funders, administrators, and any other authorities) may be different from how you respond to the needs of local audiences (such as local service users or providers). For example:

- There may be differences in the scope and detail—more about detailed areas needing change and improvement for locals; more about reporting in a more abstracted way (on things you take for granted) for central people.
- Another difference may be the kind of study called for—open and change-oriented for local people; ticking off against a checklist of goals in a service agreement or standards manual for central people.

Sometimes, however, these requirements can be reversed. Central authorities *may* assist local services to be change-oriented or responsive to users. The Victorian Education Department's School Improvement Plan, the State Salinity Plan, the Victorian District Health Councils and the Australian Taxation Office's restructuring called 'People Action' are good examples. Private Trusts or Community Foundations' Deeds of Trust may commit them to welfare or justice activities and not give them the right to withdraw. This can mean they have a greater commitment to local efforts to use evaluation for improvement.

On the other hand, local service users and providers will sometimes merely want to monitor performance using some standard criteria or broad statistics. Examples of this would be when Committees

* These comments also apply to those who spend private monies such as Trusts or Community Foundations. In their case the forms of accountability are more discretionary and there is no system of public accountability via elected representatives.

THE MINISTER
POLICY DEVELOPMENT AND CENTRAL MANAGEMENT
NOTORIOUS MISTS OF CONTRADICTION
LOCAL AND REGIONAL ADMINISTRATION
FRONT LINE SERVICE PROVIDERS
THE PEOPLE
SIMON KNEEBONE

'HEARING THE VOICE OF THE CRITICAL REFERENCE GROUP'

of Management use the Community Health Accreditation and Standards Program manual (CHASP) or the micro-computer Community Health Information and Research System (pcCHIRS), circulate quarterly statistics reports or write up an Annual Report for their members.

There is, nevertheless, an overall trend at the moment to evaluation being used more as an '*audit*' or '*review' mechanism* by centralised administering authorities (as well as some local service managers) who primarily want to be assured that funds are being used for the purposes for which they were provided, and that any particular service is doing what it said it would do. Local users and providers generally remain primarily interested in using evaluation as an *improvement mechanism* to check how or why something 'worked' or (didn't work), and then to see how to do it better.

Some evaluation theorists would go so far as to say that audit or assurance activities are not evaluation at all, and that they aren't evaluating whether the services are actually any good, but only whether they are being done as promised, according to frameworks of pre-agreed indicators. However, because such frameworks are intended to operate as implicitly valued objectives (which relate back to meeting service user's needs) then formal 'top down' evaluation-against-objectives techniques are examined in this chapter along with the more developmental 'bottom up' everyday kinds of approaches. The extent of the implicit value of objectives frameworks will rest on the strength of the previous cycles of research that led to them being framed. Where this previous research was weak or badly theorised, or inadequately grounded in critical reference groups' perspectives, then so also will the objectives frameworks be flawed. Sometimes the higher purposes or philosophical principles are better carriers of accrued wisdom about value than the more specified aims and targets.

It can now be seen from the previous chapter that these two approaches are two different perspectives on the same evaluative research cycle—one looking 'back' at previously recommended and enacted practices and checking to see if they happened; the other looking 'forward' to a problem-posing and problem-solving effort and as-yet unexplored and potential future practices. The bulk of this chapter examines these two different approaches to evaluation—recognising that *both* might be required by *either* local or central audiences and ideally should be integrated into one effort (while recognising that an 'audit review' approach might more often be favoured centrally and an 'open inquiry' approach be more often favoured locally).

EVALUATION FOR REPORTING AND ACCOUNTABILITY

Before moving on to consider the two approaches in more detail, it is worth pausing a moment to consider the separate matter of evaluation being used as a reporting and accountability mechanism. That is, to consider the matter of evaluation processes and findings being used by those who are 'local' and knowledgeable about what is going on and being done, to inform those who are 'central' or elsewhere and who do not know directly what is going on and being done.

The key practical issue from the perspective of the local level is, 'How can central or other audiences best know what is being done down here without us spending a disproportionate amount of time documenting, recording, and reporting?'

THE DEPARTMENT AS VIEWED FROM THE COMMUNITY
THE COMMUNITY AS VIEWED FROM THE DEPARTMENT

The key practical issue from the central level is, 'How can we best know that local users and providers are getting and giving the best services or activities possible (a) given the available total pot of money, and (b) given the total range of needs and demands'.

A key political issue is that evaluation-for-accountability generates an inevitable pressure to demonstrate achievement and to show progress towards defined goals. There are natural pressures to play down areas where there are problems, show things in their best light and narrowly orient to set achievement indicators. Evaluation-for-improvement, on the other hand, assumes there is room for improvement, or the possibility of better achievement indicators, and thus concentrates on where there are still discrepancies between intentions and practice. People need to feel free to share fears, worries, and vulnerabilities, come up with problems, work out solutions and carry out 'in-flight correction' (Lynton Brown's term), and then report on taking all these actions for accountability purposes. This process can be suppressed by constant inspectorial surveillance or close adherence to set achievement objectives. Interestingly, service agreements work as a genuine technique of evaluation for their first year or two when they are seen clearly as experimental and provisional. Once pinned down they largely become techniques for promising not only more of the same, but also the achievable rather than the desirable.

While the local audiences may always prefer to be more preoccupied with a dynamic 'case study' of local quality, and central audiences may be more preoccupied with counting and comparing services, there are nevertheless several possible strategies of mutual benefit to both local and central levels, to try to close this gap in perspective.

Direct contact

Direct contact is where the central audiences make direct site visits. For all its drawbacks, the old 'inspector' systems (for example, in schools and infant welfare centres) had the irreplaceable value of giving direct observational data, and a chance to question and explore. The best of the old inspectors would have been 'critical friends', using a quasi-anthropological but collaborative approach to gaining understanding, although the 'friendship' would always be limited by powers to cut funds, affect promotion, etc. But, in turn, these powers are limited by the need to ensure needs are met. The previous Education Minister's field visits with her Chief Executive Officer to schools are another example of direct contact. On-site presentations of local reports in relation to service agreements for a Victorian Government funding scheme is another recent example.

Vertical slice

Vertical slice is a variation of direct contact which involves officers at all levels from 'top' to 'bottom' meeting in small groups to collaborate on policy development and service problem-solving. This has some shared features of focus groups, although some vertical slice groups may be ongoing. This approach exposes to each other's perspective those both furthest from and closest to both Ministerial policy-making level and management, as well as to critical reference groups such as consumers 'on the ground'.

Network or tree

A network or tree is often a feature of more conventional management structures—whether corporate or hierarchical bureaucratic—and involves those at the very centre (or 'top') putting in place an intelligence network that means that there is an assured chain of links from them to the periphery (or 'bottom'). For example, there could be regional officers who do direct site visits and have good local knowledge, and central officers who have direct contact with these regional officers, and the central managers who have direct access to these central officers and so on. Certainty and reassurance lie in knowing that others know. A major drawback is 'editing' that might take place going up the line (as in the famous pass-the-message-along-the-line group dynamic exercise), and inappropriate or poorly informed direction going down the line.

Records/written documents

The unsatisfactory tendency is for central agencies to collect volumes of statistics which are stored: formerly in endless filing cabinets and now on endless computer disks, but rarely consulted except if a special query arises. Sometimes services and community groups experience this as being a little like having to take aspirin every day in case their funder gets a headache! Such reporting should be minimised in the interests of service efficiency.

To provide illuminative insights into what is done, natural records—such as those the service or activity would generate as a matter of course, for example, annual reports, etc.—could be collected more easily. (Their quality may be enhanced by the central agency providing some consultant resourcing.) Narrative forms of 'story-telling' reporting may also be more illuminative ('We did this and found that, and decided then to try, and that led to . . .', etc.) than resorting to surveys with their many possible distortions. Visual presentations, videos, photos, etc. may all also have their place.

To provide comparative planning data, central agencies should consider what is the minimum they need to know in order to divide up funds *between* regions, or know whether a policy is being met. Thus region-relevant data should be sought. *Within* a region, staff should consider what is the minimum they need to know in order to divide up funds or know if policy is being met within the region. This would condition the kind of data at this level. This approach would overcome the kind of problems typified by the herculean efforts once made by the national WELSTAT agency to collect standardised case information, continuously, about every single individual encounter between a service provider and service user, in all services within a program, across the whole of Australia.

Structural assurances

Structural assurances might involve the central agency putting in place service agreements requiring a set of sensible requirements and commitments that are regularly subject to change and revision in the light of higher purposes or long-term goals. Short-term operational objectives are always means to these ends and should never be treated only as ends in themselves. They should not be overly detailed, but should provide a framework for looking at a year or two or three years of activity with a view to making a little more conscious and explicit where the local people are coming from and heading to, and why. Practice has demonstrated that such written agreements work best if they are in a context of direct contact between central and local audiences (including direct contact with consumers). One structural assurance might be to expect (and require) sensible reporting on putting in place more organic, grounded and change-oriented local inquiry-type evaluation.

WHAT IF YOU ALREADY KNOW THE VALUE OF WHAT YOU ARE DOING?

Like all research, no useful evaluation can be carried out in the absence of a genuine unanswered question. What is essential is that you work out whether you have a problem without a known answer, or whether you already know the answer. If you have an unresolved problem, you will then engage in the exciting business of setting out on a voyage of discovery—an inquiry into the unknown. If you already know the answers (or can know them pretty easily), then you will engage in the less-exciting but sometimes just as satisfying business of marshalling existing data or understandings—a careful exercise in validation. We face a kind of fork in our path. Diagram 1 (on pages 40 and 41) sets this out.

So work out the answer to the question 'Why do we want to evaluate?' Keep going through the process in Diagram 1 until you have satisfied yourself that you either have to do a problem-posing evaluation, or a validation/documentation evaluation. In terms of the evaluative research process cycle (see the wall chart at the back of the book), the difference is between embarking on a new cycle of conscious evaluation, and reporting on a cycle of evaluation already carried out (although perhaps not so consciously).

Either way, you will find that the question we started with—'What do I think of my service (or whatever)? How is it going?'—gets asked, but this time you will be clear about what has preceded the question and whether you have an answer or not.

EMBARKING ON NEW EVALUATION—OPEN INQUIRY AND AUDIT REVIEW

If, on the other hand, you cannot yet say that you already know the value of what you are considering, we return to consider in more detail the two approaches to evaluation: change and improvement-oriented inquiry or a check on whether or not we have done what we said we'd do (such as in a statement of objectives).

Recalling that evaluation proceeds from a sensed discrepancy between the way things are and an image or description of what was expected, we can see that 'what was expected' might be either:

- Something that was *explicitly* and *consciously* expected—something we realised we wanted and knew we were looking for, maybe even that we had written down and planned to do,
  or
- Something that was *implicitly* but not *consciously* expected—something we only realise in retrospect was what we must have wanted, desired or hoped for (or not desired or wanted). That is, something we register mentally as a welcome or unwelcome surprise.

Reviewing on the basis of previous conclusions

When we are comparing the world to what we consciously planned or expected, what we are actually doing is looking back over our shoulder at the

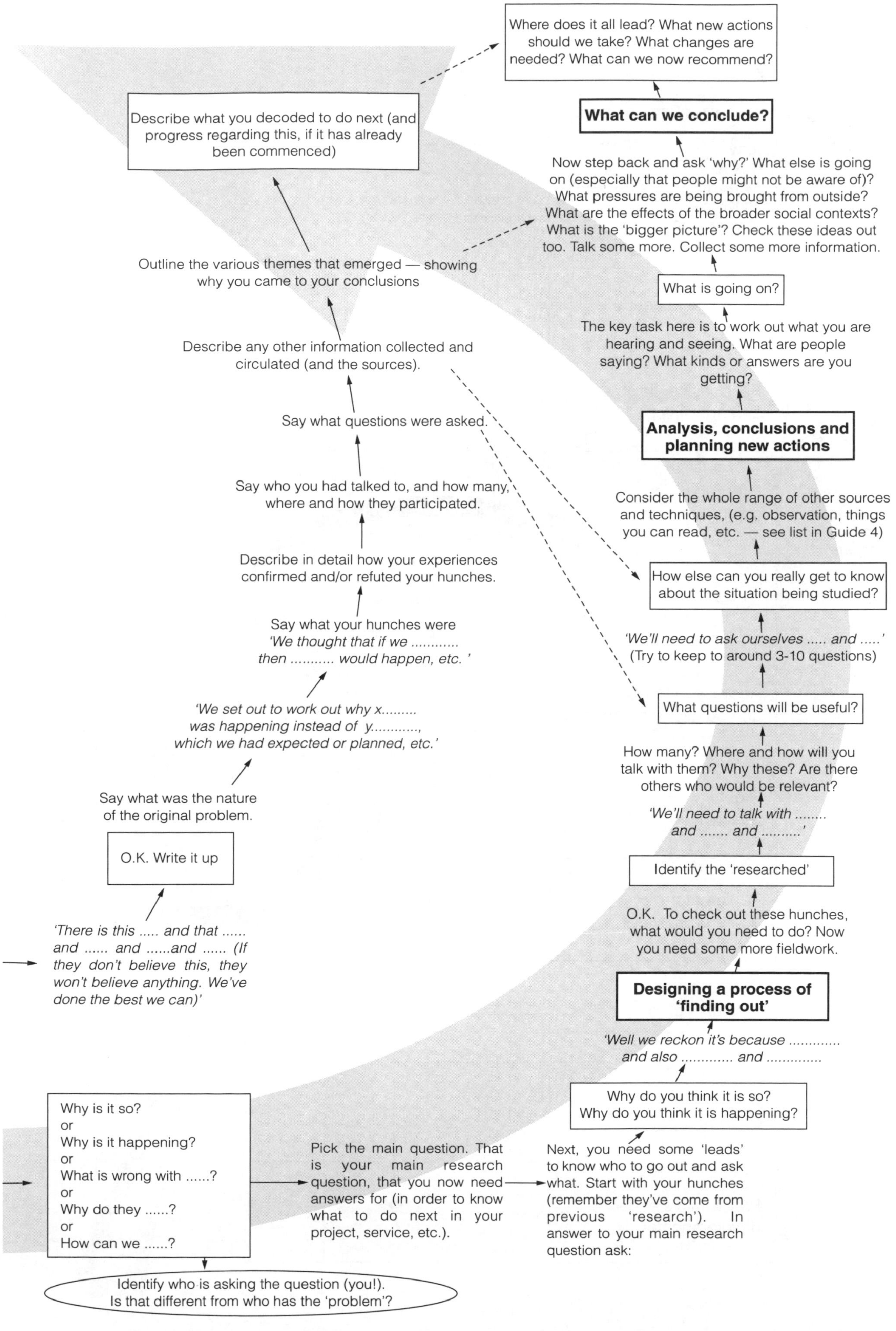
Why is it so?
or
Why is it happening?
or
What is wrong with ......?
or
Why do they ......?
or
How can we ......?
Identify who is asking the question (you!). Is that different from who has the 'problem'?
Pick the main question. That is your main research question, that you now need answers for (in order to know what to do next in your project, service, etc.).
Next, you need some 'leads' to know who to go out and ask what. Start with your hunches (remember they've come from previous 'research'). In answer to your main research question ask:
Why do you think it is so? Why do you think it is happening?
'Well we reckon it's because .... and also .... and ....
Designing a process of 'finding out'
O.K. To check out these hunches, what would you need to do? Now you need some more fieldwork.
Identify the 'researched'
'We'll need to talk with .... and .... and ....'
How many? Where and how will you talk with them? Why these? Are there others who would be relevant?
What questions will be useful?
'We'll need to ask ourselves ..... and .....' (Try to keep to around 3-10 questions)
How else can you really get to know about the situation being studied?
Consider the whole range of other sources and techniques, (e.g. observation, things you can read, etc. — see list in Guide 4)
Analysis, conclusions and planning new actions
The key task here is to work out what you are hearing and seeing. What are people saying? What kinds or answers are you getting?
What is going on?
Now step back and ask 'why?' What else is going on (especially that people might not be aware of)? What pressures are being brought from outside? What are the effects of the broader social contexts? What is the 'bigger picture'? Check these ideas out too. Talk some more. Collect some more information.
What can we conclude?
Where does it all lead? What new actions should we take? What changes are needed? What can we now recommend?
'There is this ..... and that ...... and ...... and ......and ...... (If they don't believe this, they won't believe anything. We've done the best we can)'
O.K. Write it up
Say what was the nature of the original problem.
'We set out to work out why x......... was happening instead of y..........., which we had expected or planned, etc.'
Say what your hunches were 'We thought that if we .... then .... would happen, etc.'
Describe in detail how your experiences confirmed and/or refuted your hunches.
Say who you had talked to, and how many, where and how they participated.
Say what questions were asked.
Describe any other information collected and circulated (and the sources).
Outline the various themes that emerged — showing why you came to your conclusions
Describe what you decoded to do next (and progress regarding this, if it has already been commenced)

DIAGRAM 2
FRAMEWORK OF PRINCIPLES AND ACTIVITY OBJECTIVES

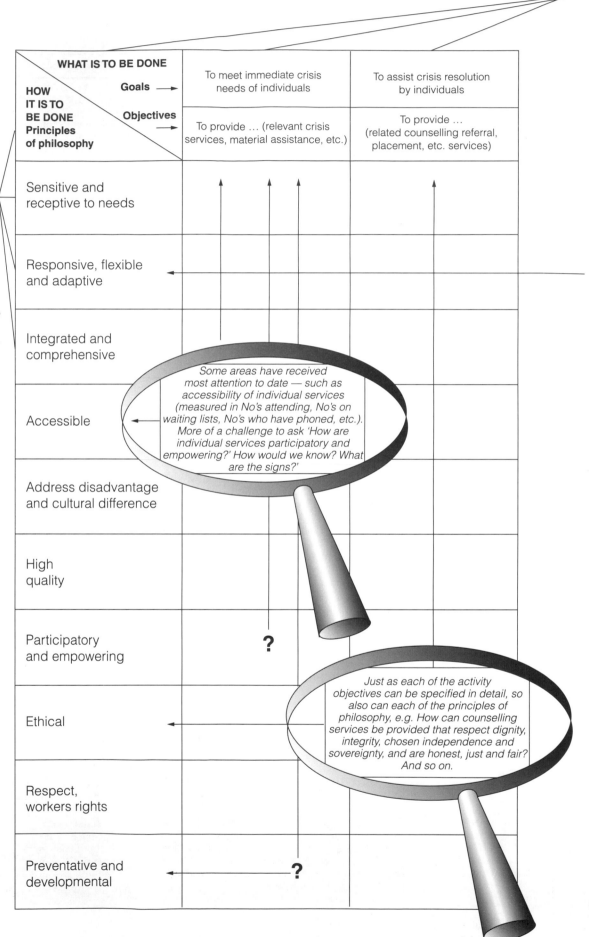

WHAT IS TO BE DONE / HOW IT IS TO BE DONE — Principles of philosophy		
Goals →	To meet immediate crisis needs of individuals	To assist crisis resolution by individuals
Objectives →	To provide … (relevant crisis services, material assistance, etc.)	To provide … (related counselling referral, placement, etc. services)
Sensitive and receptive to needs		
Responsive, flexible and adaptive		
Integrated and comprehensive		
Accessible		
Address disadvantage and cultural difference		
High quality		
Participatory and empowering		
Ethical		
Respect, workers rights		
Preventative and developmental		

This is a typical set of principles reflecting over-arching valued ways of doing things (which in turn are part of the rationale for the most over-arching process of an organisation or effort — see large-scale, long-term purposes described in Diagram 5)

Some areas have received most attention to date — such as accessibility of individual services (measured in No's attending, No's on waiting lists, No's who have phoned, etc.). More of a challenge to ask 'How are individual services participatory and empowering?' How would we know? What are the signs?'

Just as each of the activity objectives can be specified in detail, so also can each of the principles of philosophy, e.g. How can counselling services be provided that respect dignity, integrity, chosen independence and sovereignty, and are honest, just and fair? And so on.

This is a typical set of activity goals and objectives which classifies the range of valued things to do (sometimes called 'performance areas'). The grid can be used to 'cross' principles of philosophy with objectives to produce operational aims, relevant indicators and targets for achievement

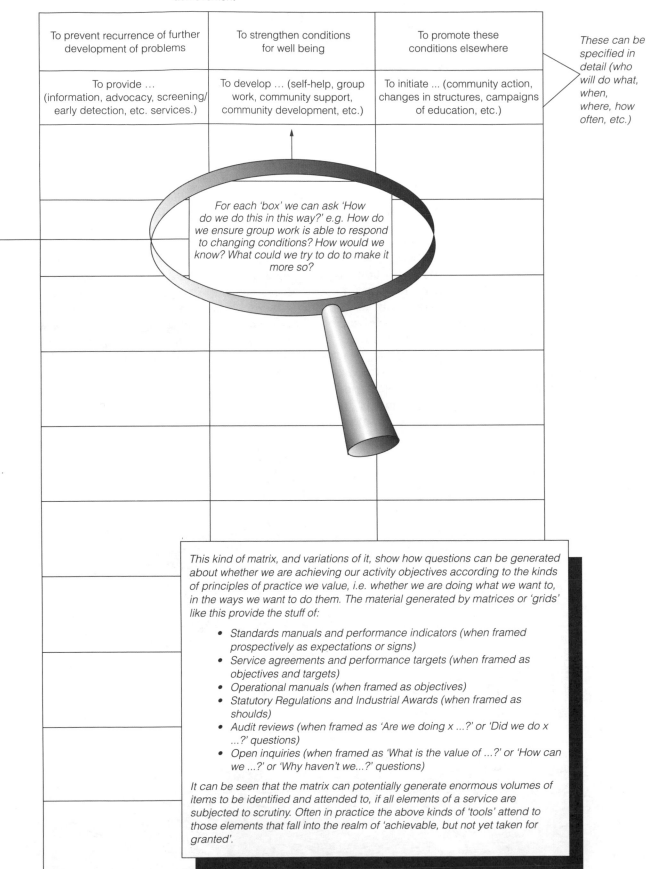

To prevent recurrence of further development of problems	To strengthen conditions for well being	To promote these conditions elsewhere
To provide … (information, advocacy, screening/ early detection, etc. services.)	To develop … (self-help, group work, community support, community development, etc.)	To initiate ... (community action, changes in structures, campaigns of education, etc.)

These can be specified in detail (who will do what, when, where, how often, etc.)

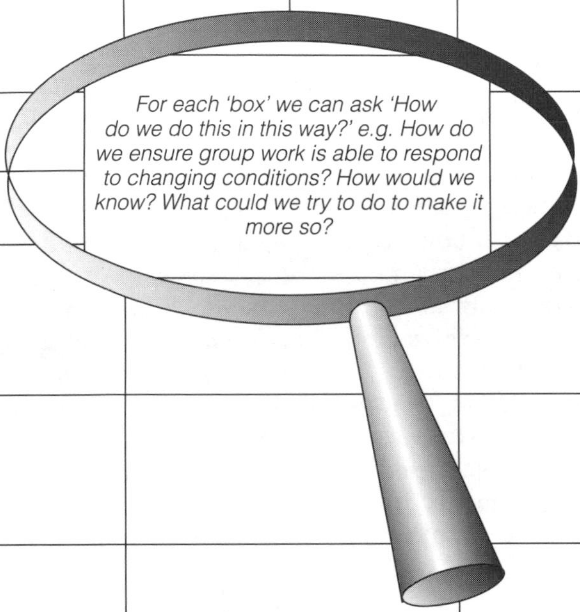
For each 'box' we can ask 'How do we do this in this way?' e.g. How do we ensure group work is able to respond to changing conditions? How would we know? What could we try to do to make it more so?

This kind of matrix, and variations of it, show how questions can be generated about whether we are achieving our activity objectives according to the kinds of principles of practice we value, i.e. whether we are doing what we want to, in the ways we want to do them. The material generated by matrices or 'grids' like this provide the stuff of:

- *Standards manuals and performance indicators (when framed prospectively as expectations or signs)*
- *Service agreements and performance targets (when framed as objectives and targets)*
- *Operational manuals (when framed as objectives)*
- *Statutory Regulations and Industrial Awards (when framed as shoulds)*
- *Audit reviews (when framed as 'Are we doing x ...?' or 'Did we do x ...?' questions)*
- *Open inquiries (when framed as 'What is the value of ...?' or 'How can we ...?' or 'Why haven't we...?' questions)*

It can be seen that the matrix can potentially generate enormous volumes of items to be identified and attended to, if all elements of a service are subjected to scrutiny. Often in practice the above kinds of 'tools' attend to those elements that fall into the realm of 'achievable, but not yet taken for granted'.

possible useful resource, and not the only guiding determinant of the future.

There is such a lot of talk about 'in-built evaluation', but this is what it means: a perpetual process of learning from our experience in the light of our guiding purposes or philosophy (the 'why'), in conjunction with a check against a memory or reminder of what we thought we were doing, or had hoped or intended to do (the 'what').

Let's compare the two approaches side by side. Diagram 3 (opposite) sets out a picture of the characteristics of each of the two approaches.

Putting it together

You may find you want to do an evaluation that combines *both* these kinds of evaluation. That's terrific! You stand a chance of both reassuring yourself that your service is doing what you thought it was doing (and finding the gaps if you have missed something)—and also of breaking some new ground that might suggest even better ways of doing it.

Some of us have been experimenting explicitly with how to do both in a single evaluation process and have found that, if we start with the 'old cycle conclusions' evaluation-against-objectives, it often has an effect of closing down our minds. We've found it very hard then to try to open our minds up again to the more creative exercise of problem-identification and thinking of ideas for improvement. That is, people often seem to slip their minds into the well-ploughed furrows of familiar objectives and actions, and forget to notice or remember the other little observations or insights or nagging little uneasy feelings that offer to break out of these furrows and plough some new ground.

To effectively do both within the one evaluation exercise, firstly, it seems to work better to start with the 'big picture', the open discussion ('What are we doing here?'), the let's-listen-to-the-fresh-voice-of-the-critical reference group, the brainstorming-what-are-we-here-for type approach. This sets aside, for the time being, all the previous answers given to that question, and also puts to one side the carefully prepared service agreement-type documents that have, to-date, prescribed and proscribed service practice. Instead it just relies on people's native wit and local knowledge and what is at the forefront of their own naturally inquiring minds: that is, the ideas already accrued through people's various belief and value systems.

We do actually already know heaps—particularly about why we are doing things! It's just that it's stored on various mental computer files and the existing programs don't always retrieve them!

Secondly, the systematic 'ticking off' exercise can then be conducted—showing where things are or are not, have or haven't been achieved. You may find that the open inquiry start may have covered some

1... 2... 3... 4...
- OFF ON AN OPEN INQUIRY!
KNOWN WATERS
UNCHARTED WATERS
CRITICAL REFERENCE GROUP
SK.

(*continues page 47*)

DIAGRAM 3
TWO APPROACHES TO EVALUATION

OPEN OR INQUIRY EVALUATION

- Inquiry—'to seek'
- Starts with the questions:
  How are we going? How is this service or activity, etc. going?
  Is it working? In what ways?
  What do we think of this service? What is its value?
- Asks the comparative questions:
  What are we doing?
  and
  Is that good or bad? (What's working? What's not working?)
  What are the signs of this?
- Then asks problem-posing and problem-solving questions:
  How could we improve things?
  How could we do more of what we are doing right?
  How can we let go of the things we don't want to be doing?
- Implies asking: *What are the needs?*
- The questions are 'opening up' questions implying the need to build theory from diverse sources. (There isn't necessarily a concrete picture of what the answer would look like at the outset.) The process will involve repeatedly asking the question *Why are we doing this?* until the fullest and most satisfying set of explanations is achieved.
- Starts with immediate or obvious 'problematisation' (either of good features or of bad features)—leaves non-problematic as taken for granted.
- Examines practice in order to be able to extract assumptions and intentions. Can then develop new and improved evaluative criteria:
  - Thus can ask about possible new goals, objectives, aims and activities that might differ from current ones.
  - Is developmental (or feedback or 'cybernetic' systemic).
  - Is improvement and change-oriented.
- Requires a questioning, intuitive, observant (interpretive), inquisitive, imaginative, speculative and creative mind.
  - Use of logic of discovery.
  - Feels more like an art.
  - Aiming at excellence of achievement.
  - Looks for 'meaningfuls'.
- Relies on who is/are the inquirer/s.

AUDIT REVIEW EVALUATION

- Audit—'to check'
- Starts with the questions:
  Have we done what we set out to do?
  Is this service, activity, etc. meeting its objectives?
- Asks the comparative questions:
  What did we set out to achieve?
  and
  What are the signs we have done this?
- Then asks the gap-filling and 'irrelevance'-eliminating questions:
  What are we not doing (that we intended to do)?
  What are we doing that we shouldn't be (that we didn't intend to)?
- Implies already assuming what are the needs.
- The questions are 'narrowing down' questions, implying the need to test theory from pre-existing sources. (The correct answers are already known and are merely being checked for their existence and implementation). The process will involve repeatedly asking the questions, *Are we doing this?, Are we doing that?* until the full set of possible aimed-for activities have been checked for.
- Sets out systematically to problematise all possible activities—leaves 'nothing' as taken for granted (except matters not covered by goals, objectives and aims).
- Examines practice in the light of objectives (applies known evaluative criteria):
  - Thus starts and ends with existing goals, objectives, aims and activities.
  - Is closed and linear systemic.
  - Is status-quo (or frozen snapshot) oriented.
- Requires a systematic, orderly, observant (monitoring), fastidious, highly organised, analytical mind.
  - Use of logic of accounting.
  - Feels more like a craft.
  - Aiming at competence of performance.
  - Looks for 'measurables'.
- Relies on the quality of previously agreed-upon goals, objectives and aims (and level of consensus previously reached).

DIAGRAM 4
SIMPLE QUESTIONNAIRES USING THE TWO APPROACHES

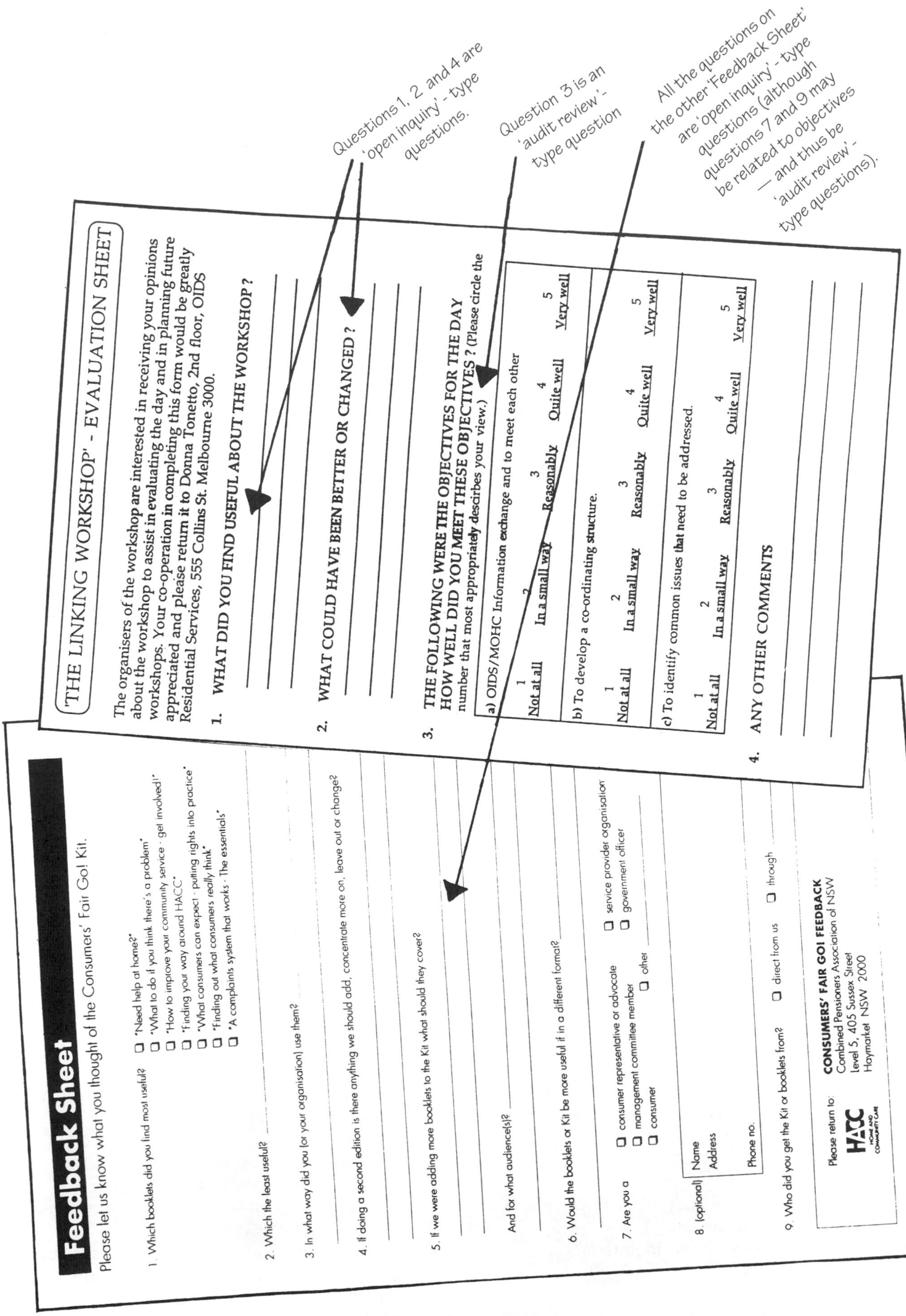

Questions 1, 2 and 4 are 'open inquiry' - type questions.
Question 3 is an 'audit review' - type question
All the questions on the other 'Feedback Sheet' are 'open inquiry' - type questions (although questions 7 and 9 may be related to objectives — and thus be 'audit review' - type questions).

'THE LINKING WORKSHOP' - EVALUATION SHEET

The organisers of the workshop are interested in receiving your opinions about the workshop to assist in evaluating the day and in planning future workshops. Your co-operation in completing this form would be greatly appreciated and please return it to Donna Tonetto, 2nd floor, OIDS Residential Services, 555 Collins St. Melbourne 3000.

1. WHAT DID YOU FIND USEFUL ABOUT THE WORKSHOP ?

2. WHAT COULD HAVE BEEN BETTER OR CHANGED ?

3. THE FOLLOWING WERE THE OBJECTIVES FOR THE DAY HOW WELL DID YOU MEET THESE OBJECTIVES ? (Please circle the number that most appropriately describes your view.)

a) OIDS/MOHC Information exchange and to meet each other

1	2	3	4	5
Not at all	In a small way	Reasonably	Quite well	Very well

b) To develop a co-ordinating structure.

1	2	3	4	5
Not at all	In a small way	Reasonably	Quite well	Very well

c) To identify common issues that need to be addressed.

1	2	3	4	5
Not at all	In a small way	Reasonably	Quite well	Very well

4. ANY OTHER COMMENTS

Feedback Sheet

Please let us know what you thought of the Consumers' Fair Go! Kit.

1. Which booklets did you find most useful?
   - ❑ "Need help at home?"
   - ❑ "What to do if you think there's a problem"
   - ❑ "How to improve your community service - get involved!"
   - ❑ "Finding your way around HACC"
   - ❑ "What consumers can expect - putting rights into practice"
   - ❑ "Finding out what consumers really think"
   - ❑ "A complaints system that works - The essentials"
2. Which the least useful?
3. In what way did you (or your organisation) use them?
4. If doing a second edition is there anything we should add, concentrate more on, leave out or change?
5. If we were adding more booklets to the Kit what should they cover?

   And for what audience(s)?
6. Would the booklets or Kit be more useful if in a different format?
7. Are you a ❑ consumer representative or advocate ❑ management committee member ❑ consumer ❑ other ❑ service provider organisation ❑ government officer
8. (optional) Name Address Phone no.
9. Who did you get the Kit or booklets from? ❑ direct from us ❑ through

Please return to: CONSUMERS' FAIR GO! FEEDBACK
Combined Pensioners Association of NSW
Level 5, 405 Sussex Street
Haymarket NSW 2000

HACC HOME AND COMMUNITY CARE

of this, but you will still have retained the 'gold' once the gravel of current practice and objectives are panned off. For example, a large residential agency for people with disabilities commenced the re-writing of its service agreement with a lengthy discussion of what single sentence they thought best represented what they were on about. When they had finished and they compared it to their existing Mission Statement, they found they had made an important conceptual leap from seeing themselves as providers of sheltered care to providers of home-like accommodation.

In another example, the volunteer staff of a community information service explored open questions about their work—and the issue of gender arose (almost all the volunteers were women, the coordinators were male, the service-users were women, etc.), yet when they turned to see whether they were meeting their formal organisational objectives, there was no mention of the gender issue.

Diagram 4 shows a couple of very simple one page evaluation sheets that have used the two approaches consecutively. Other examples in Chapter 4 show this too. A good example of the two approaches, taken from the area of education, would be the difference between a teacher evaluating a student's work (using an inquiry approach) by reading an essay written by the student, and evaluating by marking a multiple-choice examination (audit review).

If you are doing a largish effort, it can sometimes work if there is a division of labour around the two tasks. Those whose minds work more happily in an audit review mode could together assess a service against a set of objectives, extracted either from previously written, formal statements of intention, or from 'reading off' the objectives from the kinds of services or activities components provided. Another group of more inquisitive souls with a nose for 'problematisation' (both negative and positive) could ferret around for the issues (the word issues is almost always a euphemism for 'problems'!) and start applying a 'Why, Why, Why', inquiry mode of questioning to understand better the elements that need to be replicated or improved.

When the two groups eventually come back together, they might find a fair degree of overlap, but it will be the areas that don't overlap which will point in the direction of positive change, and the areas that do overlap will confirm the validity of the original research on which the service was based.

The two approaches in more detail

'Audit review'-type evaluation is currently tremendously popular and has, in some ways, got a little out of balance with the open inquiry approach. In order for it to resume its place within a more comprehensive and workable built-in evaluation program, it may be helpful to examine the context of its recent rise to prominence, and then examine the drawbacks and strengths of each of the two approaches in more detail. If this level of detail is not of interest to you, feel free to skip to the summaries in Guides 5 and 6 at the end of the section, and then move on to Chapter 4.

The popularity of audit review style evaluation may stem from the historical combination of two important factors: the introduction of new forms of human services in the 1970s, combined with a desire to constrain their growth (due to economic pressures).

The new forms emerged in the 1960s and 1970s when there was a particularly active phase of 'open inquiry' and consequent change in our views of how human services should be conducted. This was in many cases a change from where modern professionals 'knew best', and intervened, often dramatically, in the lives of their patients, clients and other subject peoples.

Ironically these characteristics were associated with a way of providing human services that had been the goals and objectives of an earlier era intent on creating a modern society in which 'social problems' were dealt with in an enlightened, well-organised, efficient and utilitarian manner. This was in contrast to an even earlier nineteenth century era when such 'problems' were left to fend for themselves apart from the vestiges of feudal charity.

In the post-World War Two period, 'evaluation' (rarely formalised or funded as such) by client populations and their sympathetic young professional advocates resulted in a rejection of this well-meaning but often damaging approach. There was a shift towards understanding the social, political and economic conditions which created and shaped disadvantage as a social category (rather than seeing it purely as personal misfortune or wilfulness). Responsibility for people's individual situations became a social matter—commencing with the introduction of government health, education and welfare and social security schemes and finally coming to rest in a set of understandings about how services should be provided to protect and promote people's dignity, self-determination and empowerment.

In the 1980s these became the set of human services program principles or goals and objectives with which we are now so familiar (see Diagram 2 for an example).

Secondly, however, and coinciding with this development, came the end of the comfortable economic conditions which had underpinned it. More money in the economy of the 1960s and early 1970s had seen the expansion of secondary and tertiary education, the growth of a well-paid, credentialled workforce, an intolerance of the 'residue' of poverty and disadvantage, and a determination to release and resource a range of incarcerated groups, including people with physical, intellectual and psychiatric disabilities.

However, the economic recession, and subsequent restructuring of industry and consequent demands for government resourcing of business recovery and debt, has led to financial stringency with the 'luxury' of social justice being largely postponed to await further growth in a competitive economy. Martin Rein has described the shift from the vision of the social workers, to the vision of the economist at the height of the boom in the late 1960s and early 1970s when a Guaranteed Minimum Income seemed desirable and possible, and finally to the vision of the auditors. This latter 'vision' has accompanied an era of 'managerialism', as the private sector moved ruthlessly to maximise output and minimise production costs, and the public sector moved to control spending growth and contain the social demand of a populace who had come to expect that their human needs would be met.

Thus the two groups—those who wished to ensure services were now targeting needs and abiding by more humane principles, and those who wished to ensure that no new services were funded and indeed that some real decreases in funding levels could be attained (we should perhaps see the word 'ration' every time we are told an approach is 'rational'!)—formed an alliance to introduce the techniques of Management by Objectives and Management for Results and related techniques (for example, program budgeting, performance indicators and targets).

This might explain some of the ambivalence with which audit review evaluation is often greeted by local service providers or users. On the one hand it seems terribly sensible and indeed helpful to check that one is doing the (good) things we set out to do, or getting the (good) services we were led to expect. But on the other hand, the 'rationality' of such a closed system approach may take further change and development off the agenda. Yet not only growth, but also improvement and development that is within current budgetary restraints may be impeded if our current objectives are insufficient, inadequate or inappropriate.

Interestingly, some of the most recent developments in managerialism (such as Management for Excellence) have been away from the excesses of tightly centrally controlled, technical rationalism (that had everyone constantly accounting in advance for everything they were going to do, and being held rigidly to doing every one of those promised things, and unable to do anything unanticipated). The shift at least partially seems to have been away from total reliance on 'top down' motivation and command-and-control management and appearances of 'performance', towards more 'bottom up' autonomous and participatory self-management, inspirational leadership and an emphasis on achievement within a broad organisational philosophy. In important ways this involves a shift from the excesses of an audit review approach towards utilising some of the characteristics of open inquiry, such as creativity and insight, and sensitively re-touching base with the 'customer' in a search for excellence.

Drawbacks of only evaluating against objectives and targets

While some of our services' higher principles and philosophy and long-term goals are the result of decades of painstaking theory and practice, we only need to consider how the shorter-term objectives and specific indicators and targets that are meant to implement them were settled on, to realise that some more change might still be desirable! Reflect for a moment on any set of objectives, indicators and targets with which you might be familiar. Would you say:

- That everybody really understands them?
- That they are really understandable?
- That they represent a high level of consensus?
- That they have proved to be easy to put into practice, and it is obvious how to do this?
- That you could actually tell whether they had or had not been met?
- That they are not overly ambitious or alternatively, too narrow?
- That the critical reference groups they are intended to serve are completely happy with them (or would be if they knew about them!).
- That they are internally consistent, logical, unambivalent, and unambiguous?
- That everyone is completely committed to all of them?
- That the community needs that they address haven't changed at all since they were written?

Yes, Yes, Yes! Terrific—you're perfect! No need to change as yet. On the other hand, if you have been chuckling out loud, then you might be remembering: how the new committee threw together the objectives one night; or a consultant came in to do the service agreement; or your service manager met with the funding body and, after endless debate and discussion, you 'got up' a few good objectives and you let 'them' get up some of theirs for the sake of peace and to get the funding application or service agreement in before the closing date; or how the objectives were made so vague and general no one could disagree, or so ambitious as to be unachievable; or how the terminology and needs addressed have already become outdated by subsequent events and trends; or how the pressures of everyday work have meant there hasn't been a chance of doing some of the planned activities.

Yet there should be no embarrassment about change and there ought to be nothing wrong with disagreement between people in a service (conflict being one sign of freedom). We should remember that in terms of the ongoing evaluation research cycle (see the wall chart in the back of the book), the goals and objectives that are a result of going round the cycle once are, in practice, merely theoretical predictions (if we do x, y, z, then needs will be met). They are only as reliable as the research that led to them, and moreover depend on no changes in the original conditions. It is only when we put them to the test of practice in the light of the higher purposes or broader philosophical values of the critical reference group that we can see if we've actually got things right, and how we need to adapt further.

As the slogan goes: 'The future is made, not predicted'—so we *must* retain a capacity to reform, change, develop and improve or else risk the same ossification that the community workers of the 1960s and 1970s were objecting to in the services of the 1940s and 1950s. And this means treating service goals, objectives and targets as valuable expressions of intention and purpose but as always *provisional* and not fixed for all time. If they are provisional then they are 'alive'. They can be discussed until there is consensus. And once there is consensus we can regularly check to see the consensus is sustained.

A drawback of audit review evaluation is that it can result in a preoccupation with measuring the discrepancy between formal objectives and practice. Some services have taken the opportunity of annual service agreements to adjust aims and activities to be more and more modest or achievable to make their 'performance' apparent—while avoiding the harder and more risky business of innovating to do better.

An open inquiry evaluation can offer to break some of the bands of this iron cage of overly rationalistic audit review evaluation, and free up a more positive frame of mind devoted to solving pressing problems and developing exciting new solutions.

While it is often an enjoyable, reassuring and largely valuable exercise when one first goes through an exercise like that sketched in Diagram 2, a drawback of audit review-type evaluation is that it can eventually feel somewhat rigid, limited, even mechanistic, and can be tedious about detail to the point of boredom. It is actually quite hard—even while worthwhile—to have to consider every little element of a service, especially all the bits that are going well enough and would otherwise be taken for granted. (It would be a bit like being stopped to evaluate your reading speed and comprehension levels every time you asked yourself whether you were enjoying reading a novel.)

Sometimes this kind of evaluation—such as that implicit in a service agreement—also becomes repetitive or confusing as each part of a service is considered under several different headings in regard to its contributions to several different objectives. It is rare that one service or even a part of a service is only meeting one objective particularly if an integrated approach is highly valued (possibly as an objective!). This might make audit review-type evaluations messy, but the messiness may actually be in exchange for meaningfulness. Alternatively, to be accomplished strictly within its own relentless logic, it calls for a mind a little like a computer. Minds not quite so logically programmed can get into terrible messes, sometimes mixing up objectives with principles of philosophy, or indicators with aims, and so on.

Yet, despite all the massive detail, and attention to systematically and logically evaluating 'all' elements of a service, the more glaring problem with evaluating a service against its objectives is that almost all the really interesting, colourful, 'thick', rich and juicy fabric of a service may actually lie outside the written-down objectives.

To give an example: if you were to evaluate this book, *Everyday Evaluation on the Run*, there are an enormous number of things that might come to mind:

- How it makes you feel, what it touches off in you, where it connects, where it doesn't.
- The language, terminology, grammar.
- The appearance of the book, the colours, typeface.
- Observations about the cartoons.
- The style of writing, the examples used.
- Whether you knew any of the people in the acknowledgements, what you think of the women to whom it is dedicated.
- Comparisons you make between it and *Do It Yourself Social Research*.
- Reflections on other evaluation literature you might have read

. . . and you would barely have touched the surface of the colossal array of potential 'data' and 'evidence' on which you might quite unconsciously be drawing to evaluate it.

If you took longer (or I interviewed you!), you might expand into considering:

- Its use in your own workplace or when evaluating services you have used or situations you have been in.
- Some other people who could use it, or who might find it difficult.
- If you had already talked to others who had read it you might recall their comments and compare them with your own thoughts. They might have mentioned its size and thickness, or cost, or value to students, or things it hadn't even occurred to you to think of

and so on and on.

From this wide range of potential aspects, you might volunteer some that you had particularly noticed which relate to your needs and interests. This would give strong clues about what is of value or not of value. This approach, by inquiring about only those elements of *interest*, could then focus the evaluation on the elements needing change or replication. On the other hand, if you wanted to do a really thorough open inquiry evaluation, you could ask, 'What do you think' of all or many of the widest possible range of aspects.

Both these exercises ('What did you think of the book?' and 'What did you think of this aspect of the book, and that aspect of the book, and this, and this, and this, and that, and that, and that . . .') would give you a grounded evaluation from the reader's own perspective. You could then extract their purposes and intentions and compare them with your own.

If, however, you started with your purposes and intentions and only checked for these ('We set out to do x and y and z: did you experience x, did you achieve y, and was z understood?') you may well have missed out on valuable insights about values, needs and interests you had not realised were there but were not catered for.

Sometimes our objectives are relatively cryptic—particularly those for more-distant audiences such as funding bodies. For this book there were four simple operational objectives (or targets):

1 To write a book with the title *Everyday Evaluation on the Run*.
2 To have it in camera-ready form for the printer by a specified date.
3 To print 5000 copies.
4 And to have it purchased (including by critical reference groups).

The answers to a basic evaluation of the success of these objectives are, more or less, 'Yes', 'three months late', 'Yes, plus a further 5000 copies in the second reprint' and 'Yes'. Evaluation of this kind strikes many agencies as not quite getting at the full meaning of their work. It is perhaps a little like describing Beethoven's Fifth Symphony as 22 minutes and 19 seconds long! Now if you're a central program manager who has to ensure that a performance of five pieces of music will fit into the program time, then this may be the only evaluation that is required. But if you're asking about the general value of the piece to an audience, then something of the 'colour' and meaning may have been lost! We don't actually know from this exercise what the value of these things are—except by reference to the framework of philosophy and goals based on previously generated theory (If this . . . , then that . . .).

The flaw in assuming that one's operationalisation of objectives will necessarily bring about one's higher purposes or intentions might also be illustrated by the example of this book. It turned out that writing a popular and accessible book on evaluation was more difficult and time-consuming than originally thought. Ideally it should have been left to develop to a further stage, however, the funding service agreement set tight limits around it and constrained its capacity to meet its overall purposes and guiding goal.

Alternatively, you might have proceeded to set objectives (and indicators, and measurable targets) for every one of the large range of possible aspects (listed in point form above). Yet would one necessarily want to record formally *all* this mass of details as part of a rational and extensive standards or objectives-based evaluation framework at all, much less in advance? Or would this be a bit like counting all the leaves to know if it is autumn?! Perhaps too much rationality of this kind locks us too tightly into a new iron cage.

As well, even if any or all of these tightly prescribed objectives were achieved, this may *not* guarantee their value. And if they *weren't* achieved, it does not mean this was necessarily a bad outcome. This is the problem of a false positive or false negative.

Often a service will generate an activity which will suddenly take off and head in a really brilliant direction. When evaluated against its formal objectives, such a development may be merely recorded as relevant to objective 'A', or it may even go unrecorded for want of a relevant category. But if the tight restriction of pre-existing audit review evaluation could be released, and a lot of attention devoted to that single successful instance, enormous ground might be covered that might have relevant repercussions for other areas of the service and may even lead to new or reframed objectives.

For example, a service may contribute a stall to a local community festival. If evaluated against a formal objective (and listed in terms of a service agreement performance indicator), it may appear as a rather weak 'community education' intervention. On the other hand, if it is examined for what effects (related to unexplicated intentions) it might have had, those who sat on the stall all day might have returned with insightful stories drawn from the half dozen remarkable encounters with several members of the public who might never otherwise have approached the services with their stories. These stories may have been tip-offs regarding the parlous state of unmet needs in a local private nursing home for the aged, or the germ of an idea about the possible volume of hoarded, unused and dangerous prescribed drugs in people's medicine cabinets at home.

Rather than the stall educating the community, the community had used it to educate the service! This insight might lead to the next stall being explicitly run as a 'person in the street' study, or being replaced by an even more effective way of tapping community views. As well, another consequence may have been to have the stall appear in the background of a photo in the local paper the following week—reminding a single member of the public to want to join up. Again, when measured against a numerical 'performance indicator', it may not look very valuable. A manager may even move to abandon it in future. But say this single new recruit goes on to lead a successful campaign against the dumping of toxic chemicals in the local creek. And what if, with that new-found confidence, she stands for local government? It might then be interesting to explore what it was about the stall that encouraged residents to talk, what characteristics of the workers allowed them to listen and hear, etc.

It is this kind of locally contextualised, meaningful information that may allow a more valid evaluation to be done of that service's activities, yet one can see why such grounded material is both so important and also so elusive:

- Effects may be long term.
- Effects may only be known about by 'chance' (or by having excellent local contacts) or be intuited.
- Effects may only be connected to the original activity by a fine thread that may meander and not follow straight cause–effect lines.
- Effects may never be able to be traced, but only anticipated 'in theory' (the theory having already been established in painstaking practice, involving time-consuming and expensive follow-up that cannot be repeated over and over again).

There is the now-famous example of the American War on Poverty's pre-school children's Operation Headstart, followed by Operation Homestart—which was evaluated as ineffective using an experimental design within several years of implementation, and subsequently abandoned. Twenty years later the evidence has come in that children who went through those programs have done significantly better in terms of education and job success. We don't require every teacher to check on their students twenty years down the track (interesting though it may be to be invited to their pupil's school reunions!), yet we can be more or less confident of the value of a year of teaching in the here and now because we have already established strong theory from previous cycles of evaluative research pitched at the appropriate level and the appropriate relationships between practices.

The Australian example of Community Health Centres being evaluated several years after inception and shown not to have made an impact also underlines this point. There is an additional point that can be made here which is not so much that such services are unevaluable (until they have operated for twenty years) although this may also be true—but that there are varying indicators of success, and that these indicators match differing levels of intention. As a writer I check today's output against an intention to produce so many pages about such-and-such a topic—not against whether I have managed to demystify modern Western science to statistically significant extents! If a community group is funded to produce a newsletter for Heart Week, we don't usefully evaluate it by checking the blood pressure of the population before and after its production.

Drawbacks of open inquiry evaluation

The fundamental drawback of open inquiry evaluation lies in its capacity to overlook matters that are not obvious to the inquirer. Audit review evaluation will ask about 'all' elements (that are covered by existing intentions), and if those existing objectives are comprehensive, then the evaluation will also be comprehensive. However, open inquiry evaluation is generally only able to be problem-focused. This makes it terribly important to ask, 'Whose problems?' and 'Are the problems important?'. If the problems are those of staff, then they must be checked to see if they reflect what is problematic to critical reference groups. Or if the problems are minor compared to the 'white horse on the table' that everyone is too polite or too afraid to mention, then the evaluation may also be misdirected. Or if the voice of the critical reference group is not being heard, then the inquiry might also miss its mark.

This again emphasises the importance of genuinely admitting critical reference groups and those with other relevant perspectives to guide the process and direction of inquiry. Users can introduce perceptions of situations that might never otherwise occur to staff; and can alert to discrepancies of priority or presumption that also might not have been obvious to staff.

Open inquiry approaches to evaluation require tolerance of considerable uncertainty, and a realisation that evaluation essentially remains a matter of judgement. We can perhaps see why quantification is so strongly associated with audit review styles of evaluation. When one has firmly decided on clear objectives, and may even have converted the signs of achievement into clear performance indicators, and even worked out precise standards to be achieved, then one can try to detail with considerable precision the extent of compliance (or discrepancy). Sometimes this precision can be expressed without scaling or ranking, such as where questions call for Yes/No answers. For example, if the standard for a 'participation' objective is the presence of a community Committee of Management—it either exists or it doesn't. Or it can be expressed in terms of how often or how many (people through the door, projects accomplished, etc); or performances and actions can be ranked, graded, scaled, etc., or scored.

For much everyday evaluation, a simple sense or feeling of discrepancy may be adequate (like the shepherd who knows there's a sheep missing without counting them all, or the service user who knows she is in pain or is being treated disrespectfully without needing a device to measure it). However, whenever the extent, degree or amount of discrepancy between a goal or standard and an actual performance becomes crucial, then human beings prefer the reassurance of certainty. Even when such matters of judgement remain matters of judgement, we seem to like to imagine that they aren't! For example, when there's huge prize money at stake, we like to 'know' that the swimmer really 'won' the electronically measured race at 24.003621 seconds and the swimmer who 'only' got there at 24.003622 seconds was definitely second.

When there are scarce budget funds to be distributed among a lot of starving services, the apportioning-type evaluation that says that this service is a '6.3' and the one that loses half its budget was only a '5.8' gives us a sense of 'the right thing' having been done. Usually, but not always, there seems to be safety in numbers (especially if you're a 6.3).* Objectifying in this way may also make it easier for managers to avoid being confronted by the moral and ethical implications of their judgements.

If the managers having to make these budgetary decisions cannot get out and about to observe services first-hand (and acquire direct naturalistic data), nor have in place a local and regional network of people who can reliably compare their naturalistic data, then they may rely more and more on abstracted numerical data. The further consequences of this may be twofold:

- Those services that are longer-established and have refined their practices so tightly as to be able to time tasks and cost them to the smallest unit and attach a numerical value related to an assessment of needs will do well (even if the practices are no longer worthwhile or meritorious in relation to new more relevant values relating to current community needs).
- Those services that are newest and most innovative (and may be addressing vital and creative ways of doing things), but are still charting their paths and working out what counts as success and what doesn't, will be most vulnerable.

In Canada, the first services to be cut in a tight economic climate just happened to be the most recently established: services such as those experimenting with self-determination, empowerment and participation of native Indian and minority groups; and low-income groups. There are similar experiences in Australia, the UK and USA as well.

Nevertheless, even the newest and most creative projects can, with some modest assistance, self-evaluate around their own particular signs of success that are meaningful within local contexts. Over time, and with consensus discussion, these can form into more reliable and comparable signs.

However, not even the most useful evaluative statistics can necessarily be guaranteed a guernsey!** Even when abstracted numbers do bear meaning, they may be rejected—or abolished! For some years, through the Australian Federal Government's WELSTAT program (a kind of mega social welfare standardised statistics-collection agency), national emergency relief statistics were collected. Every agency in the country painstakingly kept records of age, sex, family status and income source of every applicant. Such data enabled the often-quoted statistic that nine out of every ten applicants had been or were awaiting a Department of Social Security pension or benefit. The collection of these statistics was defunded in June 1988.

Guides 5 and 6 on pages 53 and 54 summarise the previous discussion.

Questions that address each of the two approaches

To return to our point about doing both approaches, comprehensive evaluation would pursue two sets of questions with both service users and service providers. Note these are not the precise questions you or your group might ask (or might ask of yourselves)! They would have to be tailored to your own situation, and they can all be expanded or contracted in detail depending on your time and purposes. What this section tries to convey is the logic of the two different kinds of questions that flow from the two approaches that have been discussed.

With users or critical reference groups

OPEN INQUIRY QUESTIONS

These are the kinds of questions which ask, 'What is the value of this service or activity to you?', 'What is not of value to you?' or 'Is the service or activity working for you?' ('What works?' or 'What doesn't work?').

If these kinds of questions are too broad, you could then break down the service or activity into aspects or elements—'What is the value of X to you?' or 'What is not of value to you about X?' (or Y or Z) or 'Is element X working?', 'Is element Y working?', 'Is element Z working?' and so on.

Then you would pursue context by asking, 'Why is that?', 'Can you talk more about that?', etc.

You should get a picture of what is being done (description of activity or service), how this is known (description of the signs) and why it is working or not working (explanation for it). You may need to ask (or ask yourselves) 'Why?' several times to get a full explanation. An example of an exchange that captures all three elements would be:

* Sometimes the ambivalent term 'measures' is used. But this has several possible meanings including:
- Size or quantity.
- Degree, extent, amount.
- Unit of capacity.
- That by which a thing is computed.
- Suitable action.

Unless quantification is intended, less ambivalent terms are 'indicators' or 'signs'.

** Australianism for being included or being given a place in the team (as in winning the right to wear a football team sweatshirt).

GUIDE 5
STRENGTHS AND WEAKNESSES OF THE TWO APPROACHES

	Strengths	Weaknesses
Audit Review	• Will call attention to 'all' matters previously thought to be valued/required—and submit them for attention and check if they have been implemented. Within this framework it can give a sense of illumination to areas that may have been overlooked or forgotten.	• Doesn't discriminate between still-valuable and appropriate matters and now not-so-valuable and even irrelevant and outdated matters (doesn't identify how to change/improve; may lead to preoccupation with mere appearances of performance).
	• Validity will be high if prior research base was strong.	• Validity will be low if prior research establishing their value was flimsy, or thin on evidence, etc.
	• Can be comprehensive and reassure that much is being done.	• Can be tedious and wastefully time-consuming.
	• Will identify matters not yet attended to within the existing framework (gaps).	• Will not identify (without resort to inquiry mode) why these matters have not been implemented, or whether they should have been, or still should be; nor identify any gaps outside the framework (for example, unmet needs).
	• Can affirm previously-reached agreements and consensus; can strengthen collective sense of direction.	• Can't assist much if the objectives don't represent consensus or effective agreement, or if they are only superficial, or 'paper over' conflict, or if the certainty is trivial, or irrelevant or meaningless or leaves out the issues of critical reference groups.
	• Can feel very comfortable.	• Can give a feeling of complacency. May encourage inappropriate conserving of the status quo.
Open inquiry	• Problem-identifying focus increases the chances of problem-solving outcomes, change for improvement and in areas identified as important.	• Problem-focus may overlook important matters that no-one has yet identified as a problem.
	• Assists innovation and creativity and dynamism in special areas (depth).	• May not be systematic and comprehensive for all areas (scope).
	• Sense of exhilaration at a journey into the unknown.	• Involves uncertainty, suspension of judgement, lack of clarity, and possibly apparent 'irrationality', disagreement and conflict.
	• Meaningful rather than abstract, involving rather than excluding.	
	• Identifies what is of value, merit, worth or significance.	

Q. *'Can you say what the value of the self-help group has been for you (or us)?'*

A. 'Well, the meetings of the self-help group I attend are good.'

Q. *'Can you say why?'*

A. 'Oh well, I suppose it's helped me recover from my grief quite a lot.'

Q. *'What are the signs of that for you?'*

A. 'Um well, I feel much brighter the day after the meetings! And it just feels less alone when your thoughts drift back—you just know that others have the same thoughts, and that you can move on from them. Some like me take longer, but there's a woman at the group—she only came once—but she's sort of my personal inspiration. I just remember how she's handled it. It gives me a picture of where I want to get to.'

Q. *'What about the different aspects of the groups—what about the group leader? What about the time, the venue, the topics, etc.?'*

GUIDE 6

WHAT TO DO TO IMPROVE THE TWO APPROACHES

AUDIT REVIEW

- When doing audit against objectives, always ensure there is a method of also collecting some records about matters that will require further inquiry, for example, especially where there is feedback about faulty or outdated objectives, problematic implementation that might imply difficulties with current objectives, and matters that are otherwise silent or have no obvious place in the current framework.
- To strengthen chances of validity, put in place a parallel process for open inquiry.
- To mitigate false certainty, recognise the need to move to some kind of change, and publicly identify the existing framework as *provisional* only.
- To overcome tedium and wasteful time consumption, keep a full audit review for only occasional use (for example, annual or two- or even three-yearly), and supplement it with frequent, ongoing, built-in problem-solving inquiry evaluation. Focus annual reviews on the areas for change and improvement that have come out of open inquiry.

OPEN INQUIRY

- To identify important matters that no one has yet seen as problematic and touch base with the critical reference group: work out ways for them to speak in their own undistorted voice and be heard without too many intervening sound barriers; encourage and respect even unconventional and (in the first place) unsystematic forms of input; don't be too quick to judge it as unrepresentative—even the most lone consumer voice may turn out to be the canary in the mine; later you can check the extent of the view ('Somebody has suggested that . . . What do you think?).

  Seek out comparable situations or groups: have they identified problems you haven't? (Again, check out the value to your critical reference groups). Draw on as many sources of different perceptions as you can: read the literature, think up analogies or metaphors that might be useful.
- Evaluate against higher-order intentions: for example, you may be able to tick off successfully that you have put an equal opportunity officer in every TAFE (Technical and Further Education) college—but has it really decreased women's inequality?

- To counter lack of thoroughness, make sure that, periodically, a systematic review *is* done, but probably less often rather than more. Constant, clarifying, problem-solving evaluation shapes an organisation in the right direction and decreases the chances of elements of a whole enterprise ending up in the wrong place.
- To tolerate uncertainty, recognise the desire to move to some level of agreement and treat what is possible as provisional. Strengthen the chances that uncertain local efforts are known about by those who require greater certainty so that some kind of interim informed judgement can be made about their value. For example, a group may be reluctant to say precisely when a project will be completed or what its effects are, but it can be known that those doing it have a track record for completing projects, or it is known that the project is addressing a notoriously difficult but vital topic. Remember that the more innovative the effort, the longer it will need to prove itself—possibly even years or decades. Measuring Aboriginal blood pressure before and after a twelve month project where a community worker is attempting to assist Aboriginal communities identify the conditions for improving health may be unhelpful. If it took 200 years of disempowering by white societies, it may take 200 years of resourcing to show identifiable effects of effort. Generate fuller descriptive narratives where abstracted statistics do not make sense.

There may be context matters that need to be clarified ('Which self-help group?'; 'How did you come to join it?'; 'What were the signs or effects of the grief?', etc.). Or you might want to get more detail on how often the person comes to the group and so on, but the focus of all contextualising questions is to further illuminate the value of the group to them. The answers imply their own goals and objectives as well as higher purposes, intentions and background needs.

Then draw out what was or would be desired and why: 'What would you (or we) have preferred?', or 'What would be preferable in future?', or 'What would you (or we) like to see change?', or 'How could it be improved?' Again, ask about 'Why?', that is, what effects might be expected, and why these changes might be improvements. These questions even further clarify the implicit goals and objectives as well as higher purposes, intentions and background needs.

AUDIT REVIEW QUESTIONS

These kinds of questions test for whether the objectives of those who planned or carried out the service or activity were realised. You might say: 'The service or activity was trying to do x, y, z. Can you (or we) say whether you think these things are happening or have happened?'. At the same time, open inquiry questions could be asked about whether these objectives are of relevance or value to the person: 'Can you say whether that was a worthwhile thing to try to achieve?'; 'What else would be of importance or more important to you?'. For example:

Q. *The self-help group's organiser is trying to provide a group that achieves a number of purposes. Please comment on the following*:

(a) *Have you found the group friendly and approachable? (How much, in what ways? etc.)*
Is this important to you?

(b) *Have you found you have learned more about the condition/situation, etc. (that is common to the group)?*
Is learning more about it of interest to you?

(c) *Do you have contact with any of the group members outside meetings?*
Would contact outside the group be of value to you?

(d) *Do you feel more in control of your situation as a result of being in the group?*
Is that important to you?

Finally, examine any similarities and/or differences between the two kinds of material resulting.

With providers and other parties

The format for questions is the same for providers and other parties as it is for users or critical reference groups above—with the exception that they must be in the context of clarifying whose valuing is sought.

OPEN INQUIRY QUESTIONS

As soon as you move to questioning providers or other parties, you are asking about their perceptions of value that may be judged by criteria which relate to themselves *or* to co-workers, *or* to funders or administrators *or* to users or critical reference groups. There are three ways of approaching this:

- You can either frame all questions in terms of the critical reference groups on the assumption that this is the fundamental purpose of their activity (for example, 'Is this service working well for the critical reference group?').
- You can ask for people's own evaluations and then ask questions to identify who are the reference groups implied in the answers. You may then need to ask explicitly about value to critical reference groups.
- You can ask what value they think it has for the critical reference group, then ask what value they think the critical reference group would place on it, then ask what they think any other parties would think of it.

Each of these different approaches reflects different purposes and contexts for asking. You would have to think carefully whether your choice might strengthen the assumption that their effort or work is for critical reference groups, or whether it might strengthen the assumption that other parties can judge what's best for critical reference groups, possibly without reference to or respect for critical reference groups' views.

AUDIT REVIEW/QUESTIONS

These questions are also the same as for users or critical reference groups (as above) but in the context of identifying:

- What are the purposes and intentions ('What are you or were you trying to do?') or what are the goals, objectives, indicators and targets set by *you or your service* that you are using or have been using? ('What did you set out to do/What were you meant to be doing?')
- Are they or were they put into practice (again: in whose eyes—yours? The critical reference groups'? Others'?)—and was this valuable? (This reverts to an *open inquiry* question.) Break it down into separate components and ask about each one—see Diagram 2 ('Did you do X?; Did you do Y?'; etc.—and 'Was this valuable, important, worthwhile?' etc.).

DOING
EVALUATION

chapter 4

DEVELOPING A CULTURE OF EVALUATION

INTRODUCTION

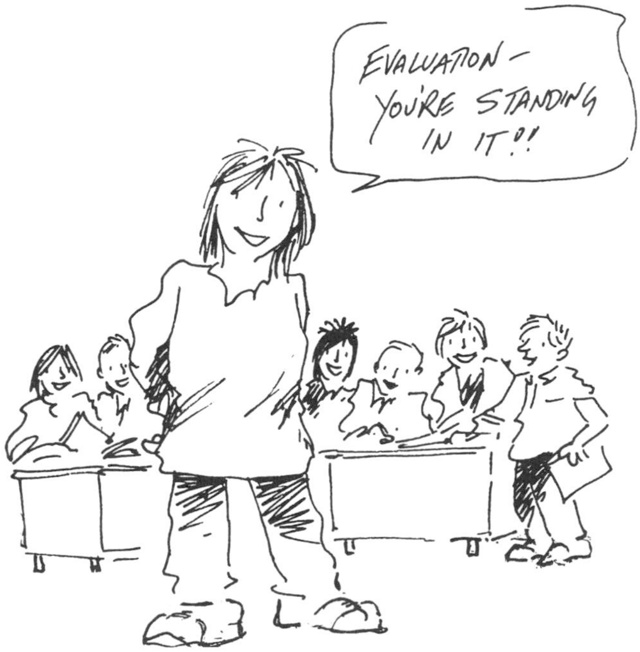
EVALUATION – YOU'RE STANDING IN IT!!

Now where to start? Well, the best place to start is where you are right now! You've already been acquiring all kinds of insights and understandings about your situation or service—right from when you had your first experience of it. Every day we take *new* actions—whether they are the same as or different from those taken the day before, we are constantly making decisions about what next to do. Most of us daily do things slightly differently, making regular small adaptations or creative responses to what we do. None of these fruits of our 'everyday-type evaluation' should be wasted.

But we're doing or experiencing heaps of things! Some of them seem trivial, some are big and deep. So the first thing is to have a think about the different levels or scales of activity and their accompanying different degrees of purpose.

We have seen how we evaluate small pieces of the world all the time: 'Today is going well'; 'That meeting was a disaster'; 'This newspaper had a lot in it'; 'The computer printout was the wrong one'; 'I liked what that woman said'.

We evaluate larger pieces of the world less often: 'This year has been a good year'; 'Our group is, unfortunately, starting to drift apart'; 'This shopping centre seems to be changing'. Similarly, our reasons for evaluating may differ from those for daily problem-solving to those for broader reflect-and-reviews.

Wherever you start, you could reflect for a moment on your starting point's relation to the whole, and then proceed to evaluate it in relation to its level of purpose consistent with that whole. If this balance between level of activity and level of purpose is not achieved, you can find yourself, for example, evaluating this minor piece of a community development process directly against an ultimate purpose of eliminating unemployment, or evaluating this book only against whether it is close to 100 pages long or whether it has improved human services! As mentioned earlier, audit review approaches often scramble levels of purpose or intention with levels of activity (such as when a community group's Heart Week Newsletter is evaluated to see if it brought down the population's blood pressure).

IF I GET THE PHOTOCOPIER FIXED BEFORE LUNCHTIME WILL THAT HELP DECREASE DOMESTIC VIOLENCE IN THE MODERN WESTERN WORLD?

Whether informal and implicit or formal and written-down, these levels need to be identified so that activities or services are evaluated as successful or not at their level. At the same time there can be recourse to higher and lower levels to check for consistency and effectiveness. For example, say at a lower level of 'operationalisation' we find that people are reporting happily having completed a course of learning about community living for people with disabilities. The material was relevant and the students come away knowing how to live in the community—but did they then move out into their own flats or houses? And if they did—were they able to live happily as ordinary community members? And so on—up to the highest levels of purpose.

Now as noted before, this is *not* to say that a single evaluation needs to accomplish all of this in one study. There may well be a complete fallacy in saying that if the students didn't move out into the community, then the course had failed. (This indicates the philosophical problem of thinking that things clearly 'cause' other things.) There may have been a problem with Real Estate Agents' practices. It may also be wrong to assume that if the students *did* move out, then the course had worked. Perhaps they learned how from another source. Evidence needs to be sought for signs that the learning in the course related to the immediate purposes of the course (whether expressed as objectives or not). Diagram 5 (on the following page) illustrates this matter of 'levels' of study and evaluation.

Keeping in mind this matter of levels of purpose (which derive from and express values and interests), it may be helpful to think of these levels as corresponding with levels of practice. For example, we would expect to change our fundamental purposes rarely. Maybe only a few times in a lifetime. Our big goals may last for a period of many years. Our more immediate objectives may be on a scale of one to three years or so. Our short-term aims may be for a span of months. Our very immediate purposes may be to do things that are this month's, this week's, or today's tasks.

It is important to practice continual cycles of reflection, clarification of what it is we value and why, and the reaching of agreement about how we might change and improve what we are doing in the light of this. We can also practise reaching conclusions about what we are doing that is going well and should be sustained. This can be practised on *all* our actions, from today's right through to this week's, this month's, this year's, this decade's and this lifetime's. What we reflect on at each of these levels of time is the corresponding level of practice in relation to its place in the hierarchy of immediate and broader purposes and intentions. This means always keeping an eye out for the big picture—while breaking the big picture down into little bits that are consistent with achieving it.

At present there is a bewildering range of ways presented for people to carry out evaluation, such as summative, formative, input, process, output, or outcome evaluation (see Chapter 5 for these and many others!). Many of these kinds of evaluation actually focus more on a particular stage of the matter being evaluated and split it off as a separate thing. They might talk of doing 'an' evaluation, as if it is always just a step, stage, or finite action.

It may be more useful, in terms of trying to build in evaluation as a more naturalistic element of ordinary activities, to talk of developing a 'culture of evaluation'. By this I mean—just as we might talk about an 'ethnic culture'—it might be useful to think of evaluation as activities and a way of thinking permeating every kind and level of our actions, and giving constant rise to particular kinds of questions and observations and, it is hoped, regular spirited exchanges between 'members' of that culture! The following kinds of opportunities could be seized, which, if considered 'in toto', might comprise a comprehensive program of built-in evaluation:

- **Daily informal personal reflection**
- **Weekly spans**
- **Special effort evaluations of particular aspects of practice or activities**
- **Monthly collective problem-pooling sessions**
- **Annual what-have-we-achieved and where-are-we-heading-next-year workshops**
- **Comprehensive program 'stocktakes' every three to ten years or more**

As noted in the fieldwork section of Chapter 2—for the practical purpose of designing evaluation activities (from a tiny scaled-down version for daily personal reflection, right up to a large scaled-up version for a major program stocktake)—and to

DIAGRAM 5
LEVELS OF EVALUATION RELATED TO PURPOSES

Time Scale	Open inquiry questions	Example	Audit review questions
large-scale long-term	What do we ultimately want to work towards with all of our effort over the lifetime of an organisation or a community of interest?	Action Research Issues Association's purpose: The strengthening of an emancipatory and just culture in which situations identified by critical reference groups (e.g. resulting from discrimination or disability) can be overcome.	Have we worked towards our mission? Have we contributed to strengthening an emancipatory and just culture, etc.? (Remembering that many others are taking different actions to achieve the same ends)
	What do we intend to do to achieve this ultimate state?	To strengthen new paradigm science — viz participatory action (or critical interpretive) research methodology.	
	What will we do to achieve this fundamental purpose?	Develop, support, promote and popularise this methodology.	Have we contributed to our goals?
	What practical actions will we aim to carry out to meet these goals?	Develop models and methods and collect good examples of practice. Publish and circulate accessible written materials about them. Set up discussions and networks for the exchange of ideas and experience of them. Assist those with a critical reference group perspective to carry them out — either directly or by providing or referring them to other resources, etc.	Have we been meeting our aims?
	What can we do to meet these aims?	Establish an association of members who meet. Set up a centre which seeks funding for specific projects in each of these areas (e.g. write a book on self evaluation, run workshops, have a phone advisory service, establish networks of Friends of Participatory Action Research, Researchers in Community Health, Teachers of Participatory Action Research, contribute sessions to courses and conferences, publish directories, prepare annotated bibliographies, write articles, work with particular groups to assist them to their own participatory action research).	Have we met our objectives? Have we met our targets?
medium-scale medium-term	What do we need to do to realise these objectives?	Call together an initial meeting of interested people ... thereafter the detailed description of all the levels and increasingly tiny actions needed to put into practice all of the above would take up pages and pages rather than the single paragraph available! Nevertheless, every activity objective can be broken down into its constituent bits — ranging right down to the making of phone calls and buying pens to writing the submissions, to paying bills, painting furniture, keeping records and learning new word processing packages, to booking rooms, designing letterhead, getting cost quotes, having meetings, buying stationery, keeping ledgers, paying the rent, writing more funding submissions, doing back-ups, reading reports, correcting drafts, making tea and coffee, recycling paper, fixing the stapler, fixing the printer, talking to groups, making appointments, changing appointments, drawing posters, writing pamphlets, preparing minutes, doing mail outs, talking to visitors, travelling to and fro, writing invoices and receipts, talking over dinner meetings, looking up the dictionary, dialling phone numbers, speaking to audiences, assembling overhead projectors, using the photocopier, fixing the photocopier, writing reports, reading articles, reading books, writing commentaries, getting them typed, arranging chairs for a meeting, questioning people, observing, listening, fixing the photocopier, making diagrams, examining maps, looking at the clocks, looking up the phone book, answering the phone, emptying the rubbish and writing things on the whiteboard, etc.	Are the minutiae of the things we do related to our objectives?
small-scale/ short-term			

An alternate 'open inquiry' mode of arriving at purposes is to commence by asking 'Why are we doing this?' And then working up through all the answers, asking 'Why?' then 'Why?' and 'Why?' until the largest scale and longest term purposes are arrived at.

While it is appropriate to check that highly specific actions are still identifiably consistent with the highest level of purposes, it is ineffective and inappropriate to try to test them by seeking direct evidence that fixing the photocopier 'caused' a more emancipatory culture! Instead, by establishing a network of corresponding assumptions, each 'knot' in the net needs only to establish its relationship to the 'knots' closest to it.

reiterate, we need to be able to assemble the following for each of these levels of activity:

Q. *What are our experiences and what is their value?*

This involves being able to get a picture of each element of what is being evaluated (who, does what, to whom, when, where, why and how), and getting a sense of why these elements have come to be as they are (history, context, rationale, purposes).

At the same time, it involves being able to get a picture of what everyone thinks of or feels about each of these elements (the value of who does what, to whom, when, where, why and how and with what effects—intended or unintended, desired or undesired), making sure that the views of the critical reference group are fully heard and recorded, as well as those of all others with an interest in the evaluation or that which is being evaluated. This involves getting people to identify and describe the discrepancies they experience between the 'existing' and what they 'wanted' (or expected)—to the extent needed to satisfy the audience.

Q. *What are valued experiences and how can we experience them in future?*

This involves getting a set of ideas, images and descriptions of what would be better—and why. That is, it involves ways of working out how to get from the actual 'here' to the desired 'there' that are practicable, realistic, and about which people are enthusiastic.

DAILY INFORMAL PERSONAL REFLECTION

Daily informal personal evaluation is the essential basic building-block of any successful self-evaluating group, service or organisation. Groups, services and organisations don't actually evaluate—the individuals in them do. Yet evaluation, even 'personal' evaluation, is always social. Every sharp observation we might make, every insight we might generate, and every adjustment we might make to our individual practice, will always have its roots in the common social soil of language, ideas, skills, and practices that are shared by us with workmates, friends, families and neighbours, past and present.

The better we are at daily informal reflection and the more of us that do it, the better we will—as part of the groups and the services we work with—be able to think clearly about the value of what we are doing and wanting to do collectively. In turn, the better this effort is at the local level, the better the quality of information that regional and central levels will be able to rely on.

We need to make time and space in our busy lives for this sort of reflective activity. One form of daily reflective evaluation is to stop, whenever we feel either uncomfortable, uneasy, or any other 'problematic' feeling, or alternatively, whenever we feel inexplicably or surprisingly pleased, happy or satisfied. Stop and ask:

> *'What happened?' or 'What's troubling me here?'*
> *'What is happening, and what had I expected or wanted?'*
> *'What was the context?'*
> *'Why are things not right? (or amazingly right!)'*
> *'What must I have expected? Why didn't what I expected, happen?'*
> *'Should it have happened—or was it better it didn't?'*
> *'How can I avoid or change or repeat the situation next time?'*

But how can we see clearly that which we are so closely involved in? Seeing the trees *and* the

...I THINK I SENSE A DISCREPANCY COMING ON...
VERY URGENT
WAS URGENT
URGENT - NOW HISTORICAL RECORDS

forests, seeing the remarkable individual instances as well as seeing the unremarkable patterns, trying to be frogs jumping into pots of hot water and jumping out rather than slowly being boiled alive!—these are the knacks we need to cultivate. Noticing the discrepancies, seeing, hearing, listening, observing. Then thinking quietly about it. Reflecting. Asking ourselves, 'What is making me feel uneasy here?', or 'Why does this seem such a surprise?'. Talking about it among ourselves. Working up hunches. Testing them out. Asking questions. Trying out our ideas. Running them past each other. Modifying them. Watching some more. Observing. Listening. Hearing.

The wise old owl sat on the oak,
The more he sat, the less he spoke.
The less he spoke the more he heard,
We should be like that wise old bird!

Another form of daily reflective evaluation is to routinely try to 'problematise' things that aren't obviously making us feel uneasy (or elated). Think about what times in an ordinary day's activity would be good to stop and reflect. Perhaps to write down some of your thoughts and observations. After a meeting? After an interview? After a visit? After a class? Even if only for a minute or two. Stop and ask:

'How did that go? Why?'
'Did it go as I expected or intended? Why?'
'Is there anything I could do? Or do differently? Or change?'

Give it a go! Start with the things you can see around you. Some candidates for daily on-the-run reflection might include:

1 The filing system that has spread out of the files and is creeping up the walls.
2 The constantly ringing phone that never lets any work get done.
3 The huge pile of daily tasks that never get done.
4 The delete key on your computer you keep mistaking for the 'save file' key!

Reflection

For each of these tiny pots of hot water, firstly we frogs have to *notice* the discrepancy! We have to actually let it stop us in our tracks, and then plan to do something about it. Articulate it as a question: 'Is this situation not working well?', or 'Is this the best way of doing this?' Secondly, we have to ask what is the value of this, especially to those whose interests are to be served—how does it assist or impede our critical reference groups getting what they need? What *do* they need?—the information buried two feet in the pile? Do they need to talk on the phone (or would an alternative be just as effective)—or do they need us to be doing the 'work' more? Does mixing up the computer keys slow you down and leave less time for other work with your groups?

Work out which are the best questions

1 What is the value of all these files? What are they? What have I been saving and why (describe context, history, etc.)? How do I feel about the situation? What would be my preferred vision? Do I need all these files? If yes, do I need more filing cabinets? If no, which should go out, which stay? Why?
2 What is the value of these phone calls? What do they consist of? How do I feel about them? Why does the phone ring (context of calls)? What can I envisage as a better alternative? What is the comparative value of the work that doesn't get done? If other work is as or more important than calls, can I do both? (Or decrease the calls?) How?
3 The huge pile of daily tasks—what does it consist of? What is the value of each? How do I feel about my workload? What would I prefer? Can I list them in order of value? Do they all need to be done? If yes—how? If no—how can I let some of them go?
4 Is this mistake slowing me down? Yes! How can I avoid mixing up these two keys on my computer?

Do the 'fieldwork'

1 Take time to examine either the whole pile or a typical sample of it. Assess each item. While you're doing that, reflect on how you came to be in this mess! Remember what propelled you to keep adding to the pile (context, history). Check the state of your filing cabinets.
2 Log a day's phone calls. Collect information on the time of call, length of call, who called and why. Do this in conjunction with evaluation 'project' number (3) below, on your daily task load.
3 Examine the evidence of a day's tasks. How do you know what you have to do in a day? Keep a list for a few days. Are all the day's tasks listed in one place?
4 Observe how it is that you hit the key by mistake.

Analyse the 'data' or your experiences

1 You decide some of it is useful but most is worthless. You also conclude you thought some

of it *might* be useful for 'later'—but you didn't know what for, so didn't know where to put it. The filing cabinet turned out to be nearly full and you'd never ordered a new one. Or you conclude you could have filed it all, but other things seemed more important at the time.

2 You are surprised to find the 'constant' ringing was only eight calls. Almost all of them were directly important to your work—indeed they appear to be your most crucial way of operating, (information in, information out). Only one was super urgent. You realise that the most stress comes from the first two hours of the day.

3 You ask two other people like you what they make of your day's tasks list. They faint at the thought of accomplishing so much/they ask why so many tasks look like they'd take weeks or months rather than a day. You realise why you feel so weighed down.

4 You conclude that if you could somehow mark the 'delete' key, the problem could be solved.

Make recommendations to yourself for action

1 You decide that only some of the information is critical to your activities. For one week, you will try to decide to throw out things that you now realise are highly unlikely to be useful, and you will set aside two hours on Friday afternoon *for sure* to file it all. You order a new filing cabinet. You also decide to spend one hour every Monday morning *for sure* going through the existing files to throw things out. You will try this for three weeks. You write it in your diary. You do not make appointments at the same times.

2 You let your group know that you are going to start early and not take phone calls till 10.00 a.m. You put the message on the answering machine. You learn not to answer the machine for those first two hours while you burn through the most important of your daily tasks.

3 You only put on the daily task list those things you can and should get through in one day. You have a longer term list which you revise each month.

4 You put a red spot sticker on the delete key.

Monitor the action for further discrepancy

1 You find you are getting on top of it—but that it still depends on there not being a crisis or other pressure-of-work that sends filing down the list of priorities. You resolve to be more aware of this and, at the end of the year, set aside time to cull and reorganise the files in the light of changes to the nature of your work.

2 It works. Problem solved.

3 You realise you need a very short daily list and that it would be better to have a list that goes over several weeks. You pencil in a priority number in the left-hand margin against today's items. The longer term list goes over several months, even to a year. Items from this are assessed and transferred to the days-and-weeks list.

4 You have never hit the wrong key again and feel very secure!

Now these examples are a fraction overdone for such personal and micro situations but they show the logic of evaluation. Most everyday evaluation on the run might be even less formal that this. Some evaluations might take a full 30 seconds from start to finish—or even two seconds. The examples above are the closest in a typical line of vision. Try it on more significant matters such as your interaction with group members at meetings, or your choice of reading matter, or your assessment of the uneasy effect a single conversation has just had on you. Try assessing the next new task you are going to carry out—the pamphlet you are about to write, the interview you just conducted, the letter you have just written, the launch for which you are choosing a speaker. From all of this you will reach your own conclusions and develop your own useable 'practice wisdom'!

WEEKLY SPANS

Using the same process of reflection–fieldwork–analysis–action, some of the above might be extended to a weekly review. Things that could do with a slightly longer lapse of time might be the kinds of practices that need longer to reveal themselves, and if one were to introduce change it would take about another week to reveal a range of effects. Good examples might be someone providing care to an older person with Alzheimer's disease, or a young woman seeking help because she is having trouble looking after her new baby, or a teacher with a rowdy classroom, or a community artist working on a mural. The same process applies: the asking of the evaluative questions, the 'touching base' with criteria for success set by the needs of the relevant critical reference groups, the careful observing and documenting of actions and effects or outcomes, the consideration of context, the drawing of conclusions and assessment of possible new actions—with slightly longer for each cycle of inquiry.

With these kinds of practice evaluations, diary-type records might be particularly helpful. Some examples follow.

The teacher consultant's diary

See Diagram 6 (on the following page) for an example of a teacher's journal recording her reflections over a series of several weeks.

DIAGRAM 6
THE TEACHER CONSULTANT'S DIARY

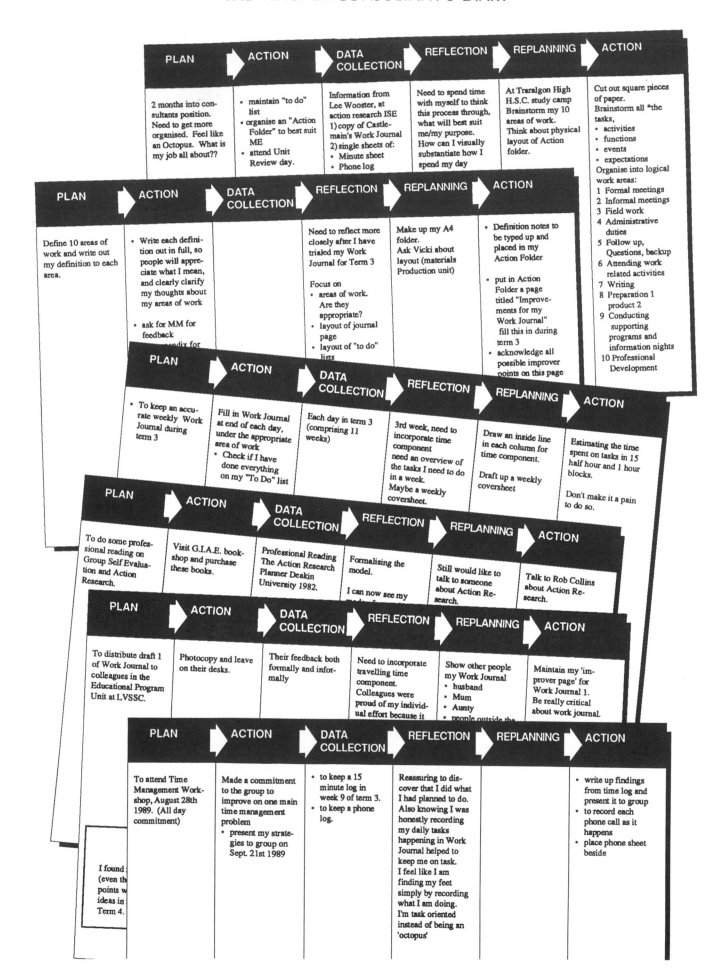

PLAN	ACTION	DATA COLLECTION	REFLECTION	REPLANNING	ACTION
2 months into consultants position. Need to get more organised. Feel like an Octopus. What is my job all about??	• maintain "to do" list • organise an "Action Folder" to best suit ME • attend Unit Review day.	Information from Lee Wooster, at action research ISE 1) copy of Castlemain's Work Journal 2) single sheets of: • Minute sheet • Phone log	Need to spend time with myself to think this process through, what will best suit me/my purpose. How can I visually substantiate how I spend my day	At Traralgon High H.S.C. study camp Brainstorm my 10 areas of work. Think about physical layout of Action folder.	Cut out square pieces of paper. Brainstorm all *the tasks, • activities • functions • events • expectations Organise into logical work areas: 1 Formal meetings 2 Informal meetings 3 Field work 4 Administrative duties 5 Follow up, Questions, backup 6 Attending work related activities 7 Writing 8 Preparation 1 product 2 9 Conducting supporting programs and information nights 10 Professional Development

PLAN	ACTION	DATA COLLECTION	REFLECTION	REPLANNING	ACTION
Define 10 areas of work and write out my definition to each area.	• Write each definition out in full, so people will appreciate what I mean, and clearly clarify my thoughts about my areas of work • ask for MM for feedback …endix for		Need to reflect more closely after I have trialed my Work Journal for Term 3 Focus on • areas of work. Are they appropriate? • layout of journal page • layout of "to do" lists	Make up my A4 folder. Ask Vicki about layout (materials Production unit)	• Definition notes to be typed up and placed in my Action Folder • put in Action Folder a page titled "Improvements for my Work Journal" fill this in during term 3 • acknowledge all possible improver points on this page

PLAN	ACTION	DATA COLLECTION	REFLECTION	REPLANNING	ACTION
• To keep an accurate weekly Work Journal during term 3	Fill in Work Journal at end of each day, under the appropriate area of work • Check if I have done everything on my "To Do" list	Each day in term 3 (comprising 11 weeks)	3rd week, need to incorporate time component need an overview of the tasks I need to do in a week. Maybe a weekly coversheet.	Draw an inside line in each column for time component. Draft up a weekly coversheet	Estimating the time spent on tasks in 15 half hour and 1 hour blocks. Don't make it a pain to do so.

PLAN	ACTION	DATA COLLECTION	REFLECTION	REPLANNING	ACTION
To do some professional reading on Group Self Evaluation and Action Research.	Visit G.I.A.E. bookshop and purchase these books.	Professional Reading The Action Research Planner Deakin University 1982.	Formalising the model. I can now see my …	Still would like to talk to someone about Action Research.	Talk to Rob Collins about Action Research.

PLAN	ACTION	DATA COLLECTION	REFLECTION	REPLANNING	ACTION
To distribute draft 1 of Work Journal to colleagues in the Educational Program Unit at LVSSC.	Photocopy and leave on their desks.	Their feedback both formally and informally	Need to incorporate travelling time component. Colleagues were proud of my individual effort because it …	Show other people my Work Journal • husband • Mum • Aunty • people outside the …	Maintain my 'improver page' for Work Journal 1. Be really critical about work journal.

PLAN	ACTION	DATA COLLECTION	REFLECTION	REPLANNING	ACTION
To attend Time Management Workshop, August 28th 1989. (All day commitment)	Made a commitment to the group to improve on one main time management problem • present my strategies to group on Sept. 21st 1989	• to keep a 15 minute log in week 9 of term 3. • to keep a phone log.	Reassuring to discover that I did what I had planned to do. Also knowing I was honestly recording my daily tasks happening in Work Journal helped to keep me on task. I feel like I am finding my feet simply by recording what I am doing. I'm task oriented instead of being an 'octopus'		• write up findings from time log and present it to group • to record each phone call as it happens • place phone sheet beside

I found … (even th… points w… ideas in … Term 4.

The carer for a person with Alzheimer's disease

Monday — *The sound of the TV on full blast drives me round the bend. I decide it will have to go, or be strictly limited, or I won't be able to continue. Dear Bill—he doesn't seem to have a clue what he's watching. He never can tell me who's related to who on those dreadful soaps. I think there really is no value in it.*

Tuesday — *Last night we were watching 'Mr Chips' and Bill cried.*

Wednesday — *I've been thinking about Bill crying about 'Mr Chips' and suddenly wondered whether he is making some sense of all this endless TV he watches. Is it possible?*

Thursday — *Decided to ask the Alzheimer self-help group coordinator about what brain function is possible, and she said thinking goes but feeling stays.*

Friday — *I feel ever so slightly less bothered by the sound of the TV. I've decided to try a little experiment. I asked Bill to point to his favourite videos, and they all had soppy sentimental aspects to them.*

Saturday — *Experiment number 2: I brought home 'Never Ending Journey' and sure enough, he sat glued to it. I think I'm onto something. He always was such a loving man despite being such an apparent toughie—maybe I haven't lost as much of him as I thought.*

Sunday — *I wonder if I could get over feeling embarrassed about talking about emotions with him and get a response from him about his beloved tellie programs? Now I wonder why he likes that 'Playschool' so much, all through the week? Perhaps I shouldn't keep rubbishing him about it!*

Other weekly efforts

There are other ways to build in evaluation on a weekly basis, for example, if you are involved on a daily basis in your activity you might consider an end-of-the-week ritual of finishing an hour early and having a drink together to chew over the week's work. Use these times to share successes and disasters, worries and observations.

Some records or statistics may be cumulative and need attention on a weekly basis. Do they tell you anything on a weekly basis? Are there any other records you could usefully be collecting?

Maybe you meet weekly. Most meetings now keep 'action by' records (who'll do what by when, etc.) which provide little audit review mechanisms. There should always be chances to raise new issues (AOB—any other business—is one traditional way).

Try reviewing your calendar planner or diary once a week. How does this week compare with last? What is it telling you about what your priorities have been in practice? What would you have preferred? What would you like to do more of or less of next week? A duty lawyer in a legal service decided for one week to phone every client she'd seen over a week, two months earlier, to see how they'd gone. She was so impressed by the value of the feedback she built it in to her routine case management.

SPECIAL EFFORT EVALUATIONS OF PARTICULAR ASPECTS OF PRACTICE OR ACTIVITIES

WORKSHOP

A special effort evaluation uses the same process—but scaled up. You might still be able to do it more or less 'on your own', or you may consciously want to involve several others. Firstly you might seek confirmation of your unease and even of your beginning hunches, and choose another person or several to talk over the matter that you are either troubled by, or feel in the dark about, or wish to 'problematise' (even though it may not appear to be a problem). Identify what it is you want to evaluate and see if they share your interest. Say why you wanted to evaluate it. Maybe take it to the whole group or a staff meeting. Alternatively, the group you are part of may have already 'commissioned' it after a monthly meeting where it was decided to focus on the particular topic.

Start by posing yourselves the questions: How is it going? Is it working? What do we think of it? Systematically pool all your versions of the issues—what you are experiencing and what you had expected or hoped for or planned.

Assess the evidence. What more do you need to know? What would count as firmer evidence for or against your hunches? What do your critical reference groups think? How do you know? What is the strength of this evidence? How could you collect more? Does it already exist? Should you have been logging it or keeping notes? Can you now do so (say for a trial period)? Is there a quick way to ask people, such as the ubiquitous 'one pager', or discussion with them in a group?

Some examples of the kinds of 'pieces' of practice one might want to evaluate at this level follow:

- *A quick evaluation of a physiotherapist's pre-natal exercise class or an ongoing evaluation of a series of workshops held to convey a consumer perspective to professional carers of people with Alzheimer's.*
- *An assessment of the value of a campaign to stop a federal funding cut to home and community care services.*
- *A consideration of the value of a newsletter to members of a group.*

A group-work class, or a series of workshops

Group work or workshops might call for slightly more formal kinds and slightly more extensive amounts of information. The usual response is to reach for a questionnaire! But let's look at what a wealth of 'data' are already available to us. To take the examples above: the class and workshops have already been developed in response to all kinds of 'data'—perceptions, observation, feedback—possibly built up over quite a long period of time. As well, you are continuing to get such input every time you hold them. Let's 'unpack' these observations. Perhaps write them down. Keep pushing yourself from the initial question, 'How do I think they are going'. Whatever your response, ask: 'What makes me think that?' and 'What are the signs of that?'.

You might make the following kinds of observations.

'I think they are going well because:

- *People keep coming. Lots of people keep coming, including many of the same people.*
- *People not only come on time, many come early for more chat.*
- *People seem enthusiastic—there's lots of happy conversation; people's faces are animated; there are not many silences.*
- *People seem to be confident enough to ask questions, they ask relevant questions; most of the discussion is on the topics planned.*
- *I overheard conversations in which people said how helpful the sessions had been and how comfortable they felt coming there.*
- *I met some of the people again at a later date and they gave examples of how they had used what they had learned.'*

Now 'interrogate' these signs. Are they all good signs? Could they mean other than what you think they mean? To give another example, you might not want to be too quick to reject noisy conviviality as disruptive of learning—it may be the necessary condition for it; or silence as a sign of disinterest—it may be a sign of intense concentration. On the other hand you might be wrong! Ask someone else what they think. Can they think of alternative interpretations? Asking other people usually generates fresh ways of seeing. If you have time, check your records, or keep records for a while, so you can assure yourself (and others) of your impressions.

You could then be even more systematic and go more deeply into the various elements of the classes or workshops. What do people seem to think about, or how do they respond to each of the different aspects. Write a list of the elements (who, what, when, where, why) of your session:

- The material conveyed by the convenors.
- Style of presentation.
- Venue.
- Size of group.
- Length of time of sessions.
- The times of day.
- The rationale behind each element.

Here you are starting to generate as full as possible a description of what is done and why. Now ask, for each element, how the critical reference group seems to be responding, or what they are getting out of it. Only when you have exhausted this, shift to what *you* were trying to achieve—*your* intentions, rationale, purposes or 'objectives' or standards (as opposed to what people actually seem to get out of it). You will probably find that much of what people did (or didn't) get out of it will relate to your intentions (you'd have done a less effective job of your previous 'research' if that were not the case!).

However, you might—by suspending these expectations in an 'open inquiry' mode—have noticed that people were getting something else out of it you hadn't planned or realised (or getting more out of some things and valuing other things less than you would have thought). You can then assess whether those needs are ones you can respond to by returning to the more fundamental philosophical purposes of your activities. For example, the physiotherapist may find that in describing what she thinks the women using her exercise classes are getting out of them (or what she hopes they will get out of them) she finds herself 'forgetting' to mention the exercises! The exercises may have become effective means to all sorts of other related ends, rather than continuing to be the most centrally important ends in themselves.

Moving beyond what you already know (just from searching your memory), you might want to touch base in an even more systematic, thorough and comprehensive way. Here, you will do best to build naturalistically on the kinds of ways people already use to express their own personal evaluations. You might ask the whole group to discuss the value of the sessions. You will undoubtedly get some good feedback (the 'you' factor again). So ask people to suggest improvements, or mention some of your own doubts or hunches; then watch carefully for people's responses. Check also with a sharp eye any who are quiet or seem ambivalent or reluctant. Maybe catch them later and say how you were really looking for ways to improve the sessions and are they sure they can't suggest anything at all. (It often 'loosens up' evaluation if you ask about how to change or improve things, rather than just what people think of them. People's valuations are then implicit in their suggestions.) Ask several of the more articulate to judge how they think *others* saw it—again stressing your need for any observations that might help you.

Here, you are trying to supply as much 'permission' to express unmet needs as possible. Do you visit (follow up) any of the attenders? Talk to them in their everyday situation—at home or on the job? See if they can identify ways they have actually used what they learned. Use any opportunity to research their needs further by observing how they go about whatever it was you were trying to teach them more about. For a pre-birth exercise class, see if you can attend a few of the births. Take notes.

If it is a sensitive, disempowered or otherwise culturally different area (such as foster care, acute psychiatric hospital practice, or non-English speaking) you may need to employ a member of the relevant group to conduct the discussion and collect people's responses for you. That may need some self-confidence, but the effect will be worth it if people realise how serious you are about hearing from them.

Take time for you or your group to reflect on all these encounters. You might want to be even more rigorous—and, just as an occasional one-off, ask *all* (or a hefty sample) of those attending what they thought. Or follow up later to see if they can identify ways they applied what they learned (remembering that just because some people can't identify their practice with particular messages they have heard, doesn't necessarily mean that they didn't actually absorb anything). In trying to establish the value of a practice, one of the joys of evaluation can be in trying to establish links between practice and effects. Given the difficulty of this, we should never waste time trying to redemonstrate effects that others have already painstakingly established.

If you do decide to try to tap everyone's view, you may resort to the apparent ease of a pen and paper question sheet. Mostly, these supply less useful information if they are of the 'Did you enjoy this: yes or no?' or 'Were your expectations met?' variety. People's responses are generally far more complex than this. For example, a verbal response might be:

> *'Well, yes, I quite liked the workshop because at morning-tea time I met someone who turned out to be a neighbour I didn't know. But I didn't learn anything much that I didn't already know in Session One, although I quite enjoyed it. Session Two I didn't enjoy because it made me feel really uncomfortable about some things I'd been doing without realising their effect; and the afternoon session interested me greatly although it wasn't what I'd come to hear.'*

Here we can see that hanging an evaluation only on 'enjoyment' or on prior objectives might result in material that turns out to be highly ambivalent. 'Enjoyment' turns out to be a good indicator—but of an unintended factor in one case (the neighbour), and a bad indicator in another (where discomfort was associated with generating a valuable perception of discrepancy). Thus, a written tick-the-box response may have rated Session One highly, and Session Two lowly, and missed entirely on knowing of the valuable encounter at the tea break. Nevertheless, we can carefully ask a set of questions that touch on most possibilities and, provided we realise that written responses give only the most abstracted and partial feedback, then even abstract and partial written feedback can have its uses.

The other thing to keep in mind is that, just as the use of all other techniques needs to get at both how people see the world in relation to *their* needs and interests, and also how they see the world in relation to *your* intentions and objectives (that ultimately are meant to relate back to critical reference groups' needs and interests), so also should question sheets (and their face to face versions—interviews) capture both open inquiry and audit review elements. Diagram 4 showed a very simple sheet that tried to do this. Diagram 7 (on the following page) shows a slightly more detailed version that sets out to check more purposively for what the session-providers were trying to convey. None of this, however, substitutes for observation and reflective conversation—what we might call in-depth naturalistic or interpretive 'fieldwork'. An example is that which a physiotherapist used to check whether her careful choice of music was contributing to a comfortable and relaxed and ethnically relevant environment (rather than to a Jane Fonda leotards-and-fashionable-aerobics-type exercise class), or which she used to evaluate her use of the term 'sinking into the mat' compared to 'floating in the air'. These are the kinds of things questionnaires will not be able to explore in such sophisticated depth.

DIAGRAM 7
ALZHEIMER'S WORKSHOP FEEDBACK SHEET

Alzheimer Society of Victoria

Title of seminar..

Workshop held for: ....

...................................; date: ..../..../....

Evaluating This Workshop

Identifying information (your name or a codeword)

....

In order to help the workshop leaders understand the usefulness of this workshop to participants, we ask you to respond to the following questions.

QUESTION ONE - To be answered before the workshop starts,

1. What are 3 things you would like to get out of today?

(i) ....

(ii) ....

(iii) ....

REMAINING QUESTIONS - To be answered after the workshop,

2. Were there things in the seminar today that helped you understand Alzheimers disease? (Tick one answer)

Yes: - a lot ❑

Yes: - a little ❑

No: - not much ❑

Can you say how?

....

....

....

Can you give one or two examples that relate to your own personal experience? (eg. "Now I understand why Mrs. so and so did ....")

....

....

....

....

3. Has the seminar given you any new ideas on how you could handle some things differently?

Yes ❑

Not sure ❑

No: - not really ❑

If yes can you give an example of how?

....

....

4. What stood out as the most interesting thing or things that were said today? (If you can remember something in particular that was said, please write that.)

....

....

5. Any particular comments to help us improve our seminars?

....

....

....

Thank you.

Please hand this in at the front registration desk.

Following are some of the ways to improve how we ask written-down questions so as to get more useful, extensive, rich or meaningful responses:

- Have in mind what people are likely to be thinking about when they pick up your question sheet. Maybe they have just had a session of ideas and information, and are now keen to get off home before peak hour. Don't automatically ask about age, occupation, ethnicity or gender. (If you really need to know how many Greek-born men aged between 39 and 60 who were factory workers do or don't think such and such, and your sample size is big enough, then leave those 'characteristics' questions till last.)

  Do start with a question that 'leads' the person in to evaluative thinking. This might be the kind of question that would parallel a naturalistic question between two friends emerging from the session who might ask each other, 'Well, what did you think of that?'. You might ask, 'Can you say what you thought of today's session?' or 'Can you rate today's session on a scale of 1 [least] to 10 [most] in terms of how much you got out of it?'. These may not be tremendously valuable questions in themselves.*
- Rather than ask 'Did you enjoy or find suitable the venue (or the time or music or discussions)?' etc., ask 'Were there good things about the venue (time/music/discussion)?' and 'Were there bad things about the venue (time/music/discussion)?'. Don't ask the question in the form 'What were the good or bad things about the venue (time/music/discussion)?' unless you are sure there were some.
- Encourage all possible 'nay-saying', for example, by saying 'We are keen to improve' or 'We are going to make changes. Tell us how', or include a finish-the-sentence item, 'If only it had been more . . .' or 'Next time it would be good to . . .'.
- Specify elements of the session to jog people's memories. Don't just ask 'Was the workshop worthwhile?'; ask 'Can you comment on when A spoke?, or on the discussion group about aspect B?, or on the exercise regarding C?'.
- Always have a space for people to volunteer things you haven't asked about ('Any other comments?' or just 'Comments'). If that seems too blunt, instead, say encouragingly, 'Is there anything else you can think to tell us?' or 'Any other comment that comes to mind?'. This is an important 'open inquiry' element.
- If you can keep it down to one page (or two sides at most) you will be rewarded by more of them being filled in and returned. As a rule of thumb, try not to ask more than five questions. And remember that you will have only scratched the surface of everything you could have asked in relation to everything you were trying to achieve!

Michael Patton has some quite good and detailed things to say about asking questions (see the Further Useful Reading at the end of this book), although I personally don't always follow his rule about not asking people 'why'. I've found people can often give quite illuminating explanations for why they think things. Alternatively, explore with questions like 'Can you say a bit more about that?' or 'What do you think was going on there?'.

The campaign

To assess the campaign, the coordinator or coordinating group might ask themself, 'How's it been going?'. Maybe there's an answer in the negative: 'Frustrating' or 'Problematic', or the positive: 'Good' or 'Terrific'. Now is the chance to say, 'Well, what have we done?', and get down on paper everything that has been done so far (descriptions of each element of practice). These might include:

- Working with the local Council, including working with adjoining sub-regional local Councils to get a joint position.
- Getting the Community Health Centre Committee of Management to do the same with other Community Health Centre Committees of Management.
- Raising awareness among staff.
- Getting local press coverage.

Now if documented fully enough, each strand of action can then be assessed. By breaking it down into elements it may be found that in some cases there was in practice a very satisfactory pay off for effort but that with one particular element of the work there had been nothing like the realisation of expectations. This is where the full contextual explanation (gained by asking why, then why, then why, till the situation is better revealed) can be sought out in order to assess the next possible range of actions. That is, the context and history illuminates the value of the expectations (or evaluation criteria), and suggests whether a new strategy should be tried (a different element of practice). Ideas for this can be sought by touching base with the critical reference group, particularly if informed by an understanding of the factors blocking success. Creativity and imagination are needed, as always, at this point of the evaluation cycle.

* Although the rating may have some reliability given that most people have gone through an education system that taught us the meanings of 'marks out of ten'! (And a slightly wider scale gives people more room to discriminate than a small one of three or five items.) A binary Yes/No scale generally means an even more drastic loss of depth of meaning when asking about extents or matters with contexts that are not self-evident. Most people hate being confined to a simple Yes/No question ('Do you enjoy life? Yes or No') unless it is of an easily answerable kind (such as 'Did you attend X? Yes or No').

The newsletter

To assess the newsletter, the group producing it may like to start with a group self-evaluation—pooling their own ideas and reasons for pride or suspicion! Asking 'What do we think of it, and why?' *may* yield some hunches.

A readership survey by pencil and paper question sheet conveniently included in the next issue may yield some further insights—but other more fruitful, more naturalistic signs might first be sought:

- Have people been known to mention to each other things raised in the newsletter?
- Are there ways of knowing if people hand their copies on to be read by others?
- Are there signs that readers have, for example, got together as a group to discuss any of the articles in it?
- Have people reported being usefully informed by it?
- Have any of the information sources that are referred to in the newsletter experienced greater demand? Have those making the demand mentioned the newsletter as their source of information?

Some suggestions of methods follow:

- Can members of the group each undertake to phone or meet with half a dozen people to get some feedback on the last issue? See if people can recall anything of it. Then go through it page by page asking 'Did you see that?'; 'Did you read that?'; 'What did you think of this?'; 'What did you think of that cartoon?'; 'Was that interesting or not?'.
- Would it help to collect examples of other newsletters and compare and contrast them?
- Try a simple 'Would you like to keep receiving this newsletter? Please cut-off-and-return-slip' in the next issue (although you will still have to interpret the response rate!).
- Pick a small random or purposive cross-sectional (cluster) sample of readers and get them to come in for a group discussion. (Offer light refreshment!) Brainstorm reactions and ideas. Alternatively, pick a selected sample of people who are known always to have opinions and/or bright ideas and/or reliable perceptions of what other people think.

Try to cross-check for opinions and actual usage. For example, people might object to a paternalistic tone but nevertheless find that some of the practical information contained in the newsletter was very useful. You may need just to 'be around' people to learn these kinds of things.

Start with a broad opening-up question like 'Do you like getting the newsletter? Can you say why?'. Or, if it requires a choice to get it (for example, to pay a subscription), you could ask 'Why do you keep subscribing?' and 'If you ever stopped subscribing, why might that be?'.

Questions like 'Do you read it?' may be less useful. Instead, try to pin down actual contextualised practice. Ask 'Which bits do you specially read or enjoy?', 'When or where do you read it', or 'How much time would you typically spend reading it?', or 'Do you:

- skim read it?'
- skim and read one or two pieces?'
- read most of it?'
- read all of it?'
- Other . . .?'

Ask about specific use made of it. For example: 'Can you recall making use of anything from the last issue/last few issues?', 'Have you ever followed its advice/or . . . [whatever's relevant] . . .?'. If the newsletter follows a regular format or there have been major themes or articles, list the format or some of the themes or articles and ask people to say whether they read it/them; get them to rate them out of ten, or rank the sections in the format from favourite to least favourite. Ask people 'Why', if that seems a useful thing to do. Sometimes people may reveal needs you had no idea they had (even if it's that the newsletter is exactly the right size for the bottom of the cocky's cage!).

IT KEEPS ME UP TO DATE
NEWSLETTER
SK

List possible areas for change (illustrations, cartoons, more or less of whatever) and get people to express opinions about them. Later, when these ideas have been pooled, people could rate or rank any options that seem worth considering.

If you're having trouble settling on a few questions (don't ask more than a page or two sides' worth) then go out and talk more to people to try out questions and get a better idea of what is 'askable and answerable'.

Finally, in an open inquiry mode that reconsiders the higher purposes of the newsletter, you might conduct a broader discussion about preferred general style or 'feel'. You may want to also consider other ways (alternative to newsletters) for keeping in touch with members, and assess them in comparison to (or as well as) the newsletter.

MONTHLY COLLECTIVE PROBLEM-POOLING SESSIONS

Tabling discrepancies

Sometimes a monthly time devoted to tabling and logging evaluative comments about issues that are preoccupying or puzzling people (or simply to raise 'How are we going'-type questions in various areas) is a way of beginning to strengthen an everyday evaluation program. For example:

- New issues can be raised when people haven't yet reached committed conclusions. Often, the longer that issues can be held and reflected on at this stage the better.
- Issues about which there is clear consensus can be identified for action, and future reporting back (what action? by whom? by when?).
- Issues about which there is divided opinion can be placed (and possibly kept) on the table for people to think about and return to the following month with suggestions. Too-early conclusions or votes should generally be resisted as they often store up dissatisfaction. Maximum time for reflection and imaginative solution-generation should be given.
- Issues which reappear over and over again without resolution may be referred to a special group evaluation exercise that could then report back to a monthly session.
- Issues which can be left for an annual inquiry-review could be placed on notice for handling at that time.

The discussion about group self-evaluation in Chapter 5 is relevant here. Think about the people-resources in your group with a view to maximising the value of this kind of monthly effort. Think about who are the 'organic' or 'indigenous' researchers in your group:

> *Who's good at asking critical questions?*
> ('Why are we doing it like this?', 'What about considering . . .?', 'Has anyone asked our users?')
> *Who's good at developing hunches?*
> ('Well I reckon it's because . . .', 'I've been thinking there might be a link between . . . and . . .', 'I've noticed that every time we . . . then . . .')
> *Who's good at observing?*
> ('The other day I was sitting watching . . . and I could see that . . .', 'Did you see how when she . . ., then he . . .?')
> *Who's sceptical?*
> ('What makes you think that?' 'But it could be because . . .', 'Do we really know that for sure?', 'What if . . .', 'I'm not so sure. It might more be a matter of . . .')
> *Who's creative and imaginative?*
> ('Perhaps we could try . . .', 'I've had an idea!', 'What about . . .', 'This is a bit unorthodox, but what if we . . .')
> *Who's good at judging which are good ideas?*
> ('That idea would work because . . .', 'We could try idea X first, and idea Y if X works', 'I can't see that idea working at this stage because . . .')

Some people are good at identifying these traits—either in themselves or in other people. It's a bit of an art. 'Elect' people to these roles by a modified pencil and paper 'Delphi' technique if necessary! Watch how people accomplish these skills. Later the jobs can be rotated when everyone gets the hang of them.

Reporting on reflective evaluations

Such monthly sessions could also be used by people to report on personal or small group self-evaluations, with the fruits of this labour being shared. The emphasis of these should be on what was learned and on any improvements planned or made as a result. Reports on development are often very illuminating and set a valuable tone for others to try the same kind of exercise: *'Firstly we noticed that . . . Then we decided this was a fruitful direction to pursue. Then we tried it and found . . . That showed us we needed to do more of . . . and less of . . . So we considered X, Y and Z and thought that because of . . . then X would be best. Now we're about to give X a go'*. You could have a different person or project or program component each month.

This kind of evaluation work comes very close to what some might call *staff development* or even *organisational development*. The essential elements of these two concepts are indeed shared.

'Business as usual' (and all the congealed interests and power relation and familiar ways that that entails!) will threaten to swamp these sessions—exactly like everyday busy-ness threatens individual self-reflection efforts. The same discipline and determination will be required to preserve even the smallest monthly reflective times.

Whether the discussion is in a monthly meeting or in small group spot evaluations it should be shaped to suit your scope and purposes. If interest flags and few people are attending, try a more interest-oriented approach to things that people are Really Interested in.

What *are* people *really interested* in right now? Work on that. Try bi-monthly or quarterly, if that works better.

ANNUAL WHAT-HAVE-WE-ACHIEVED-TO-DATE AND WHERE-ARE-WE-HEADING-NEXT-YEAR EFFORTS

Discussion meetings

Although discussion meetings could serve a formal function of checking practice against intentions, the discussions—which could be held at the group's ordinary first or last general meeting of the year, or at a special residential workshop up to two days long—should commence with an 'open inquiry'-style session. During this session, people might firstly discuss their general reflections and evaluation of the previous year's work, and then elaborate, or they might alternatively start by envisioning the future.

Inquiry review

Each person might report very briefly on the value of what has been done or what they've been doing during the past year. This needs to avoid being a familiar descriptive litany, for example, by being told as a story of change from the previous year. People could do some reflective preparation for this, prior to coming. This supplies a 'collective memory' as a point of shared reference. The ideas, suggestions and questions of the group could then be contributed to each of the other members.

Envisioning the future

People could then set aside their current activities or formal objectives, and, by orientating themselves to the situation of the critical reference group, volunteer their visions for the future of the general enterprise, and for the specific contributions they could make. This could be placed in the context of a directional change from a point in the past, and towards a point in the future. Here people are actually articulating their deepest and most important values, standards or templates—some of which they may not have put into words before. Brainstorm these ideas. Get them all out before examining them with a view to practicability.

Identifying what needs to be done

People could then talk about the steps necessary. People might like to brainstorm or volunteer ideas about what they think is either blocking or would enable their achieving the situations they want for the future. This kind of discussion could be assisted by the techniques of Group self-evaluation and Force-field analysis described in Chapter 5.

THIS WAY

Deciding on achievable steps

The final consensus may be a mixture of:

- Some more of the same.

- Some changed practices (some completed, some improved, some abandoned).
- Some entirely new practices.

It will relate to a revised and more articulated general vision, informed by more ideas that will have developed during the course of the workshop. The fine details can then be settled by going through any previous formulation of the group's purposes and intentions, philosophy, objectives and targets—such as a service agreement. If conducted with a view to revising the funding service agreement, each clause of the agreement can be revised in the light of the open inquiry—adding, subtracting and revising. The group then ends with a *new* articulation of their formal plan for the coming year.

Other annual efforts

There is a range of other kinds of evaluation that can be done on a yearly cycle, many of which we may not have thought of as such! For example, they can include:

- The annual office clean-up.
- Cleaning out your desk and unfinished in-tray before or over the holiday break.
- Revising your own or the organisation's filing system.
- Rearranging the furniture.
- Going through last year's diary and putting the dates in your next year's diary.
- Updating your teledex or address book.

The *Self-evaluation Kit* prepared by Gai Wilson (cited in the Further Useful Reading section) is used for a special effort evaluation by local Citizens Advice Bureaus—particularly as an annual audit on progress by local bureaus in implementing standing objectives. The cancer support groups' example (see Diagram 8 on following page) has been built in to the groups' annual calender of meetings as a way of providing more 'bottom up' inquiry information on what participants' hopes and purposes are, and also feedback on ways to improve and develop the groups.

COMPREHENSIVE PROGRAM STOCKTAKES EVERY 3–5 YEARS OR SO

There is something of an ascending scale from personal reflection on components of activities (and even elements of components), to activities that make up services or campaigns, to programs made up of services. Just as it would be disastrous to leave small daily problems to build up for years (we've all seen examples of that!), it is equally disastrous to attempt total program reviews regularly, or even annually.

Indeed, if regular daily, weekly, monthly and small-scale special-purpose evaluation is practised, many of the big, total, disruptive program reviews of the recent past might become unnecessary. Total program reviews may continue to be useful in retrieving programs out of large, deep, routine ruts or, alternatively, to defend programs against sudden or irrational or uninformed external threat (requiring extensive documentation and justification for audiences that are completely isolated from the local practice). They will also still be useful when standing back at a very long distance is not possible either on a regular basis or without some longitudinal or time series-type records.

A current flaw of most major program reviews is that they attempt to reproduce all elements of evaluation from the local and micro right up to the central. But program reviews should evaluate whole programs—not every tiny element of every service that comprises the program.

The following is an example of a committee self-evaluation of a funding program, where three years of the committee having funded many projects gave them a perspective that would otherwise have been difficult to achieve. As the program was of modest size it was possible to evaluate specific elements, although this material largely confirmed what was already known (from more regular feedback sources) about these. It was the program re-design that was the real breakthrough, and even this had already emerged from daily practice. The main value of the program review was to formalise the process of reaching consensus about the desirability of taking this direction.

A three-year evaluation of a grants program

The Australian Consumers' Health Forum wanted to know whether its research grants program was working. It approached the matter by using several sources of understanding to illuminate the various levels of intention: from the most general and philosophical (how to strengthen the voice of health consumers *per se*), to middle-level purposes (how to develop a health consumer research sector), to more specified levels (how to empower consumer, community and self-help groups to carry out their own value-driven efforts to 'find out'), through to the highly specific (how to assist groups to do their own participatory action research and evaluation).

It assembled a rough picture of the elements of the program using a logic or organising-framework based around consumers' sequential or chronological experience of the program, that is to say, first hearing of it, barriers faced in preparing and submitting an application, experience of the Forum's staff, application form/kit, assessment procedure, notification of outcome, any changes made to the group's budget, presentation of cheques ceremony, ethics procedures, administrative matters, alternative sources of funding approached, outcomes of project and unexpected things learned from the project. As well, both *open*

DIAGRAM 8
CANCER SELF-HELP GROUPS' ANNUAL REVIEW QUESTIONS

ANNUAL REVIEW OF OUR GROUP

It's the start of the year, and we thought it would be good to reflect on what we've got out of being part of our mutual support group, and what worked over the past year, and what hasn't.

Anti-Cancer Council of Victoria Recognised Cancer Support Group/Service

Procedure:

We start by each filling in the questions ourselves. Then we will pin them all to the wall. You do not need to put your name on it. We will then read each other's contributions, and then come back into the group to discuss them further and decide on how to do things this year.

This gives us all a chance both to have our say and also to see every one else's ideas - thus pooling our collective wisdom!

---

1 Why do we come to the group? What do we hope to get out of it?

....

....

2 What were our first impressions when we came to our very first meeting?

....

....

3 What have been the best things about the group?

....

....

4 What have we found less useful ...

....

5 Has being part of the group had an effect on us? (e.g. on what we do, or feel, or think?) *Give actual examples.*

....

....

....

6 If we didn't come to the group, what would be the effects on us?

The good things that we would miss (the disadvantages of not coming).

....

....

The drawbacks of coming that we would not miss (the advantages of not coming).

....

....

7 Are there ways we can think that the Anti Cancer Council could help us? (e.g. support, ideas about something, courses, leaflets, contact person, feedback about other groups and their activities, etc.)

....

....

8 What would we like the group to do this year? (e.g. speakers and talks, activities, outings, visiting people with cancer, public speaking, support work). *Give new ideas as well as say what existing things should be continued.*

....

....

9 Any other comments you'd like to add?

....

....

Take your time. When finished, pin your sheets up on the wall and then read each other person's contribution. If the other sheets make you think of new things - bring these ideas into the group discussion which will follow.

inquiry questions (general impressions, specific impressions related to the elements of the program, plus ideas for change), and also *audit review* questions were asked which checked against the Forum's objectives (namely, active consumer control over the project, emphasis on prevention rather than treatment, action research rather than purely academic/theoretical knowledge, multiplier effects, the addressing of oppression or disadvantage, the giving of voice to consumers, good geographic spread, and the addressing of issues of gender).

In this way it not only examined highly specific elements but also enabled a major shift in the program to be recommended (that is, a shift from all the money going to projects proposed from the field to dividing the funds into three buckets—one to respond to proposals from the field, one for strategic projects identified centrally from the Forum's experience of the myriad needed efforts that would advance the whole field, and one for a network of local people and written resources to assist groups to prepare better proposals and carry out more effective research and evaluation themselves).

The evaluation drew on the following multiple sources of understanding (using a range of techniques):

- Past and current members of the Grants Committee itself (questionnaires followed by feedback and group discussions, plus participant-observation).
- Past and current members of the Grants Committee secretariat (individual discussions, questionnaires followed by group discussions, plus participant-observation).
- Successful grant recipients from all three years (questionnaires, individual and group discussions).
- Unsuccessful applicants whose proposals had been ranked worthy of funding (questionnaires, individual and group discussions).
- A previous research study of the full field of potential applicants' needs for research resources, barriers faced in applying, etc. (on-site visits, observation, small group and individual discussions, content analysis of groups' research studies).
- Use of file material on decisions made each year, and other written materials generated by the program (newspaper advertisements, pro formas, various letters sent to applicants and grant recipients at various stages of the process, correspondence with the Minister, grants processing procedures, etc.).
- A content analysis of three years of sequential files on projects awarded funds, initially to examine progress, but—by using an open inquiry mode—also to become aware of themes and issues emerging from groups' experiences. (Files included initial application, subsequent correspondence, progress and final reports, groups' own evaluation reports, and any output—reports, pamphlets, publications, posters, videos, etc.)
- Attendance at a cheque presentation ceremony, and attendance at a grant recipient's performance of a funded health education play (performed by young people who had been paid out of the grant as peer action researchers).

This national evaluation work was substantial enough to have been a specially funded project in its own right, however it was not farmed out to an external evaluator. Instead, the Grants Committee Chairperson—herself a consumer representative—conducted the evaluation as a group self-evaluation, providing also her reflections on three years' experience. Nevertheless, despite these excellent conditions, and despite it being well-received by the rest of the Forum and by external audiences (who had either an interest in the program or a sceptical view of it), the evaluation probably did not substantially result in an outcome different from what could have been achieved from a less elaborate and more built-in informal exercise. It may, however, have provided more confidence and reduced some uncertainty about reaching these same conclusions.

CONCLUDING REMARKS

Experienced evaluators heading towards the end of long careers in the evaluation business often report that they see less and less need for large formal evaluation exercises. Instead, they often find themselves opting more and more for smaller-scale, more built-in, naturalistic, more responsive or utilisation-focused approaches. Some end up calling their work staff development or training, finding it to be integral to, and even indistinguishable from OD (organisational development). What remains of value, however, is the use of the process of 'new paradigm' science and its constituent characteristics:

- Explicitly naming the 'discrepancies' or problems, and consciously formulating questions.
- Ensuring the effort is driven by the values and interests of those who have the problems, and who are to benefit from the exercise.
- Rigorously, thoroughly and comprehensively gathering new perceptions and context-based understandings.
- Self-sceptical development of theory.
- Re-valuing of actions and formulation of new and practical actions.
- Implementing and monitoring of these actions as part of an ongoing cyclical process of learning from our experience.

It is useful at times to think of what we are doing as 'research' and even 'science' because it magnifies the self-conscious and purposive aspects of our efforts. Everyday intuitive research and evaluation which is not raised to this level of self-consciousness *may* be equally effective. For example, people we recognise as 'naturally' effective or competent—the good nurse, the gifted teacher, the outstanding community worker, the spectacularly successful self-help group, the very 'professional' community group (when the word 'professional' is not used in its pejorative sense!), or the influential campaign workers—all operate as intuitive scientists of their own practice. Those, including peers, service-users or managers, who recognise their value are also fine intuitive evaluators!

However, those of us who can see as-yet imperfect states of affairs, who see continuing injustice or disadvantage, and have not yet happened on the most effective way of taking action, may be impatient to speed up our chances of 'getting it right'. Resorting to more conscious, theorised and articulated practice can offer to short-cut some of our otherwise slower processes of learning. No miracles. Just a few less pots of water to boil to death in!

THE EVALUATION INDUSTRY'S TOOLBOX

chapter 5

MODELS AND TECHNIQUES

TOOL BOX
PTY LTD
SK

INTRODUCTION

Everyday evaluators will probably rarely need to resort to the professionals' toolbox—the contents of which range from useful but sophisticated attempts to capture and codify all or some of the nuances of logic and definition that are possible, right through to confusing jargon and mystified 'snake oil'. Thus, rather than a smorgasbord from which you should feel you have to choose, this section of the book is a cook's tour through a range of terminology that you might occasionally have reason to wonder about. There is also a list of questions you might usefully ask of the different approaches.

This chapter concentrates on:

- The chief *models* of evaluation processes (general design or pattern, or framework of logic and content).
- Some associated *techniques* (specific methods of gathering data, hearing people's experiences or ways of engaging with the social worlds to be understood).
- Some major *methodologies* or 'paradigms' of knowledge (fundamental orienting philosophies of science).

Terms already described in *Do It Yourself Social Research* are not repeated here (with a couple of exceptions).

The models, techniques and methodologies in this chapter are in alphabetical order for easy reference; however, some major theorists have attempted to classify models and techniques and paradigms into typologies which give some idea of either their logical connections or their genealogies (lineage or ancestry). At the end of this introductory section to the chapter, several book references are listed for the enthusiast who wishes to delve deeper.

In the hope of giving readers a compass by which to navigate this chapter, frequent references are made to the framework and terminology already used in this *Everyday Evaluation on the Run* book. Some of these terms are denoted by being in *italics.*

Cross-references to related models, techniques or methodologies within this chapter are in CAPITAL LETTERS.

INDEX

-I'VE GOT AN IMMEDIATE NEED FOR AN ACCESSIBLE, EVERYDAY VIEW OUT THE WINDOW...

What is presented in this chapter is a glimpse into what the academics and heavies in the field are up to, as well as giving a small insight into the debates that rage in the professional evaluation community. It also offers deeper insight into the whole business of evaluation—a little like learning a language by seeing how it is used by many different speakers.

However, as this book is for the small-scale everyday evaluator with a need for immediate, accessible, everyday evaluation processes, this section may be a little overwhelming! If, at any point, this happens, then **immediately stop reading** and return to contemplating either the foldout wall chart at the back of the book, or the view out of your window!

EVALUATING THE EVALUATION APPROACHES

Attempts have been made to try to classify this bewildering array of models, approaches and techniques into similar or related groupings. However, there is often either a lot of overlap or else some models only attend to one particular aspect of evaluation. One would really need a 3-D map on which to try to plot a full picture (and even then, some of the techniques would have to move back and forth between one category and another). References in which these different classifications are discussed are listed below. It might be more helpful to pose questions of each as a way of identifying where an approach stands in relation to your situation and purposes.

Questions regarding whose values drive the evaluation method

Q. *Who is this evaluation method oriented towards?*
A. Anyone? Managers? Clients? Stakeholders? Program staff? Critical or other reference groups? All of these?
Q. *What are the purposes of this evaluation method?*
Q. *Why has this evaluation method been decided upon?*

Questions about the conduct of this evaluation method

Q. *Who will be able to carry it out?*
Q. *How will the evaluation method be used?*
Q. *Who will be familiar with it—or need to know more?*
Q. *What are likely to be the outcomes of using this method?*

REFERENCES DESCRIBING CLASSIFICATIONS OF EVALUATION MODELS

EVALUATION TRAINING & SERVICES PTY LTD *Evaluation Models and Strategies* Melbourne:1986

GUBA, Egon G. *Toward a Methodology of Naturalistic Inquiry in Educational Evaluation* CSE, University of California, Los Angeles:1978

HOUSE, Ernest R. 'Assumptions Underlying Evaluation Models' Chapter 3 in George MADAUS, Michael SCRIVEN, Daniel L. STUFFLEBEAM *Evaluation Models* Kluwer-Nijhof Publishing, The Hague:1983

OWEN, John M. *Program Evaluation—Forms and Approaches* Allen & Unwin, St Leonards, NSW:1993

PATTON, Michael Quinn *Utilization-Focused Evaluation* Sagé, Beverly Hills, California:1978

PATTON, Michael Quinn *Qualitative Evaluation Methods* Sage, Beverly Hills, California:1980

STUFFLEBEAM, Daniel L. and William J. WEBSTER 'An Analysis of Alternative Approaches to Evaluation' Chapter 2 in George MADAUS, Michael SCRIVEN, Daniel L. STUFFLEBEAM *Evaluation Models* Kluwer-Nijhof Publishing, The Hague:1983

Accountability

To be accountable means to account *for* that for which one is responsible, and *to* those to whom one is responsible. In its most archetypical form it involves being able to say how funds have been spent on what they were *meant* to be spent on. However, to show, account for, demonstrate or report on *what* has been done (which has a pre-agreed value) is conceptually different from working out what is its *value* in order to ensure that worthwhile and valuable things are indeed being done. This latter may better be termed evaluation for improvement. Thus, strictly speaking, to demonstrate accountability is to report retrospectively on *audit review* results; but to evaluate is to embark prospectively on *open inquiry* processes to identify the value or worth of something. The increase in talk of 'need for accountability' largely reflects the development of gaps between those who know and those who should know or who want to know. If those who do not know are the critical reference groups, then this should serve as a sign that something is wrong in the everyday practice of the work. If those who do not know are those representing broader constituencies or other interested parties, then accountability may be experienced as 'power over' rather than 'power for' (critical reference groups). 'Accountability' thus seems often to be an ambivalent term.

Action research, action evaluation

Action research is not merely research which it is hoped will be followed by action! It is action which is *intentionally* researched and modified, leading to the next stage of action which is then again *intentionally* examined for further change, and so on *as part of the research itself.* Everyday evaluators might call it trial and error—a kind of NATURALISTIC experimental approach over a longish period of time. Life itself is a kind of action research project when you think about it!

In this way, research can be thought of as following a cycle or spiral of action, reflection, questioning, researching hunches, drawing conclusions, evaluating options and planning further action, then taking the new action, and reflecting again and so on. The spiral, it is hoped, goes up towards improvement—but it can also go down (if people compound their errors).

Much conventional and academic research proceeds as if it starts with hunches or hypotheses and ends with conclusions, but this is an inadequate formulation of the full research process for two reasons. Firstly, it does not take seriously the matter of the value-driven and experience-based sources of the hunches—which are terribly important to getting both *meaningful*, and *relevant* or *useful* hunches. And secondly, it does not take seriously the matter of putting the conclusions to the practical test (with their value being judged ultimately by those whose interests were to be served by the evaluation in the first place).

Some theorists believe that evaluation stands separate from research—however, this book has argued that the two elements are part of an integrated action evaluation process, and are bound together by the *purposes* of the exercise (and thus by the *critical* reference group who has those purposes, needs, interests or values). In practice, whenever we try to describe a 'fact' we find we are constructing a description of the world in which we have some kind of a value-interest, whether mild, strong, positive, or negative. So also, wherever we try to describe a value we find we are describing value-states or valued-activities. That is, just as there is no such thing as a value-free fact (or value-free research to come up with them), there is also no such thing as a fact-free value (in that our values are valued-states we have learned about through endless previous cycles of everyday action research or action learning).

In a way, social research or social science has as much to learn from the value-explicit nature of its evaluation elements, as evaluation has to learn from the evidence-seeking and hunch-testing nature of its essential research process. The 17 tenets of action research on the page opposite are drawn from McTaggart:1989.

References:

KEMMIS, Stephen and Robin McTAGGART *The Action Research Planner* Deakin University, Geelong, Victoria:1988

LEWIN, Kurt 'Action Research and Minority Problems' in *Journal of Social Issues* Vol. 2. pp. 34–46:1946

McTAGGART, Robin 'Principles for Participatory Action Research' Paper for Participatory Action Research Encounter, Nicaragua:1989

STRINGER, Ernest *Action Research* Sage Publications, Thousand Oaks, California:1996

Advocacy evaluation

This is a model for internal evaluation within an organisation that is half-way between people doing it themselves, and bringing in an external evaluator. It involves designating one person who is part of the organisation as the evaluator. The role shifts from a traditional one of neutral expert to that of active organisational change agent. Important elements include using an advocacy philosophy; ensuring the evaluator is optimally located in the organisation; and selecting for the role imaginative, iconoclastic people who possess extensive 'operational' experience and are good listeners, communicators and negotiators. Case studies show high rates of implementation of recommendations and a shift from preoccupation with 'quantity' to 'quality'. The approach, emphasising

Principles for Participatory Action Research

A paper presented to the 3er Encuentro Mundial Investigacion Participativa (The Third World Encounter on Participatory Research), Managua, Nicaragua, September 3-9, 1989.

1 Participatory action research is an approach to *improving social practice* by *changing* it and learning from the consequences of change.

2 Participatory action research is contingent on *authentic participation*: a spiral of cycles of *planning, action,* (implementing plans), *observing* (systematically), *reflecting* ... and then re-planning, further implementation, observing and reflecting. One good way to begin a participatory action research project is to collect some initial data in an area of general interest (a reconnaissance), then to reflect, and then to make a plan for changed action; another way to begin is to make an exploratory change, collect data of what happens, reflect, and then build more refined plans for action. In both cases, issues and understandings, on the one hand, and the practices themselves, on the other, develop and evolve through the participatory action research process - but only when the Lewinian self-reflective spiral is thoughtfully and systematically followed in processes of group critique.

4 Participatory action research is *collaborative*: it involves those responsible for action in improving it, widening the collaborating group from these most directly involved to as many as possible of those affected by the practices concerned.

5 Participatory action research establishes *self-critical communities* of people participating and collaborating in all phases of the research process: the planning, the action, the observation and the reflection; it aims to build communities of people committed to *enlightening* themselves about the relationship between circumstance, action and consequence in their own situation, and *emancipating* themselves from the institutional and personal constraints which limit their power to live their own legitimate educational and social values.

6 Participatory action research is a *systematic learning process* in which people act deliberately, though remaining open to surprise and responsive to opportunities. It is a process of using 'critical intelligence' to inform action, and developing it so that social action becomes *praxis* (critically informed, committed action) through which people may consistently live their social values.

7 Participatory action research involves people in *theorising* about their practices - being *inquisitive* about circumstances, action and consequences and coming to *understand* the relationship between circumstance, actions and consequences in their own lives. The theories that participatory action researchers develop may be expressed initially in the form of *rationales* for practices. They may develop these rationales by treating them as if they were no more than rationalisations, even though they may be our best current theories of how and why our social (and educational...) work is as it is. They subject these initial rationales to critical scrutiny through the participatory action research process.

8 Participatory action research requires that people put their practices, ideas and assumptions about institutions to the *test* by gathering *compelling evidence* which could convince them that their previous practices, ideas and assumptions were wrong or wrong-headed.

9 Participatory action research is open-minded about what counts as evidence (or data) - it involves not only *keeping records* which describe what is happening as accurately as possible (given the particular questions being investigated and the real-life circumstances of collecting the data) but also *collecting and analysing our own judgements, reactions and impressions* about what is going on.

10 Participatory action research involves participants in *objectification of their own experience*, for example, by keeping a *personal journal* in which participants record their progress and their reflections about two parallels sets of learnings: their learnings about the practices they are studying (how the practices - individual and collective - are developing) and their learnings about the process (the practice), of studying them (how the action research project is going).

11 Participatory action research is a *political process* because it involves us in making changes that will affect others - for this reason, it sometimes creates resistance to change, both in the participants themselves and in others.

12 Participatory action research involves people in making *critical analyses* of the situations (projects, programs, systems) in which they work: these situations are *structured* institutionally. The pattern of resistance a participatory action researcher meets in changing his or her own practices is a pattern of conflicts between the new practices and the accepted practices of the institution (accepted practices of communication, decision making and educational work). By making a critical analysis of the institution, the participatory action researcher can understand how resistances are rooted in conflicts between competing kinds of practice, competing views of social (and educational ...) positions and values, and competing views of social organisation and decision-making. This critical understanding will help the participatory action researcher to act politically towards overcoming resistances (for example, by involving others collaboratively in the research process, inviting others to explore their practices, or by working in the wider institutional context towards more rational understandings, more just processes of decision making, and more fulfilling forms of social work for all involved).

13 Participatory action research *starts small*, by working through changes which even a single person can try, and works towards extensive changes - even critiques of ideas of institutions which in turn might lead to more general reforms of projects programs or system-wide policies and practices. Participants should be able to present evidence of how they started to work on *articulating the thematic concern* which would hold their group together, and of how they *established authentically shared agreements* in the group that the thematic concern was a basis for collaborative action.

14 Participatory action starts with *small cycles* of planning, acting, observing and reflecting which can help to define issues, ideas and assumptions more clearly so that those involved can define more *powerful questions* for themselves as their work progresses.

15 Participatory action research starts with *small groups* of collaborators at the start, but widens the community of participating action researchers so that it gradually includes more and more of those involved and affected by the practices in question.

16 Participatory action research allows and requires participants to build *records* of their improvements: (a) records of their changing *activities and practices*, (b) records of the changes in the *language and discourse* in which they describe, explain and justify their practices, (c) records of the changes in the *social relationships and forms of organisation* which characterise and constrain their practices and (d) records of the development of their expertise in the conduct of *action research*. Participants must be able to demonstrate evidence of a group climate where people expect and give evidence to support each other's claims. They must show respect for the value of rigorously gathered and analysed evidence - and be able to *show and defend* evidence to convince others.

17 Participatory action research allows and requires participants to give a *reasoned justification* of their social (and educational ...) work to others because they can show how the evidence they have gathered and the critical reflection they have done have helped them to create a *developed, tested and critically examined rationale* for what they are doing. Having developed such a rationale, they may legitimately ask others to justify their own practices in terms of their own theories and the evidence of their own critical self-reflection.

Robin McTaggart, Deakin University, Geelong, Victoria 3217, Australia, [Fax (61) 52 442777].

timeliness and relevance, shares much in common with DECISION-THEORETIC or CLIENT-CENTRED, and UTILISATION-FOCUSED evaluation.

Reference:

SONNICHSEN, Richard 'Advocacy Evaluation—A Model for Internal Evaluation Offices' in *Evaluation and Program Planning* Vol 11, pp. 141–148:1988

Autocratic evaluation

This definition was developed by Barry McDonald in the education field, and can be contrasted with two other kinds of approaches defined by him: BUREAUCRATIC evaluation and DEMOCRATIC evaluation. Autocratic evaluation is a conditional service to those government agencies which have major control over the allocation of resources. It offers external validation of policy in exchange for compliance with its recommendations. Its values are derived from the evaluator's perception of the constitutional and moral obligations of the bureaucracy. The evaluator focuses upon issues of merit, and acts as expert adviser. His or her techniques of study must yield scientific proofs. His or her power base is the academic research community. The contractual arrangements guarantee non-interference by the client and the evaluator retains ownership of the study. The report is lodged in the files of the bureaucracy, but is also published in academic journals. If the recommendations are rejected, policy is not validated. The evaluator's court of appeal is the research community and higher levels in the bureaucracy. The key concepts of the autocratic evaluator are 'principle' and 'objectivity'. Its key justificatory concept is 'the responsibility of office'.

Reference:

MACDONALD, Barry 'Evaluation and the Control of Education' in D.A. TAWNEY (Ed) *Curriculum Evaluation Today—Trends and Implications* Schools Council Research Studies, London, Macmillan: 1976

Baume Report approach

In 1979 an Australian Senate Standing Committee on Social Welfare published an influential report entitled *Through a Glass Darkly: Evaluation in Australian Health and Welfare Services.* Chaired by Senator Peter Baume, the Committee's report was a meta evaluation (an evaluation of evaluation) which—despite some notable efforts to the contrary—came down heavily on the side of a shift towards a strongly rational-technical approach to evaluation involving:

- PROGRAM-BASED and OBJECTIVES-BASED evaluation.
- ZERO-BASE BUDGETING.
- QUANTITATIVE statistics and measurement focus.
- A central MANAGEMENT and funding body perspective emphasising value-for-money and accountability.

Coming as it did at the end of the 1970s with an economic recession making governments begin to panic about spending, the Baume approach to evaluation quickly took over from practices popular in the 1960s and mid 1970s. These superseded models included, along with some conventional surveys, some more PHENOMENOLOGICAL efforts (which mirrored the American NATURALISTIC critique of rational EXPERIMENTAL approaches). It was regrettable that Baume's brief had not extended to the education sector and his inquiry and subsequent recommendations did not benefit from the more advanced state of debate there.

References:

Through a Glass Darkly: Evaluation in Australian Health and Welfare Services Vol. 1 and 2, AGPS, Canberra:1979

LAWRENCE, John 'Preface' in Rosemary S. SARRI and John R. LAWRENCE *Issues in the Evaluation of Social Welfare Programs—Australian Case Illustrations* NSW University Press, Kensington, pp. iii-vii:1980

Bradshaw's typology of needs

In 1972, Jonathan Bradshaw published a modest little article in the English *New Society* journal entitled 'The Concept of Social Need'. It subsequently became overwhelmingly popular as a way of, for nearly two decades, defining 'needs'. While needs-based evaluation is recognised as a distinct school of evaluation, in practice all evaluation refers in some way to who or what it is *for*, even if this is left implicit. There is a sophisticated debate about whether we should speak of critical reference groups' 'needs', or 'values', or 'interests', however, at present there is no doubt that the vast majority of human services practice has hinged on a language or 'discourse' about 'needs'. The four ways of identifying 'needs' that Bradshaw described are:

- *Normative*: What the expert, professional, administrator or social scientist defines as need, in terms of a 'desirable' standard.
- *Felt*: Need defined as want, expressed directly by those who have it.
- *Expressed*: Need is defined here as felt need turned into action, or demand which is expressed indirectly in some way, for example, by a waiting list.
- *Comparative*: If consumers get a service in one area but not in another, it is assumed the unserviced area has an unmet need.

However, Bradshaw never intended his four categories to be *definitions* of needs, but rather as four *methods* of identifying what needs people have. That is, there aren't four different *kinds* of need, but four different ways of finding out what they are. Three out of his four, however, are *other* people's ways of judging critical reference groups' needs, with those other people occupying usually very different class and cultural backgrounds. Only one of the ways attempts to tap directly critical reference groups' *own* judgements. Bradshaw notes that even this latter way is widely considered 'unreliable' and an 'inadequate measure of "real" need'. Rather than then moving on to address either the requirement for a well-informed populace to avoid forms of 'colonialism', the approach is rejected as relying on people's 'limited perceptions' or otherwise not wanting to 'confess a loss of independence'.

One could add to and reshape some of these categories using the approach of this book:

- *Volunteered*: Where critical reference group members directly, explicitly and verbally articulate and request their needs be met.
- *Signified*: Where members of the critical reference group have not been given opportunities to, or are not otherwise confident or able to volunteer explicitly their needs verbally, but freely offer non-verbal or other signs—such as a person with Alzheimer's disease who uses body and facial signs that can be 'read' by someone using a critical reference group perspective.
- *Sought:* Where one group with a critical reference group perspective mobilises the volunteering of information from the critical reference group, which may not otherwise have been explicitly volunteered by that group.
- *Conveyed by secondary reference groups*: Where an advocacy group for critical reference group members define need with reference to the critical reference group members' volunteered experience.
- *Advocated by secondary reference groups*: Where an advocacy group for critical reference group members define need with reference to the critical reference group members' signified experience.
- *Professionally or administratively defined*: Where a person trained in a specialist body of knowledge defines need from their own point of view without direct reference to the experience of the people to whose needs that body of knowledge is meant to refer.

References:

BRADSHAW, Jonathan 'The Concept of Social Need' in *New Society* pp. 640–643, 30 March:1972

FITZGERALD, Ross (Ed) *Human Needs and Political Practice* Pergamon Press, Rushcutters Bay, New South Wales:1977

Brainstorming

This often-used technique is intended to increase a group's access to a range of ideas through free association. It is a seemingly unsophisticated technique that can be easily used by everyday evaluators—although it is often difficult to maintain the ground rule that suggestions are made *without any critical comment* being made. It involves bringing together a face to face small group (less than ten works best). The matter for which ideas are required is presented, and on a board or butcher's paper all suggestions are recorded. Apparently irrelevant, impractical or problematic suggestions can be discussed later when the group evaluates all the offerings. When used to try to generate creative and imaginative new solutions, the results of brainstorming could be listed for further thought and discussion rather than expected or relied on to come up with the best solutions immediately. Sometimes it is helpful for people to be able to go away and chew over all the problems, or the wide range of ideas and possibilities, once they have been 'put on the table' by a group, and come back later.

Reference:

RAWLINSON, Geoffrey, J. *Creative Thinking and Brainstorming* Gower, Westmead:1981.

Bureaucratic evaluation

This, along with AUTOCRATIC and DEMOCRATIC evaluation, was a term developed by Barry McDonald in the education field. He described bureaucratic evaluation as an unconditional service to those government agencies which have major control over the allocation of resources. The evaluator accepts the values of those who hold office and hold the resources, and offers information which will help them to accomplish their policy objectives. The evaluator acts as a management consultant, and his or her criterion of success is 'client' (management) satisfaction. The techniques of study must be credible to the policy-makers and not lay them open to public criticism. The evaluator has no independence, no control over the use that is made of his or her information and no court of appeal. The report is owned by the bureaucracy and lodged in its files. The key concepts of bureaucratic evaluation are 'service', 'utility' and 'efficiency'. Its key justificatory concept is the reality of power.

Reference:

MACDONALD, Barry 'Evaluation and the Control of Education' in D.A. TAWNEY (Ed) *Curriculum Evaluation Today—Trends and Implications* Schools Council Research Studies, London, Macmillan:1976

Client-centred models

These models of evaluation take the 'user' or 'commissioning agent' as their driving force. 'Users' may be defined by this approach as managers, Government departments, a funding body, or a self-help group. That is, the term 'client' is an ambiguous one which may cover any of the conceptual parties to an evaluation (those it is for—to help; those it is for—to inform, convince or influence, etc., the evaluators, the evaluated or the self-evaluating). In the literature, client-centred models might include some MANAGEMENT approaches, RESPONSIVE evaluation, STAKEHOLDER evaluation, UTILISATION-FOCUSED evaluation, and CONSUMER evaluation—that is, those approaches that directly involve in the evaluation the various groups who want the evaluation.

Collaborative evaluation

This refers to evaluation which proceeds with the DEMOCRATIC or PARTICIPATORY involvement of STAKEHOLDERS. Some or all of the various parties to evaluation come together or are brought together. For example, a collaborative evaluation in a school might involve:

- Those who it is for (in the sense of: to help), for example, students.
- Those who it is for (in the sense of deriving value from it, if the critical reference group is helped), for example, parents, teachers.
- Those it is for (in the sense of: to influence, or to convince), for example, regional departmental authorities.

The collaboration is between people with different interests or values but who have enough common ground to be able to collaborate. While the warm fuzzy meaning of 'working together in a joint enterprise' is usually intended, the secondary meaning of 'aiding the enemy occupying forces' may provide a cautionary insight! For example, if professional staff and a self-help group collaborate, or large institution managers and social workers and consumer-employed community workers collaborate, then careful provision should be made for addressing imbalances of power relations.

The great value of collaborative evaluation is the involvement of all parties who might be expected to change their practices—and who need to experience, both directly and personally, the evidence for value, merit, worth or significance and the consequent arguments for change. With a strong INTERPRETIVE or PHENOMENOLOGICAL base, such evaluation can effectively enable the mutual illumination of various parties' perceptions, world views, contexts and histories. A collaborative evaluation of psychiatric nursing practices—involving both nurses' and patients' perceptions in dialogue—might more effectively lead to change than either a patients' exposé of bad practices or a staff inventory of structural difficulties they face *per se*. It will certainly have better chances of succeeding than a managerialist evaluation that doesn't draw on the experiences of the 'troops' and civilians. Collaborative studies might run aground if one party is unable to have enough of a desire to understand another party's perceptions, or if a critical reference group can't wait any longer for another party to see their situation, and either leaves in frustration or continues in frustrated silence.

Reference:

Collaborative Inquiry, Newsletter, Centre for the Study of Organizational Change and Development, University of Bath, England.

Community Health Accreditation and Standards Program (CHASP)

As the name indicates, this is a STANDARDS PROGRAM, and contains the typical features of such an *audit review* approach. Its particular notable feature is that it has been developed 'bottom up' from the field (at least from staff). It is run by the peer organising body—the Australian Community Health Association (just as the hospitals' version is run by the Australian Hospitals Standards Association). It remains in a formative stage (for example, still posing descriptive questions rather than relying entirely on verificationist questions) and this assists it to avoid too great rigidity. As well, most questions require holistic and non-quantitative data. A typical selection of questions would be as illustrated on the page opposite.

Reference:

FRY, Denise and Lesley KING *A Manual of Standards for Community Health* AGPS, Canberra:1991

Complaints mechanisms

Complaints mechanisms range from the humble suggestion box through to highly formal semi-legalistic bodies like State Ombudspersons, or Health Services Complaints Offices. They can provide feedback to the service as well as give consumer redress. Conventionally they are a last (or later) resort when more everyday avenues are exhausted. Characteristics associated with greater success include:

- Being accessible (the suggestion box should not be under the direct watchful eye of the service provider!).
- Allowing for consumers' confidentiality or protection against reprisal if confidentiality cannot be maintained.
- Allowing the complaint to be received by others than the direct provider.
- Giving the complainant enough support to have confidence to lodge a complaint.

A CHASP Review

COMMUNITY HEALTH ACCREDITATION AND STANDARDS PROGRAMME (CHASP)

AN EXAMPLE OF A STANDARD AND ITS INDICATORS

Standard 4.4 - Accessibility and - Availability

The community health centre/service will be located and operated so that its activities are accessible and available to the community it serves.

Assessing a Standard

The CHASP Review team assesses the extent to which a community health centre/service has achieved the standard. The review team compiles and summarises its comments for each indicator, in order to assess the overall attainment of each standard.

Indicators No.	**Comments For Each Indicator** No.
4.4.1. Are the centre's premises located in a visible and convenient part of the area it serves?	*4.4.1 Centre is in main shopping area and has a prominent sign*
4.4.2. Can the centre be easily reached by public or community transport from all parts of its area?	*4.4.2. Generally yes, but residents from X Heights have no bus service to X.*
4.4.6. Does the telephone system operate efficiently, and is it answered 24 hours a day? (It may require an answering machine)	*4.4.6. Insufficient clerical assistance means a recorded message is used in lunch hour. An after hours recorded message gives information on emergency services, and how to contact the community nurse on weekend roster.*
4.4.9. Does the centre have easy access to an interpreter service that covers the languages spoken in the area served?	*4.4.9. Interpreter service available, but it's sometimes difficult to get a female Arabic interpreter for pre-natal classes.*
4.4.15. Does the health centre use other venues in the community from which to conduct its activities (e.g. homes, schools, workplaces)?	*4.4.15. Many programs conducted in schools and other community venues. Primary Medical Services provide no home visits.*

The CHASP standards have indicators that:

i) suggest how the standard may be achieved,

ii) can be used to assess the level of achievement.

The CHASP Review Report includes comments on how each standard has been achieved by the centre/service.

(Fry, Denise and Lesley King: 1991)

- Giving the receiver of the complaint power to make changes.

Reference:

'The Essentials: A Complaints System that Works' in *Consumers' Fair Go! Kit*, written by Rick Mohr and Rowan Lunney, Combined Pensioners Association of NSW, Level 5, 405 Sussex Street, Haymarket, NSW, 2000:1989

Congruency and compliance models

These terms are used in the evaluation literature to refer to evaluation models which look at whether program operations are consistent with or divergent from OBJECTIVES and PERFORMANCE INDICATORS, such as those found in SERVICE AGREEMENTS, and whether funds have been spent as agreed (not just whether they have been spent). Typical congruency and compliance models would be MANAGEMENT BY OBJECTIVES, PROGRAM BUDGETING, SERVICE AGREEMENTS, and techniques like CRITICAL PATH ANALYSIS (for example, PERT). The term 'compliance' indicates that these are generally operated as management approaches.

Reference:

ARMSTRONG, Anona *Evaluation Models and Strategies* Evaluation Training and Services Pty Ltd, Melbourne:1986

Connoisseurship model

An evaluation model from the American education camp, Elliot Eisner developed this model. It uses the special metaphor of the arts critic to represent perceptive observation drawing on experience and imaginative criticism (critique or disclosure) to reveal deeper underlying characteristics or structures. The fine nuances noticed by someone who has devoted years of attention to refining evaluative judgement in a particular area are given credit and sought out. The chief drawback is if the perception, and hence insights, have been driven by different values or interests from those involved in the current evaluative effort. There may also be a large amount of unexplicated intuition, or undocumented evidence, making it difficult for others to use the technique themselves or to cross-check the sources of the connoisseur's evaluations.

Reference:

EISNER, Elliot 'Educational Connoisseurship and Criticism—Their Form and Functions in Educational Evaluation' in George F. MADAUS, Michael SCRIVEN and Daniel F. STUFFLEBEAM (Eds) *Evaluation Models—Viewpoints on Educational and Human Services Evaluation* Kluwer-Nijhoff Publishing, The Hague, pp. 335–348:1983

Constructivist evaluation

Also termed by its theorists Egon Guba and Yvonna Lincoln 'fourth generation' evaluation, this draws on and extends radically some of the old tenets of INTERPRETIVE research and applies them to evaluation. It leaves behind the *'first generation' of evaluation which was preoccupied with measuring test results; 'second generation'* objectives-based and outcome-oriented evaluation; and *'third generation'* judgement and decision-oriented evaluation, on the grounds of their tendencies to disempower legitimate parties to the evaluation, their failure to accommodate other values, and their overcommitment to old paradigm science. Instead, it proposes that the central concern of evaluation is negotiation over, and construction of, the meanings of the value of what is being evaluated—involving the evaluators, the evaluated and evaluated for—in relation to context, and with an action orientation. The various stakeholders may, however, differ in their centrality relative to the purposes of that which is being evaluated (and there remains a risk of existing power relations determining outcomes, despite an ethics of 'dignity, integrity and privacy' and hope of enfranchisement of all stakeholders). But certainly Guba and Lincoln make the quantum leap from old paradigm to new paradigm science. The evaluator no longer evaluates, but sets in place processes that assist others to co-evaluate.

Reference:

GUBA, Egon and Yvonna LINCOLN *Fourth Generation Evaluation* Sage, London:1989

GUBA, Egon *The Paradigm Dialog* Sage, London:1990

BERGER, Peter and Thomas LUCKMANN *The Social Construction of Reality* Anchor Doubleday, New York:1967

Consumer evaluation

The formal evaluation literature regards 'consumer evaluation' as that where an expert evaluator acts as an 'enlightened surrogate consumer' and judges what is in the interests of consumers.

'Consumer studies' have also conventionally involved professional researchers going out and asking consumers for their views of services. More recently, these studies have been conducted by consumers themselves, or by their organisations, or by consumer advocacy bodies. Conventional science often considers such work to be biased and subjective, etc., however the critique of old paradigm science in conjunction with an increasing body of consumer studies, suggests that strong driving value-interests increase the pressure to accomplish relevant and valuable work. When REFLEXIVE and self-critical, they are more likely 'to get it right' because consumers literally can't afford to get it wrong. 'Bad intelligence', like the covert military operations from which the metaphor is drawn, is not in consumers' interests (even if the findings are 'liked'). Consumer evaluation, or that done by critical reference groups, may involve SELF-EVALUATION or GROUP SELF-EVALUATION, or it may 'study up' or be COLLABORATIVE. An assumption of this kind of consumer evaluation is that users of services are the ultimate arbiters of the value, merit, worth and significance of those services, since the essential indicators of service success must relate to their meeting users' needs (there being limits to how 'good' a service or intervention can be if consumers do not agree that it is).

Reference:

MOHR, Rich and Rowan LUNNEY *Consumers' Fair Go! Kit*, particularly the papers 'How to Have Your Say', 'How to Improve Your Community Service', Combined Pensioners Association of NSW:1989

Context, Input, Process, Product (CIPP)

This SYSTEMS model, developed by Daniel Stufflebeam, has been popular in education circles. It was developed in the late 1960s in reaction to Tyler's behavioural objectives-based testing and experimental designs and is based on the view that the most important purpose of evaluation is 'not to prove but to improve'. It offers four different kinds of evaluation in response to four different kinds of decision-needs:

- *Context evaluation*: This identifies strengths and weaknesses, assesses needs and judges relationships to objectives.
- *Input evaluation*: This identifies and assesses system capabilities and alternative plans (procedures, staff, budgets, strategies, etc.).
- *Process evaluation*: This assesses and guides implementation by identifying defects, refining design and procedure.
- *Product evaluation*: This identifies and assesses outcomes and relates to objectives, in order to serve 'recycling' decisions (continue, terminate, modify, refocus, etc.).

This model was initially primarily intended as an *inquiry approach* for guidance in service development and improvement, but it was later thought that it could be used also to generate records for accountability and reporting or *audit review* kinds of evaluation.

Reference:

STUFFLEBEAM, Daniel L. 'The CIPP Model for Program Evaluation' in George F. MADAUS, Michael SCRIVEN and Daniel F. STUFFLEBEAM (Eds) *Evaluation Models—Viewpoints on Educational and Human Services Evaluation* Kluwer-Nijhoff Publishing, The Hague, pp. 117–142:1983

Cost-benefit analysis, cost-effective analysis

These evaluation methods (and the associated PROGRAM BUDGETING, CRITICAL PATH ANALYSIS, and PERT methods) are ways of evaluating spending, investment and funding, but by reference to a variety of criteria such as benefit-to-population served (value for money) efficiency (maximum value for minimum money), and so on. Originating in the market economy, cost-benefit analysis has been controversial in human services where the price mechanism is less meaningful. Their 'price' is set not in the market place, but in a sense by the ballot box. As well, even when there are comparable private sector services, account has to be taken of the way in which public sector services are already partly a result of 'market failure' (that is, already having been deemed to represent inefficient resource allocation by the competitive, profit-driven market). Cost-effectiveness analysis is an attempt to relate costs to non-monetary internal criteria or to objectives. It has also been called 'performance budgeting' and this is its link with PROGRAM BUDGETING (PPBS). Thus, the nature of the debate is more about the effects of spending this much, rather than that much, or spending this much on this, rather than on that.

Reference:

LEVIN, Henry *Cost Effectiveness* Sage, Beverley Hills, California:1983

THOMPSON, Mark *Benefit Cost Analysis for Program Evaluation* Sage, Beverley Hills, California:1980

Critical path analysis

This technique, and versions of it such as PERT and GANTT scheduling, is a way to sort out and establish a kind of an evaluative framework for the chronology of implementation tasks for a service, while still at the planning stage. It is a way of setting down a description of an expected set of timed activities so that actual progress can be quickly and easily compared for any discrepancy, and rectifying action taken (or explanation made for diversion). While designed as a decision-making tool for managers, the essence of this approach can easily be applied by everyday evaluators. The technique in its simplest form can be done by pen and paper; in its more complex form (for example, for more than 100 activities)—by computer program. The danger of the computerised form is that, when calculations turn out to be wrong, everything can be adjusted by the pushing of a few keys so no apparent discrepancy remains! See PERT and GANTT for examples of how the technique looks. The critical path is the total expected time path after all calculations have been made. You can calculate worst possible scenarios (longest path) or best (shortest).

Reference:

EDUCATION DEPARTMENT OF VICTORIA 'Critical Path' in *Destination Decisions* Curriculum Branch, Chapter 7, pp. 43–46:1985

HOFFER, Joe R. 'PERT: A Tool for Managers of Human Service Programs' in F. COX et al. *Tactics and Techniques of Community Practice* F.E. Peacock, Itasca, pp. 287–298:1977

Decision-theoretic approach

This technique is aimed at clarifying the relationships among multiple goals which may represent conflicting values and interests. It can use statistical and quantitative techniques for measuring values and uncertainties regarding outcomes, and the probability of those outcomes. In its broadest sense, it is about evaluating with a view to decision-making. In its simplest sense it is accessible to everyday evaluators, that is, it encourages us to ask about the value of our decisions and also to assess new ideas with a view to what will be done in practice as a result of them.

Reference:

EDWARDS, Ward, Marcia GUTTENTAG and Kurt SNAPPER 'A Decision-Theoretic Approach to Evaluative Research' in Elmer STRUENING and Marcia GUTTENTAG (Eds) *Handbook of Evaluation Research* Vol. 1 Sage, Beverly Hills, California pp. 139–182:1975

Delphi Technique

Like its name (which alludes to a famous oracle of ancient Greece) this technique attempts to get a handle on ideas for planning for the future. Originally developed by the Rand Corporation in the 1950s, it has since been taken up in both the education and community services areas. While it reached a peak in popularity in the late 1970s it has continued to be used, particularly by managers, to elicit quickly both a range of ideas from and then also a form of consensus among a group of experts. The format involves an initial round of open-ended questionnaires seeking the issues people see as important. The results of these are circulated to all those who contributed to the original questionnaires, with a further questionnaire asking people to rank all the possibilities now before them. Convergence tends to ensue as an artefact of the technique. A drawback arises if the pool of items after the first round represent less than an ideal pool of wisdom. If better options are required and no-one could imagine viable new steps, then frustration can arise in the second round when people are forced to choose from less-than-desirable options. The second drawback is if these less-than-desirable options are then ranked and a 'numbers game' ensures everyone is then stuck with the result. That is, the 'consensus' isn't reached by discussion and empowered/informed contributions, but by imposition after someone crunches the numbers. It may be unfortunate that some of the original defining characteristics of the technique (such as the elimination of face to face contact and discussion in order to minimise the 'emotive effects of group dynamics' and also the inconvenience of geographic travel, plus its reliance on forced choices, and emphasis on involving 'experts') have always been stuck to so rigidly. Its basic format, supplemented by some group interaction, can be helpful to everyday evaluators for firstly getting a lot of individual ideas on the table, and secondly getting a group to move towards selecting from among the ideas. It can also be useful for clarification of intentions or purposes. SEARCH CONFERENCES overcome some of these drawbacks. BRAINSTORMING and NOMINAL GROUP TECHNIQUES (see *Do It Yourself Social Research*) also address similar needs.

Reference:

DELBECQ, A.L., A.H. VANDEVEN and D.M. GUSTAFSON *Group Techniques for Program Planning: A Guide to Nominal Group and Delphi Processes* Foresman and Co. Scott, USA:1975

Democratic evaluation

This is the third kind of evaluation defined by Barry MacDonald, along with AUTOCRATIC and BUREAUCRATIC evaluation. Democratic evaluation is an information service to the community about the characteristics of a program. It recognises value-pluralism and seeks to represent a range of interests in its formulation of issues. The basic value is an informed citizenry, and the evaluator acts as broker in exchanges of information between differing groups. Techniques of data-gathering and presentation must be accessible to non-specialist audiences. The main activity is the collection of definitions of, and reactions to, the program. The evaluator offers confidentiality to informants and gives them control over the use of information. The report is non-recommendatory, and the evaluator has no concept of information misuse. The evaluator engages in periodic negotiation of his or her relationships with sponsors and program participants. The criterion of success is the range of audiences served. The report aspires to best-seller status. The key concepts of democratic evaluation are 'confidentiality', 'negotiation' and 'accessibility', and the key justificatory concept is 'the right to know'.

Reference:

MACDONALD, Barry 'Evaluation and the Control of Education' in D.A. TAWNEY (Ed) *Curriculum Evaluation Today—Trends and Implications* Schools Council Research Studies, London, Macmillan:1976

Developmental evaluation

This is a term being used by a number of evaluators and evaluation consultants who have identified the value of working with services or organisations *over time* in contrast to the swoop-in-swoop-out one-off version of evaluation consultancy. By building both working relationships and trust between themselves and the organisation or service, and by building a store of experiences and skills to self-reflect and explore questions and gather data *among* those within the organisation or service, evaluation facilitators or consultants can overcome some of the wastage associated with the style of consultancy which is predominant. In ORGANISATIONAL DEVELOPMENT, it may be called 'process consulting'. It has some things in common with ACTION EVALUATION, CLIENT-CENTRED MODELS, PARTICIPATORY and REFLEXIVE evaluation.

Reference:

PATTON, Michael Quinn 'Developmental Evaluation' in *Evaluation Practice* Vol. 15, No. 3, pp. 311–319:1994

Discrepancy evaluation model (DEM)

This model, developed by Malcolm Provus in the education area, places heavy emphasis on implementation evaluation and was itself a reaction to the limited usefulness to practitioners of the assumptions of laboratory experimental designs. It seeks to identify the *discrepancies* between the actual program *performance* and the ideal program or a *standard*. It derives the description of ideals from the values of program staff and the client population served. It also argues that evaluation of even large-scale national programs must begin at the local level. Decision-makers are assisted to determine how far and in what ways a program deviates from the ideal but can still be said to have been implemented (and be meeting its fundamental criteria). To the extent to which it treats goals as surrogates for needs, and hence the discrepancy is practically between programs and goals/ideals, then it has tended to operate more often as a management tool than as a staff or consumer-driven model. See also STANDARDS programs.

References:

PROVUS, Malcolm *Discrepancy Evaluation for Educational Program Improvement and Assessment*, Berkley, California, McCutchan:1971

STEINMETZ, Andres 'The Discrepancy Evaluation Model' in George MADAUS, Michael SCRIVEN and Daniel F. STUFFLEBEAM (Eds) *Evaluation Models—Viewpoints on Educational and Human Services Evaluation* Kluwer-Nijhoff Publishing, The Hague, pp. 79–100:1983

Ecological evaluation model

This model also emerged out of educational psychology in the 1970s in reaction to the artificiality of laboratory-based experimental approaches. Like NATURALISTIC and CONSTRUCTIVIST models drawing on HERMENEUTICAL understanding, it sought to orient evaluators' attention to the settings and interactions within and between people's environments, and to understand these not as a set of interacting separate variables, but as organically or wholistically structured parts of a single 'living' context. Ultimately, its particular format fell prey to some of the features of more conventional POSITIVIST evaluation—such as those of 'objectivism', where the external non-participatory scientist still peered down a microscope (albeit at a whole duck pond rather than just the duck weed!), and did not engage actively in the process of discussion and interaction characteristic of a more INTERPRETIVE or CONSTRUCTIVIST approach.

Reference:

BRONFRENBRENNER, Urie 'The Experimental Ecology of Education' in *Educational Researcher* Vol. 5, No. 9, pp. 5–15:1976

Evaluand

That which is being evaluated.

Experimental evaluation

Laboratory-based science has yielded a model of science which has its enthusiasts in the social sciences. This model proposes that in order to know whether something has had an intended or expected effect, one should try to control all elements of a situation and only vary the one intended or expected element to see if the effect is as anticipated. In a simple everyday way we often use a quasi experimental approach whenever we use 'trial and error'. However, a full blown experimental approach tries to control all elements and only vary the 'study elements'. Thus it tries to control for all possible sources of difference by random sampling of participants to standardise the study population, having control groups (that are meant to be identical to the study group, except for the study element or intervention which is not varied), by standardising the physical environment, by attempting to eliminate any effects of the experiment or experimenter—

conducting the experiment so no-one (neither researcher nor researched) knows which group got the varied element (double blinding) and so on.

Unfortunately, as can be imagined, the method is pretty difficult to accomplish in human life with human populations—particularly if the matter being studied is a natural social process of any complexity like community development, or household formation or human service provision or processes of discrimination.

The nature of human beings as aware, self aware and mutually aware; the complexity and interdependency of 'variables'; the constant natural changeability, including that resulting inevitably from any form of research intervention (even so-called 'unobtrusive' research), not to mention the requirements of human ethics (for example, not withholding treatment from a control group when it is already suspected of having value), largely prevents this form of science from having everyday applicability. When attempted it often results in problematic science—primarily because of the reduction of meaning and validity and the giving of a false sense of certainty. Where some meaning survives, results often feel like one is 'reading braille through a doona':* yielding only abstract outlines or glimpses of the multiple and socially-constructed realities they are meant to be representing. Alternatively, it often results in predictable science since it primarily offers to verify (or falsify) hypotheses which are generally already the result of previous theory-building research or evaluation. The experimental method is frequently further confounded by adherence to POSITIVIST and expertist assumptions which deny the value of people's experiential truths and knowledge claims.

References:

CAMPBELL, D.T., and J.C. STANLEY, 'Experimental and Quasi-Experimental Designs for Research on Teaching' in N.L. GAGE (Ed) *Handbook of Research on Teaching* Chicago, Rand McNally:1963

COOK, T.D., and D.T. CAMPBELL, *Quasi-Experimentation—Design and Analysis Issues for Field Settings*, Chicago, Rand McNally:1979

GOTTMAN, John and Robert CLASEN 'Troubleshooting Guide for Research and Evaluation' in F. COX et al. *Tactics and Techniques of Community Practice* F.E. Peacock, Itasca, p. 367–370:1977

An accessible and plausible account is contained in:

HAWE, P., D. DEGELING and J. HALL *Evaluating Health Promotion—A Health Worker's Guide* MacLennan and Petty, Sydney:1990

* A Yoland Wadsworth 'original' which translates as attempting to detect meanings through thick abstraction or reductionism (as in reading braille through a feather quilt).

Explication model

This approach tries to avoid the implication of 'judgement' (often by an external 'objective' expert) that has given evaluation a negative connotation. Instead, like ILLUMINATIVE, NATURALISTIC or CONSTRUCTIVIST approaches, it tries—as the name implies—by means of clarification, INTERPRETATION and explanation, to understand and illuminate. It draws on anthropology as a source of techniques such as on-site observation, and its key strength is that it may produce more rich and detailed descriptions of both practices and intentions. Its drawback lies in its fear of being evaluative (judgemental) which may obscure the necessity of having to produce at least some kind of value-driven comparative analysis that implies that some practices and intentions are more desirable than others (for critical reference groups' purposes or needs). CONSTRUCTIONIST evaluation overcomes some of these difficulties by using an explication model but also by shifting the locus of judgement from an independent 'objective' expert back to the collective participants in the evaluated phenomena.

References:

KOPPELMAN, K.L., 'The Explication Model—An Anthropological Approach to Program Evaluation' in George MADAUS, Michael SCRIVEN and Daniel F. STUFFLEBEAM (Eds) *Evaluation Models—Viewpoints on Educational and Human Services Evaluation* Kluwer-Nijhoff Publishing, The Hague, pp. 59–64:1983

McDERMOTT, Fiona, and Priscilla PYETT *The Meaning of Treatment—An Evaluation Handbook for Alcohol and Other Drug Treatment Agencies* University of Melbourne:1990

Financial Management Improvement Program (FMIP)

The FMIP was an influential Australian Commonwealth Government budgetary *audit review* mechanism aimed at improving resource allocation decision-making in the 1980s and early 1990s. It was a highly rationalistic and comprehensive attempt to achieve performance evaluation of all programs based on identified descriptions of objectives and activities with efficiency and/or effectiveness performance indicators, tied to resource usage. It involved several related mechanisms such as PROGRAM BUDGETING and MANAGEMENT FOR RESULTS (MFR)—an extension of MANAGEMENT BY OBJECTIVES (MBO). One feature was the insertion of the expectation that new initiatives must be at the expense of old ones—thus involving apportioning-type decisions. (This relates to the popularity, particularly in the health area, of QUALYS—a tool to assist this kind of evaluation activity). It also involved the introduction of a 'user pays' principle—even where goods or services are exchanged between and even within government departments—as a way of introducing costing to assist managers to think about COST-BENEFIT evaluation. The greatest drawback for services from all this top-down *audit review* activity is that there can be a powerful 'locking-in' of services to a fixed set of objectives. Such a tremendously rationalistic effort can make it enormously difficult for change to take place in flexible response to community needs. The ponderousness of any change to PROGRAM BUDGETING categories attests to this, as does the lack of discretionary funding power when all items are 'tied down' for at least one full budget cycle. The greatest value is that, like all audit review evaluation, explicitly aware attention can be focused on the value of even the smallest backwater of activity—even if only in the simple and abstract form typical of most audit review approaches.

Reference:

LINARD, Keith 'Program Evaluation and Resource Management Improvement in the Commonwealth Public Service' *Paper* to National Evaluation Conference, Canberra:1988

Fishbowl

Fishbowl is an observational and feedback technique and involves the simple idea of staging a 'two-ring circus'—with the inner circle comprising a group discussion watched by an outer circle. At a later point in time the two groups can either swap places in entirety or exchange some members or exchange perceptions, or the outer circle reports on their observations of what the inner circle did. It is a way of organising active participation and silent witnessing that might be useful, for example, around an issue where one point of view (or more points) are not otherwise getting a good hearing. It depends a lot on the skills of those staging it and the purposes being served.

Reference:

Education Department of Victoria 'Fishbowl' in *Destination Decisions* Curriculum Branch, Chapter 13, p. 83:1985

Force-field analysis

This technique addresses the old maxim 'We act, but not under conditions of our own choosing'! It involves the written-down description of all the 'forces' or social conditions that are *for* the desired change on one side of the page, and then all the 'forces' or barriers or conditions *against* change on the other side of the page. The lists may not be the same length—some 'forces' are stronger than others. (This could be denoted in some way.) BRAINSTORMING could be used to produce the lists. Again, some of the 'forces' may not be immediately obvious and only thought of later. This kind of technique is useful at the point in the evaluation research cycle when the question has arisen, 'Why have our valued worlds not come to replace our actual worlds?' or 'Why have our actual worlds not metamorphosed into our valued worlds?'. It is also useful at the point of the cycle where possible future options are being evaluated in order to settle on a recommended new course of action. Once the forces have been described, these descriptions could be researched to fill them out in more detail (for example, not just mentioning 'professional power'—but designating exactly the elements of professional ideas or practices), or to check their strength. A drawback can be if the 'forces' are only superficially explored and 'obvious' but less effective solutions are opted-for rather than hard-to-imagine but more informed solutions.

Reference:

Education Department of Victoria 'Force Field Analysis' in *Destination Decisions* Curriculum Branch, Chapter 9, pp. 53–62:1985

Formative evaluation

Michael Scriven's conceptualisation of evaluation as FORMATIVE (or SUMMATIVE) has now become so widespread as to have supplied some household (officehold?) words in evaluation. They are not, however, two *kinds* of evaluation, but designate two roles or *functions* (and audiences) of evaluation—formative being 'for *improvement* of a skill-developing entity' (while summative is 'for *decision* about the fate of a program'). Both roles or functions are essentially performed for managers—but 'formative' presumably so managers can instruct staff and 'summative' so managers can inform funders or higher-ups! Scriven saw evaluation for formative purposes as logically subservient to evaluation for summative purposes—indeed as 'early-warning summative', and ideally done by an independent evaluator. It refers to evaluation that is generally ongoing, or of a monitoring nature with continuous feedback to amend and improve a service or activity. It may focus on 'throughput', although it would be difficult to do without some attention to effects.

Formative evaluation is not necessarily equivalent to PROCESS evaluation, or to implementation evaluation or progress evaluation (nor is summative evaluation necessarily equitable with OUTCOME or OUTPUT evaluation). Evaluation for formative purposes *may* study outputs and outcomes *to-date*; and evaluation for summative purposes may give an account of process and be unable to report on outputs or outcomes at that point in time.

Reference:

SCRIVEN, Michael *The Logic of Evaluation* Edgepress, Inverness, California:1981

Fuzzy set theory

This theory, which has no connection with 'warm fuzzy' theory, was in response to the phenomenon of so-called fuzzy goals. Rather than treat program staff's tolerance of intuitive and implicit (and possibly ambivalent, unclear, emergent or divergent) goals as problematic, it sees as desirable that there be a variety of interests and perspectives in order for people to be able to get on with things. Unlike techniques such as DELPHI, MULTI-ATTRIBUTE UTILITY MEASUREMENT and DECISION-THEORETIC as well as all goals-based approaches, which all require a clear list of specific accurate and measurable goals at the outset, fuzzy set theory is an (albeit highly mathematical-quantitative) approach to understanding 'approximate reasoning'. Fuzzy goals (fuzzy decisions and fuzzy programs) can be accepted by evaluators by a kind of reverse estimation of goals from decision problems. GOAL-FREE evaluation attempts to shift the exercise right out of preoccupation with any kind of goals clarification.

References:

ZADEH, Lofti 'Fuzzy Sets' in *Inform and Control* No. 8. pp. 338–353:1965

ZADEH, Lofti, King-sun FU, Kokichi TANAKA and Masamichi SHIMURA (Eds) *Fuzzy Sets and Their Applications to Cognitive and Decision Processes* Academic Press, New York:1975

GANTT schedules

When you read what this is you will probably be surprised to find it is a Proper Technique with A Name! This horizontal set of bar charts will be familiar to many everyday planners. It works a little like PERT as a mild CRITICAL PATH-like framework for evaluating (*audit reviewing*) progress where several or many people are sequentially or correspondingly accomplishing activities between which there are links. Unlike PERT it does not actually show the links between activities. The typical staff holiday leave schedule or volunteers' roster are examples. A GANTT chart for the Action Research Issues Centre's projects might look as per the diagram below.

Reference:

Education Department of Victoria 'Critical Path' in *Destination Decisions* Curriculum Branch, Chapter 9, pp. 43–46:1985

Goal Attainment Scaling (GAS)

This approach, like the WELL-FORMED OUTCOME MODEL, was developed in the mental health area to assist clients and therapists or nurses rate client achievement of goals on a matrix of behaviours. In this technique these are classified into five levels of outcomes from 'least likely' to 'expected' to 'best possible outcome'. Like all *audit review* approaches its strength lies in making ones' 'best guesses' conscious, and its weakness in treating these 'best guesses' as the 'right guesses'.

Reference:

KIRESUK, T.J., 'Goal Attainment Scaling at a County Mental Health Service' in *Evaluation*, Special Monograph No. 1, pp. 13–19:1973

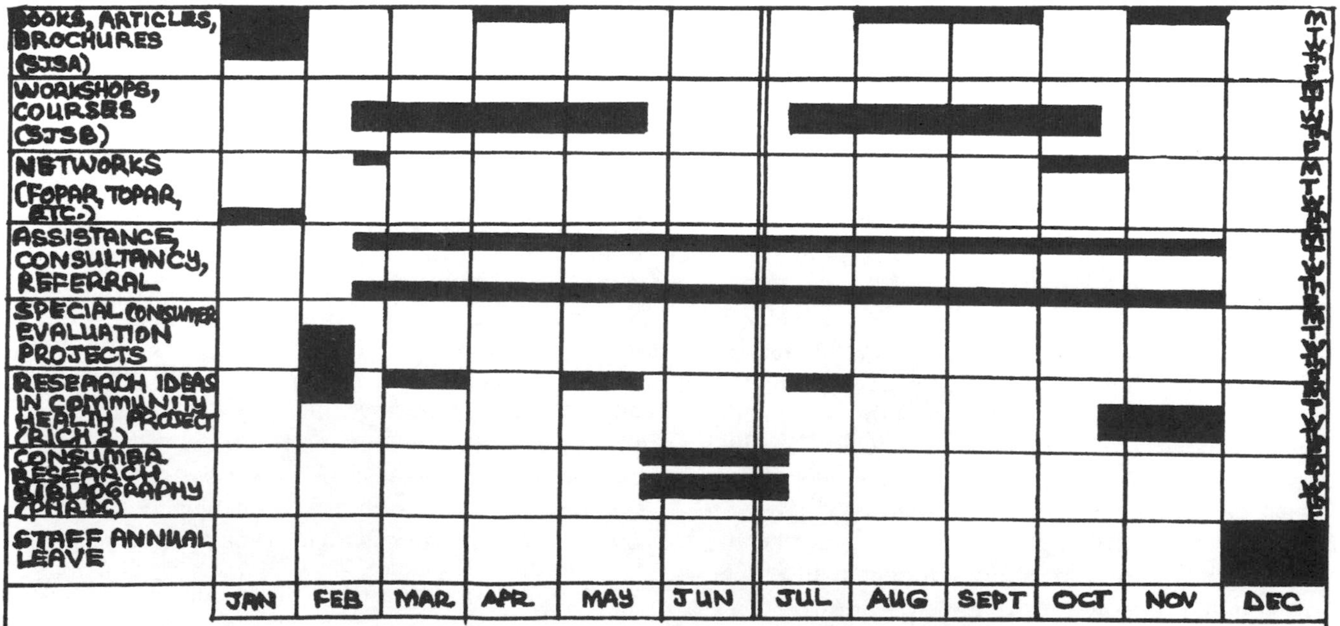
BOOKS, ARTICLES, BROCHURES (SJSA)
WORKSHOPS, COURSES (SJSB)
NETWORKS (FOPAR, TOPAR, ETC.)
ASSISTANCE, CONSULTANCY, REFERRAL
SPECIAL CONSUMER EVALUATION PROJECTS
RESEARCH IDEAS IN COMMUNITY HEALTH PROJECT (RICH 2)
CONSUMER RESEARCH BIBLIOGRAPHY (PHARC)
STAFF ANNUAL LEAVE
JAN
FEB
MAR
APR
MAY
JUN
JUL
AUG
SEPT
OCT
NOV
DEC

GANTT PLANNING CHART FOR THE ACTION RESEARCH ISSUES CENTRE

Goal-based (or objective-based) evaluation

This is evaluation which *starts* by asking what were a services' or an activities' formal explicit, written-down, pre-framed, pre-agreed goals and/or objectives and then asks whether these were fulfilled. Some believe this is not evaluation *per se* but merely a checking exercise where merit and worth cannot be treated as reducible to meeting goals. Nevertheless it can form a useful framework for detecting discrepancies if the goals are known to still be of value. That is, they will be more useful if the prior cycles of inquiry research were well done and there has been little change. Paradoxically, they will be more rigid and difficult to change as they become more and more refined. See sections in this book on the *audit review* approach to evaluation for further strengths and weaknesses. (See also Diagram 3 and Guide 5.) Examples in this annotated bibliography of related models and techniques include MANAGEMENT BY OBJECTIVES, PROGRAM BUDGETING, PERT, DISCREPANCY EVALUATION MODEL, CHASP and PASSING.

Reference:

Most standard evaluation guides, texts and manuals produced by central agencies.

Goal-free evaluation

The preoccupation with evaluating against goals and objectives statements led Michael Scriven, among others, to propose a way of trying to avoid the associated difficulties of:

- The narrowness of program objectives' coverage.
- Missing seeing the unanticipated outcomes which hitherto carried negative connotations as mere 'side-effects'—but which might actually represent crucial achievements (suggesting new priorities).
- To avoid the so called 'contamination', 'tunnel-vision' and 'perceptual biases' of the observer if the goals (particularly if laudable) are known and familiar, and channel thinking into unhelpful ruts.

While this approach may easily have lapsed into a naive inductivism (assuming that our perception is guided by no pre-formed ideas, hunches or theories), Scriven was clear that he was, in practice, evaluating 'actual effects' against a 'profile of demonstrated needs'.

Nevertheless, even needs statements are often produced in a form that implies (albeit unarticulated) some kinds of needs-meeting arrangements (and hence informal 'objectives' and 'goals'). In this sense Scriven's effort has been criticised as substituting needs for program staff's goals. Scriven also talked of 'national needs' and a wider 'decision audience' of 'national policy formulators' who define needs rather than those who have them. While this may free up the evaluator from local management or program staff control, it does not appear necessarily to bring the evaluator closer to those with the needs. Unlike the approach of this book which directs attention back to the specific and concrete expression of needs by those who have them—the critical reference groups—Scriven appears to direct attention upwards to decision-makers or experts, and to broader categories of represented needs, that in practice may turn out to be simply the evaluator's judgement of these. Local service providers are excluded from this kind of evaluation, however, if they were to be included and encouraged to reflect on their services *without reference to formal goals statements*, and examine other effects, other than those intended, then this would approximate part of what has been called an *open inquiry* approach in this book. In Scriven's version of the goal-free model there is also ambivalence over the role of the 'client'. While his approach has been called 'consumerist' rather than managerialist, he does appear to place the evaluation's point of view outside and above that of either consumers or managers.

Reference:

SCRIVEN, Michael 'Pros and Cons About Goal-Free Evaluation' *Evaluation Comment: The Journal of Educational Evaluation* Centre for the Study of Evaluation, UCLA, Vol. 3. No. 4. pp. 1–7:1972

Group self-evaluation (GSE)

Group self-evaluation incorporates the basic elements of SELF-EVALUATION but in an organised collective setting. It might be a group brought together to work collectively on exploring the fruits of individual self-evaluations (for example, a service staff meeting might work to regularly receive and offer ideas about individual staff's self-evaluation exercises) or it may be a group that together is providing the same service and which comes together to examine collectively that joint effort. As well, like self-evaluation, group self-evaluation may be an exercise in looking at one's own practices, but will generally also extend to reflection on the context and efforts of the practices of others—not in the sense of taking responsibility for what others are doing and giving them Good Advice, but in the sense of examining the effects—both enabling and frustrating (see FORCE-FIELD ANALYSIS)—of their practices. There are some important conditions for GSE working well:

- People must participate voluntarily. GSE cannot be mandated for reporting or *audit review* functions. If it is, then it will become group self-reporting (generally reporting in terms of objectives), and it will not function for *open inquiry* evaluation and improvement purposes.
- The learning which takes place can be credited to the group, but the group should resist any tendency to 'close ranks' to compel individual

members to learn particular things in particular ways. The technique for learning relies entirely on individuals swapping their experience and trusting and being trusted to ask sympathetic illuminative or *critical questions.*

'Critical' does not mean criticism. A critical question takes the form of a query about the conditions for knowledge and action—why and how people came to know what they know and do as they do. It is essential that the route to current conviction and practice is retraced and useful questions be asked to generate new conclusions or a different route to a new way of knowing. Secretly you might be convinced that someone is spending a lot of their time doing some things that are unimportant, irrelevant or downright damaging. You suspend your pre-formed conclusions in the spirit of sceptical science and you go back to the start by asking what led the person to do what they are doing. The forthcoming explanation can be further pursued by continuing to ask 'why' questions such as:

'And what led you to draw that conclusion?'
'Where did those ideas come from?'
'Did you have a lot of evidence for that?'
'Why was that evidence so convincing for you?'
'Where or when did you first start noticing that?'
'What effects did you notice?'
'Did that fully satisfy you?'

This style of questioning helps each person retrace their steps and possibly beat a new track in order to finish up in a place different to the current problematic one. People need to do this for themselves if they are to be truly committed to the new way of seeing. As the old Chinese proverb (only slightly modified!) goes:

What I am told—I forget.
What I read—I recall.
What I see—I remember.
What I do—I understand.

If the group includes no critical reference group members then a further range of 'touching base' questions can be asked such as:

'How did your students/clients/patients/community members feel about that?'
'What signs did you pick up of their reactions?'
'Were they the reactions you'd hoped for?'

The group can vary in size, formality, number of times it meets, and so on. It might be three other like-minded souls you trust to reveal something you feel very vulnerable about, or it might be five people including an outsider with a fresh perspective, or it might be ten people who include some of your greatest critics! It might be a one-off, or you might 'contract' to meet once a month for six months, or once a week for four weeks, or on an ad hoc basis whenever a member would like it.

GSE examines 'circumstance, action and consequence' in an active PARTICIPATORY and organised learning process. It has strong ACTION RESEARCH and action learning elements. While GSE has been developed for professionals working together in human services provision, there is no necessity for the approach to be limited in these ways. Service users, self-help groups, or 'slices' of mixed COLLABORATIVE groups made up of providers and users could use GSE which is at essence a reflection on '*learning by doing*'. Even groups of managers could use GSE, perhaps involving some service providers and users to get a fresh handle on their own practices. Groups operate as 'learning communities', united around shared interest, organising around joint tasks, and with a sense of solidarity around a desire to question, understand, learn and develop. Group processes do, however, need to overcome or work hard at overcoming the non-DEMOCRATIC effects of any power imbalances among members.

References:

BROWN, Lynton *Group Self-Evaluation—Learning for Improvement* Ministry of Education, Victoria:1988

BROWN, Lynton *Group Self-Evaluation—A Collection of Readings* Ministry of Education, Victoria:1990

Guttman-type scale

This has a set of items which increase on a scale along an attribute such as difficulty or favourableness. If a respondent ticks item three, it is assumed that items one and two also apply. The following example illustrates this kind of scale. It may be seen that this kind of data would leave an *audit review*-style of evaluation without much idea as to what to do to bring about change:

1 Would you object to a retarded person living in your community?
2 Would you object to a retarded person working where you work?
3 Would you object to having lunch with a retarded person at work?
4 Would you object to a retarded person coming to your home for dinner?
5 Would you object to a retarded person marrying a member of your family?

Most of the problems with scales come about from either the statement being badly worded (or conceptualised) and/or the responses being too closed, irrelevant or otherwise incurring unwanted resistance by the person who is meant to choose from among them. Another problem of this kind of survey approach is that it can contribute to reifying opinions, ideas or situations that are undesirable from the value standpoint of some disadvantaged group. Evaluation itself is not value-free, and asking particular questions in particular ways does not merely 'capture' truth-for-its-own-sake but can actually influence and increase the strength with which people may believe things that may be damaging to themselves or to others. Conventional POSITIVIST approaches are unable to evaluate their own contribution to the setting in concrete of both desirable and undesirable situations. INTERPRETIVE, CRITICAL and CONSTRUCTIVIST approaches can take these matters into account.

Reference:

GOTTMAN, John and Robert CLASEN 'Troubleshooting Guide for Research and Evaluation' in F. COX et al. *Tactics and Techniques of Community Practice* F.E. Peacock, Itasca, p. 372:1977

Hermeneutic evaluation

The term 'hermeneutic' has traditionally been used to describe the practice of Biblical exegesis, that is, what scholars do who are trying to understand and INTERPRET the stories and material of scripture in terms of the context in which they were written. In social science it has come to refer to the task of trying to put forward an understanding of a message by grasping the context from which it was sent. It implies that one cannot know or interpret the particular without knowing the whole (just as the whole can only be hermeneutically grasped by reference to the particular). For example, the value of one self-help health group's efforts may only make sense by reference not only to its own past history but also to the current and past practices of other self-help health groups, all self-help groups, the medical profession and its institutional forms, and the nature and level of community support for self-help groups. In turn, each of these other contexts may be better understood by reference to the activities and existence of that one particular self-help group. The concept of 'hermeneutic' captures the popular idea of a grain of sand being a microcosm of the universe—while it being impossible to understand fully the universe unless the grain of sand is included. When 'living' societies are studied, we can talk of a double hermeneutic whereby the 'study matter' can be contextualised by an observer and then can review and alter that contextualisation themselves!

Reference:

BAUMAN, Zygmunt *Hermeneutics and Social Science* Hutchinson, London:1978

Illuminative evaluation

This is another approach concerned with description, INTERPRETATION and understanding rather than with measurement, QUANTIFICATION and prediction. Malcolm Parlett and David Hamilton coined the term 'illuminative' to describe evaluation which takes account of the wider *contexts* in which programs (in their case, education programs) take place. It draws on social anthropology traditions, and was developed in response to the dominance of what they called the 'agricultural-botany' experimental tradition. The 'context' element of CONTEXT, INPUT, PROCESS, PRODUCT (CIPP) attempts a similar task.

Reference:

PARLETT, Malcolm and David HAMILTON, 'Evaluation as Illumination: A New Approach to the Study of Innovatory Programs' in David HAMILTON et al. (Eds) *Beyond the Numbers Game—A Reader in Educational Evaluation* pp. 6–22 Macmillan, London:1977

Impact evaluation

Impact evaluation is another SYSTEMS theory element, but which concentrates on the immediate effects of services or programs, often in terms of operational aims and objectives and principles. It differs from OUTPUTS and OUTCOMES. An impact evaluation of this book project would check to see whether the books were read (and considered to be readable, understandable and applicable to people's worlds). It might seek evidence that people reported feeling more confident and able to imagine evaluating their activities. A narrow systems theory view, however, limits us to examining an active element 'impacting' on a passive recipient. A fuller picture would include a more interactive picture of the person making active choices to receive some messages rather than others, and point towards a more INTERPRETATIVE, cultural and CONSTRUCTIVIST approach. As well, a more contextual analysis might avoid the difficulties associated with presuming that effects relate to the interventions made. That is, the 'black box' between input and output requires illumination of the context well beyond the boundaries of the service system.

Input evaluation

This was once a routine form of evaluation in the balmy days before the end of the post-war economic boom. (However, it is having a curious revival in some parts of the world where there is no evaluation of the effect of radical human services reduction and restructuring. Instead, services are deemed 'appropriately' in place if, for example, three (even if ineffectual) phone calls are made in an attempt to place someone needing care.) Input evaluation focuses on checking that a program or service commences or is supplied with, at the outset, grants, funds, staff and facilities. In the past, the mere supply of 'inputs' was deemed sufficient evidence that a program or service was effectively operating. Indeed, if adequate inquiry had been conducted beforehand, this may well have been true.

Interpretive evaluation

'Interpretive' refers to how the nature of what we are evaluating isn't in and of itself good or bad, valuable or unworthy—but that these judgements are entirely relative to the people making the judgements, who do so from their own standpoints and contexts. That is, we are faced with a task of interpreting the meaning of people's views in the context of the rest of their lives. To do this we must become like anthropologists who 'go native' or else we may miss grasping the true meanings—'true' relative to those whose meanings they are. This is also sometimes referred to as a HERMENEUTIC or CONSTRUCTIVIST task, and is what is accomplished under the heading of much QUALITATIVE evaluation.

References:

DENZIN, Norman *The Research Act in Sociology* Butterworths, London:1970

RABINOW, Paul and William SULLIVAN (Eds) *Interpretive Social Science—A Reader* University of California Press, Berkeley:1979

Judicial evaluation model (JEM)

This technique, like the ADVERSARY model (which emphasises the trial-by-jury element), draws on certain features of the legal system such as:

- Formal inquiry by a panel of peers or judges.
- Presentation of evidence (or submissions).
- Cross-examination of witnesses.

It can—if it can overcome everyone's fears and anxieties about 'kangaroo courts'—sharpen people's arguments and evidence by exposing them to critical questioning, reassuring everyone they've been heard, etc. Both techniques rely on there being genuinely opposing 'sides' to be argued. They can work a lot like debating teams. If they are to have value in everyday settings they need to tone down the formality and narrow rules governing the operation of the legal system.

Reference:

POPHAM, W. Jones and Dale CARSON 'Deep Dark Defects of the Adversary Evaluation Model' in George F. MADAUS, Michael SCRIVEN and Daniel L. STUFFLEBEAM (Eds) *Evaluation Models—Viewpoints on Educational and Human Services Evaluation*, Kluwer-Nijhoff Publishing, The Hague, pp. 205–214:1983

Likert Scales

Using Likert Scales is a way of forcing evaluative responses into selecting from pre-determined categories which represent varying degrees of discrepancy. It is typically composed of a statement, followed by a scale of five possible responses (note that layout is usually horizontal), for example:

School is fun (tick)
☐ Strongly agree
☐ Agree
☐ Neutral
☐ Disagree
☐ Strongly disagree

or

School is: (circle)	
Fun:	1
Some fun:	2
Neither:	3
Sometimes dull:	4
Dull:	5

This kind of scale is sometimes termed a semantic differential item. If the statements and wording of the possible responses are appropriate, this kind of scale may have some value. Most of the problems with scales come about from either the statement being badly worded (or conceptualised) and/or the responses being too closed, irrelevant or otherwise incurring unwanted resistance by the person who is meant to choose from among them. See GUTTMAN-TYPE SCALE for other drawbacks of written scale items.

Reference:

GOTTMAN, John and Robert CLASEN 'Troubleshooting Guide for Research and Evaluation' in F. COX et al. *Tactics and Techniques of Community Practice* F.E. Peacock, Itasca, p. 371:1977

Management by objectives (MBO)

This managerial technique is, as its name implies, of the nature described in detail in this book as evaluating activities or programs against pre-established policy or objectives (an *audit review* approach). See Diagram 2, and Diagram 3 and the section on audit review (in Chapter 3) for the major strengths and weaknesses of this. See also GOAL-BASED EVALUATION, FINANCIAL MANAGEMENT IMPROVEMENT PLAN, MANAGEMENT FOR RESULTS, PROGRAM BUDGETING.

Reference:

CARROLL, S.J. and H.L. TOSI *Management by Objectives—Applications and Research* Macmillan, New York:1973

Management for results (MFR)

This technique represented the next step beyond MANAGEMENT BY OBJECTIVES. It also used a SYSTEMS approach, and gears itself to ensuring there is:

- A formal statement of objectives (or corporate plan) for every aspect of activity.
- A formal policy for evaluating performance in these activities against objectives.
- A specific cycle ensuring all programs are regularly reviewed.
- Performance indicators, identified for programs' efficiency and effectiveness.
- Management information systems (MIS) to monitor resource inputs, program outputs, and program outcomes.
- A unit which is responsible for evaluation.
- A set of procedures for deciding on evaluation recommendations.
- Mechanisms for linking evaluation to the budget process.

It may seem that this captures some of the elements proposed in this book, however, the distinguishing features are the 'top down' manageralist nature of this exercise, the invisibility of involvement by those who provide or use the services, the rigidity of the objectives-based approach (with no mechanism for *open inquiry* and hence the possibility of change, development and improvement), the decontextualised SYSTEMS nature of the exercise, and the emphasis on Management Information Systems comprising only statistical computerised databases (and not verbal descriptive and interpretive information).

Reference:

LINARD, Keith 'Program Evaluation and Resource Management Improvement in the Commonwealth Public Service' *Paper* to National Evaluation Conference, Canberra:1998

Management for excellence

This involves a set of assumptions about the imperative need for superior customer service, constant innovation, staff involvement in creative problem-solving and inspirational leadership. These assumptions contrast with traditional management's need to control subordinates, give directions, motivate through both rewards and punishments, and centrally determine goals and measures for their achievement. Management for Excellence involves ideas about developing a culture of feedback and responsiveness, commitment, vision, and openness throughout an organisation, not just focusing on the top. The Australian Taxation Commissioner's recent stint of service on an inquiry counter reflects an element of this approach in 'touching base' and being open to new insights.

Reference:

PETERS, Tom *In Search of Excellence—Lessons from America's Best-Run Companies* Harper and Row, Sydney:1990

Multi-attribute utility measurement

This is a QUANTITATIVE technique developed to try to deal with conflict over goals (and presumably also between the differing interests and values of groups that lie behind this conflict). Translated, this extravagantly named technique means in part that the evaluator provides separate information to each competing grouping in terms of their own values. Decision-makers eventually have access to research data on issues that may not be consistent with their own values, but are consistent with those of the other relevant groups. This sophisticated kind of intelligence relies on everyone contributing so everyone can then know precisely where the differences and similarities in values between them lie. An adaptation of this technique to evaluation is called the DECISION-THEORETIC approach.

Reference:

GARDINER, Peter C. and Ward EDWARDS 'Public Values: Multi-Attribute Utility Measurement for Social Decision Making' in Martin F. KAPLIN and Steven SCHWARTZ (Eds) *Human Judgement and Decision Processes*, Academic Press, New York pp. 1–38:1975

Naturalistic inquiry (NI)

The title of this technique picks up some of the meaning of the word 'natural' in the sense of inquiring into what is usual, customary, and unaffected; and some sense of the old-fashioned 'naturalist' being someone skilled in the observation of nature as found in its habitats. That is, NI uses QUALITATIVE or 'grounded' designs which do not artificially manipulate the phenomenon or its environment, and which proceed inductively from practice to theory, rather than the other way around. As a discovery-oriented approach, it has much in common with the *open inquiry* approach described in this book. Like many of the other evaluation techniques described, it arose in reaction to the more manipulative approach to science derived from laboratory experiments. Indeed Guba and Lincoln, its most important exponents, note that it represents a paradigm shift from rationalist and positivist science which they argue has generated unused and unusable findings. The table illustrates its fundamental axioms, in contrast to those of conventional science.

They also developed criteria to assist in what they call the 'assurance of trustworthiness' of findings (in contrast to conventional science's concern with reliability and validity). Thus, in contrast to the rationalistic concerns about truth validity, applicability, consistency, and neutrality—NI's concerns are for credibility, transferability, dependability, and confirmability. They suggest a number of techniques to ensure this. Guba and Lincoln have recently carried their work a further step forward with the publication

Forms of Inquiry

	Conventional Inquiry	Naturalistic Inquiry
Philosophical base	*Logical positivism*	*Phenomenology*
Inquiry paradigm	*Experimental physics*	*Ethnography; investigative journalism*
Purpose	*Verification*	*Discovery*
Stance	*Reductionist*	*Expansionist*
Framework/design	*Preordinate/fixed*	*Emergent variable*
Style	*Intervention*	*Selection*
Reality manifold	*Singular*	*Multiple*
Value structure	*Singular*	*Pluralistic*
Setting	*Laboratory*	*Nature*
Contest	*Unrelated*	*Relevant*
Conditions	*Controlled*	*Invited interference*
Treatment	*Stable*	*Variable*
Scope	*Molecular*	*Molar*
Methods	*Objective - in sense of factual/ confirmable*	*Objective - in sense of inter-subjective agreement*

Naturalistic Inquiry (Guba, Egon: 1978)

of their book on fourth generation evaluation or CONSTRUCTIVIST methodology.

References:

GUBA, Egon G. *Toward a Methodology for Naturalistic Inquiry in Educational Evaluation* Centre for the Study of Evaluation (CSE), University of California:1978

GUBA, Egon and Yvonna S. LINCOLN 'Epistemological and Methodological Bases for Naturalistic Inquiry' Ch. 18 in George F. MADAUS, Michael SCRIVEN and Daniel F. STUFFLEBEAM (Eds) *Evaluation Models —Viewpoints on Educational and Human Services Evaluation* Kluwer Nijhoff Publishing, The Hague, pp. 311–333:1983

Neuro Linguistic Programming (NLP)

Developed by Richard Bandler and John Grinder, this approach to understanding the structure of human behaviour is currently being used as a training and development tool, as well as a therapeutic technique. It is based on the work of behaviourist Milton Erikson and the linguistic model of Noam Chomsky. Some of its basic assumptions that make it relevant to the field of evaluation are:

- Meaning (and value) lie less in what people say (or mean), than in the sense made of it by those who hear or receive the messages. Meaning is not unproblematic, but must, therefore, be discussed, negotiated and *agreed.*
- People construct their responses to the world via mental models or 'maps' of the world.
- These models or 'maps' code or filter meanings and are grounded in people's neurological responses.
- In this way, the mind and body works together in a cybernetic (energy feedback) loop.
- 'Success' and 'failure' become, therefore, 'mere' feedback for future behaviour.
- Change takes place by changing the person's own behaviour in the light of this feedback. One of the catch phrases of NLP is 'Act as if . . .'

See also WELL-FORMED OUTCOME MODEL.

Reference:

BANDLER, R. and J. GRINDER *The Structure of Magic* Science and Behaviour Books, Palo Alto, California:1975.

On-site Analysis (OSA)

This is a technique which Bob Myers, its chief exponent, saw as drawing on business management approaches to personnel, resources, time management, budgets and organisational development, and assumptions about the unit measurability of human services performance. It involves an external paid consultant facilitator trained in the technique (developed by a Canadian fund-raising organisation) coming into the service for one week, and, via a thirteen-step process with management, staff and possibly volunteers, consumers and some other external peers:

- Gathering participants' perceptions and looking at various statistical measurements (for example, how many clients are being seen a day) which

might be discrepant with expectations or objectives (for example, social workers think they should be seeing more clients each day).
- Identifying the 'problems' (for example, clients' appointment cancellations).
- Generating a solution (for example, scheduling more appointments so social workers are seeing more clients after the cancellations).
- And making a public presentation to key outsiders of a final report at the end of the five-and-a-half day session.

There is a one day follow up after twelve months.

Its two chief values lie firstly in it being conducted 'on site' in collaboration with staff (thus using some of the insights of INTERPRETIVE, HERMENEUTIC, PHENOMENOLOGICAL, DEMOCRATIC, COLLABORATIVE or anthropological research); and secondly in it involving the fresh perception of a sympathetic outsider who might more quickly problematise and challenge a situation that has been more or less tolerated, perhaps for too long. Its chief drawbacks are its reliance on:
- The outsider's selective interpretation of the statistical 'facts' (and particularly on that person's level of critical experience) to problematise what program participants had previously 'not noticed'—rather than training insiders to develop reflective skills about the meanings of their own records.
- The apparent revelatory power of 'the numbers' (the technique privileges numerical 'facts' over verbal 'perceptions').
- Its necessarily superficial approach to context and history given its short time frame.

For example, a consumer perspective, plus the depth of a more *open inquiry* approach, might provoke asking in the example given above, *why* it was that clients broke their appointments. That is, it may have pursued lines of inquiry that would lead to a different kind of service being seen as valuable rather than more of the same, and possibly for an unintentionally select group of clients (those who can tolerate a professional appointment system). On-site Analysis makes a laudable attempt to gain consensus around organisation values, but, in one week, it is not clear how the limits to consensus (entrenched power and authority relations, etc.) are overcome. Comparably carried out but not the same, are systematic review techniques like CHASP and PASSING.

Reference:

MYERS, R.J., Peter UFFORD and M.S. MAGILL *On Site Analysis—A Practical Approach to Organisational Change* O.S.C.A. Ltd, Ontario, Canada:1988

Optional Proportional System

See WADSWORTH, Yoland *Do It Yourself Social Research* Allen & Unwin, St Leonards:1997

Organisational Development (OD), Learning Organisation (LO)

This is an activity which, at its most enlightened (such as in the Australian context of union involvement and award restructuring) comes very close to an ACTION RESEARCH evaluation model with both REFLEXIVE and PARTICIPATORY, or at the very least COLLABORATIVE elements. At its best, it involves staff development activities which are designed to enhance staff's self-awareness of what they are doing, and why they are doing it—in the context of consensus-building around organisational goals (see Australian Tax Office reference below). However, in the current context, it often also refers to 'top-down' corporate restructuring of management into flatter but tighter structures, combined with program budgeting, corporate plans, computerisation and conventional staff retraining. These moves may be oriented towards increasing efficiency and central command and control rather than increasing 'grounded' quality and effectiveness and a diffused organisation of enthusiastic self-starters. Peter Senge has taken the concept further with the encouragement of 'systems thinking' (in the sense of interdependent feedback loops) in his book about learning organisations (1990).

References:

APPELBAUM, Eileen and Peter ABIN 'Computer Rationalization and the Transformation of Work—Lessons from the Insurance Industry' in Stephen WOOD (Ed) *The Transformation of Work—Skill Flexibility and the Labour Process* Unwin, Hyman, London:1989

AUSTRALIAN TAXATION OFFICE 'People Action—A Plan for Human Resource Development' The Human Resource Development Unit, Melbourne:1990

SENGE, Peter *The Fifth Discipline—The Art and Practice of the Learning Organisation* Doubleday Currency, New York:1990

Other government audit review mechanisms

Besides traditional internal accounting audits, governments use a range of evaluative mechanisms that are 'external' to the section of the government being reviewed. These include Royal Commissions, Committees of Inquiry, Ministerial consultants, Statutory Inquiry Bodies, Management Performance Reviews (often investigated by Public Service Boards), the Auditor-General's office, Parliamentary Committees of Inquiry, and interdepartmental task forces. Some of these use quasi-judicial approaches, others might use approaches verging towards *open inquiry*. Primarily, however, they involve *audit review* methods.

Reference:

LINARD, Keith 'Program Evaluation and Resource Management Improvement in the Commonwealth Public Service' *Paper* to National Evaluation Conference, Canberra:1998

Outcome evaluation

This SYSTEMS theory element concentrates on the longer term effects of services or programs. It attempts to check against broader goals or philosophical mission statements. An *audit review* outcome evaluation of this book project would try to find evidence that the use of the book was related to an increase in people's own actual evaluative activity. Evidence and actual evaluation reports produced by groups which utilised 'touching base' with critical reference groups and so on, would be sought. An *open inquiry* evaluation might ask 'What were the outcomes? (whether related to goals or not), and 'What was the value of these outcomes?'. These questions might expand the evaluation to examine matters that 'escape' being part of the 'system' under study.

Output evaluation

This is another SYSTEMS theory element but which concentrates on the more immediate 'products' of services or programs. It identifies whether these intended tangibles actually were forthcoming or produced. An *audit review* output evaluation of this book project, for example, would check to see whether the books were actually printed, delivered, published and available. An *open inquiry* evaluation might expand the evaluation by asking 'What was the output?', and 'What was the value of these outputs?' beyond the written-down expectations or intentions.

Participatory evaluation

This again refers to the inclusion of some or all the parties to an evaluation (as does COLLABORATIVE and STAKEHOLDER evaluation). Like collaborative evaluation, this can mean a pluralist kind of participation. Both these terms have arisen in reaction to the dominant form of evaluation which was conducted entirely by the external 'objective' expert using an old-paradigm form of objectifying science. The reaction of being disempowered in the evaluating and evidence-gathering processes was felt by those *most* disempowered: service providers at the level closest to 'the ground', advocates of service users, and some service users themselves. The demand to participate has been usefully conceptualised by Sherry Arnstein as involving a hierarchy of possibilities, and these can be matched to a hierarchy of possible forms of participation in evaluation (see the diagram below).

References:

ARNSTEIN, Sherry 'Ladder of Citizen Participation' in *American Institute of Planners Journal* July pp. 216–224:1969

WHYTE, W.F. (Ed) *Participatory Action Research* Sage, London:1991

PASSING technique

'PASSING' is an acronym for Program Analysis of Service Systems' Implementation of Normalisation Goals. It is a sophisticated approach to evaluating services that are for people who have stigmatised characteristics but who are meant to be moving towards integration and normalisation in mainstream community life. It is based on symbolic interactionism and role theory, and after thirty years of development, it represents a highly refined STANDARDS PROGRAM *audit review* technique. It is designed to identify where services deviate from normal settings and normal interaction (in terms of forty-two different characteristics) and to what extent (in terms of five different levels). It examines the physical settings of services, the nature of the relationships between staff and service users, activities, language, symbols and

LEVEL OF POWER	MODELS OF COMMUNITY PARTICIPATION	RELEVANT MODELS OF EVALUATION
DEGREES OF CITIZEN POWER	CITIZEN CONTROL	Critical self-evaluation or action research, reflexive
	DELEGATED POWER	Responsive, participatory
	PARTNERSHIP	Collaborative
DEGREES OF TOKENISM	PLACATION	Stakeholder (representative) Democratic
	CONSULTATION	Consultation, surveys
	INFORMING	Top down feedback, Bureaucratic
NON-PARTICIPATION	THERAPY	Depth interpretivism
	MANIPULATION	Controlled experimental, autocratic

images used. A service would, for example, rate poorly if people are still left wearing dressing gowns in the afternoon, or if the service for the elderly is named 'Sunset Home', or if adults are called 'kids' and carry around soft toys.

PASSING comprises a handbook, field manual, and criteria ratings book, and involves a certified training program before it can be used (although the written materials are available in some libraries). PASSING reviewers conduct tours of the facilities and neighbourhood, interview staff and clients, and draw on documentary materials. Like all highly refined audit review techniques, PASSING's strengths (the level of detail, the rigour and discipline, the reliability of its items, and the sheer comprehensiveness) are the other side of the coin of its potential weaknesses (inflexibility, and contextually relative validity). The apparent objectivist nature of the ratings exercises may also disguise the subjectivism of the value-driven interpretation required to make the evaluative judgements on a five point scale. As well, improvement still requires movement to an *open inquiry* mode if people are to understand *why* they are or are not doing the best thing, what to do instead, and how to get from where they are now to where they could be. An open inquiry mode is also required if any of the PASSING ratings items themselves are to be subjected to critique or change. For example, if an element of normative mainstream life is sexist or ageist, should PASSING uncritically seek to reproduce such 'normality'? Or, if the meaning of soft toys to adults turns out to be that they are a compensation for physical intimacy deprivation, what is the value of merely removing them in order to rate well on a PASSING item? This raises the question of the needs assessment that lies at the core of each item. Within a purely audit review approach, such as PASSING, there is not always a logical point of entry to re-evaluate the evaluation criteria against critical reference groups' own formulation and reformulation of their needs.

Reference:

WOLFENSBERGER, Wolf and Susan THOMAS, *PASSING Program Analysis of Service Systems' Implementation of Normalization Goals, PASS 3 Handbook*, 3rd Edition:1975; *Field Manual*, 3rd edition:1975; *PASSING Normalization Criteria and Ratings Manual*, 2nd edition:1983

Peer review

This is evaluation by peers—generally by and among fellow professionals. Peer review is a major ideological 'promise' by the professions. Professionals promise 'to do the right thing' and keep each other in line in exchange for autonomous control over their practices and rewards for service (such as high incomes). Negative peer review evaluations unfortunately can range from the vicious (such as anonymous reviews for grant applications or journal publication) through to a barely audible 'tut tut' in the case of major malpractice. The strengths of peer review lie where there is genuine collaborative intention to raise standards or correct directions so as to better meet clients' needs (such as through STANDARDS PROGRAMS like CHASP in community health, or PASSING in the disability area). The weaknesses lie where the separate class interests of professionals *as* professionals, override these and lead to weak evaluative effort and a 'closing of ranks' against external criticism (well documented by Michael Scriven in his stinging description of the 'Country Club Model of Institutional Evaluation', reference cited below).

Reference:

SCRIVEN, Michael *The Logic of Evaluation* Edgepress, Inverness, California, pp. 105–113:1981

Performance indicators (PIs)

Performance indicators are generally thought of as the *signs* we accept as meaning that someone or some service has done what was expected in terms of objectives or goals. They are now most often linked to STANDARDS programs, SERVICE AGREEMENTS, and PROGRAM BUDGETING, and *audit review* approaches. Because of this, 'indicators of performance' may differ from 'signs of achievement' (remembering that current activity objectives may not turn out to be either the only or the best ways of meeting critical reference groups' needs). PIs have also suffered greatly from having been originally developed 'top down' and hence were often initially somewhat crude or even distorting.

The metaphor of machine performance—drawn from industry—has also been perceived as less-than-human in its application to the human services sector, particularly when the pressure to quantify 'performance' led to a lot of services being evaluated according to what could be counted, rather than according to genuine and meaningful signs of effectiveness. The machine metaphor also easily led indicators to be developed in terms of SYSTEMS approaches—for example, PI's for needs-derived objectives, for inputs (resources), related to activities and outputs (workloads and efficiency), and for impacts and outcomes against objectives (effects and effectiveness).

Better indicators or signs are those developed 'bottom-up' by asking service-users and providers 'How would you know if this was a good service?' or 'What would be the signs for you of getting/giving a good service?', etc. The value of this approach is twofold—users and providers reflect usefully on what they are experiencing, and managers get grounded indicators that are more likely to inform them and reduce their uncertainty. Such indicators may not be quantitative—or may involve only modest quantification. At the service level this will be even more so, while at the managerial level all descriptive material (numerical and verbal) will be in much more summarised form. It is often the case that the more 'grounded', meaningful, negotiated and better the quality of PI's, the less likely they can be mass standardised for application to a lot of different services. Centralised program managers will always have to tolerate some level of crudity and abstraction for the sake of some kind of comparability. They should strive to remember that the performance measures on which they rely often resemble 'reading braille through a doona', and thus be tolerant of a certain level of uncertainty! Performance indicators are frequently confused with performance targets, with the terms being used interchangeably. A performance indicator for community participation may be that service-users elect a committee of management for the service. A performance target might be that all such services have elected committees by a certain time.

References:

COMMUNITY SERVICES OF VICTORIA, 'Guidelines for Developing Performance Indicators', Draft, March 1990

GUTHRIE, Hugh *Performance Indicators in TAFE* TAFE National Centre for Research and Development, Adelaide:1988

MAYO, Toni *Performance of Community Organizations* NCOSS:1990

SOCIAL JUSTICE STRATEGY UNIT 'Performance Indicators and the Social Justice Strategy—A Discussion Paper' Department of Premier and Cabinet, Victoria:1988

WYATT, T.J. and P. HALL 'Some Limitations on the Application of Performance Indicators in Public Sector Organisations' *Paper* to the National Evaluation Conference, Canberra:1987

Phenomenology

Phenomenology, like NATURALISTIC, Verstehen or INTERPRETIVE approaches, refers to a methodology (developed by Edmund Hussel) for grasping the meaning of everyday social life by studying events, activities and practice as experienced and perceived. It focuses on the business of interpreting individual's meanings as well as the *inter-subjective* construction of those meanings through their relationships and reactions to life.

tafe COLLEGE
GRADUATE SUCCESS RATE
PASS RATE
STUDENT SATISFACTION
AVERAGE CLASS SIZE
AVERAGE HOURS TAUGHT
RECURRENT COST PER SUBJECT PER STUDENT
ANNUAL GRADUATE NUMBERS
2
PERFORMANCE INDICATORS

Performance Indicators (Guthrie, Hugh: 1988)

Reference:

SCHUTZ, Alfred *The Phenomenology of the Social World* Heinemann, London:1972

Positive evaluation

This is a new non-patented, non-copyrighted technique that anyone can practice! It results from the observation of countless instances of evaluations which result in reports which concentrate on all the Things That Are A Problem! You know the sort of thing—page after page of negative conclusions about what is wrong—then at the end; either a conclusion that more research is needed, or a giant hiccup and leap to recommendations that appear to have little to do with the rest of the report but seem like good ways to go! Now, negative evaluation conclusions *may* be a necessary stage, however, this humble new approach (which shouldn't really be graced with the title of a model or technique!), is more of a plea that we spend some time examining the Things That Have Gone Right as a source of ideas for other Things That Might Go Right in future. Whenever we look at recommendations for new practice, they pretty much always stem from the evaluator making a theoretical leap from what is before her or his nose—to imagining ways (or remembering instances) that might theoretically address the conditions *missing* in the world-before-our-noses. BRAINSTORMING around solutions or desirable SCENARIOS, or creative visualisation, might give some leads out of negative evaluation. The knack is to shift from a picture of 'what is' to a picture of 'what could be'. Positive evaluation can contribute to this.

Positivist evaluation

'Positivist' is a term which is now often used in a pejorative sense to describe the fundamental philosophy of conventional or traditional science. This conventional view of science rests on two key assumptions:

- Firstly, positivist philosophy holds that the subject-matter of science (or research or evaluation) is independent of the observer (or the researcher or evaluator). That is, that there is a single, real, true, factual world 'out there' which is knowable separately from the knower. Hence the observer (or scientist) should strive to capture this truth objectively without bias or contamination and this should be done by remaining separate and uninvolved. (The observed person or people are also seen as biased and contaminated in their own opinions or views, and these should be avoided, ideally by unobtrusive research, so the researched are not aware of the study or the researcher's hypotheses.)

The INTERPRETIVE, NATURALISTIC, QUALITATIVE or CONSTRUCTIVIST critique says that this is an inappropriate and unhelpful science for the human world where subjective *and* objective meanings are socially-constructed and negotiated and multiple realities characterise human society. To try to avoid them is to avoid deep *understanding* of human phenomena. (Interestingly, modern physics makes the same arguments about the natural world, for example, relativity theory, the uncertainty principle, etc.)

- Secondly, and closely related to the first assumption, positivist philosophy holds that the reasons for pursuing science (or research or evaluation) reflect no particular purposes but ideally derive from mere curiosity for its own sake. Indeed, to admit to reasons or purposes other than 'sheer interest' is to risk biasing and contaminating inquiry with values or interests. Inquiry, seeks only to know 'what is'. Values about 'oughts' are supplied by users of the otherwise neutral information. (Hence researchers or evaluators have no logical responsibility for the use of their work—nor need to select morally defensible topics in the first place.)

The critical interpretive or value-interested critique says that the purposes of science, research or evaluation *always* derive in some way from the values and interests of those whose situation gives rise to the inquiry in the first place. That is, all inquiry is inspired by some discrepancy between an experienced and an expected state and that this sense of discrepancy is always charged with a 'valuation', whether small or large, conscious or not conscious. Hence, all knowledge is in some way 'interested'. Far from being value-laden, all research, science or evaluation is essentially *value-driven*, and the best way to avoid error or 'getting it wrong' for the purposes, is to be critically questioning or sceptical about one's own conclusions and grounds for knowing until competing explanations can be answered, or refuting evidence explained. Hence researchers and evaluators, once aware that all their work will be in some interests and not in others', must choose as best they can 'whose side (or sides) they are on', and consciously and self-sceptically focus attention on developing the best-evidenced theory possible. Got that? Sorry! It's a bit hard getting 300 years of philosophy of science into a couple of paragraphs! Well, what it boils down to meaning is that it appears *we* decide what is true and valuable—rather than it being straightforwardly inherent in *what* we are evaluating, it is inherent in what *we* value, and that, in turn, is relative to our purposes, needs, interests and past experiences.

References:

FAY, Brian *Social Theory and Political Practice* George Allen and Unwin, London:1975

BRYMAN, Alan *Quantity and Quality in Social Research* Unwin Hyman, London:1988

Process evaluation

This is evaluation that concentrates on what is done 'within' a service or program: the activities, who does what with whom, and other matters of implementation. It is the often unexplained 'black box' in a SYSTEMS theory approach to evaluation. An *audit review* process evaluation of this book project would check to see whether the Management Committee met, the writer produced drafts, whether discussions were held about the ideas and content, whether files of material were collected, etc. An *open inquiry* process evaluation may ask 'What happened?' and 'How did things unfold?' and 'Why?' and 'What was their value?'. This may take the evaluation beyond a systems approach into considering a range of unintended and unexpected events, contexts, needs, conflicts, negotiations and so on that, for example, could call into question the original goals or objectives intended to determine the process. This more dynamic feedback approach would begin to break down the artificiality of separating systems components. For example, early feedback regarding effects (or even imagined effects) could alter 'inputs' and other 'processes'.

Program budgeting (PPBS)

Program budgeting and its more ambitious version—the Planning Programming Budgeting System (developed in the US Department of Defence)—are variants of cost-effectiveness analysis and performance budgeting, and hence are approaches to evaluating value for money. This continues to be a major passion of Western governments—ever since the late 1970s and late 1980s recessions—and is a management tool designed to both contain spending within boundaries and tighten awareness of spending relative to other spending within a Department. Relativities are able to be identified by linking budgets to goals and objectives in a hierarchy of programs which are broken down into sub-programs and components. (Previously, budgeting had been by line item spending categories such as recurrent costs, salaries, capital costs, equipment, and so on). Program budgeting enables some crude but useful descriptions of the world to become more obvious, for example, if objectives are related to provision of more health promotion or prevention services, it could easily be seen that there is a huge imbalance in spending with the vast majority of money going to ill health hospital treatment. Or, if policy wished to devote more attention to women and child-care services, the evidence from program budgeting could indicate a shift in resources. On the other hand, the approach breaks down when objectives start to be altered to match the budget reality (for example, implementation of policy may now be 'over time', or when waiting list reduction policy gets converted into more-money-for-hospitals instead of, for example, more-money-to-retrain doctors to work in community based preventive practice). The technique uses an *audit review* approach.

Reference:

VICTORIAN GOVERNMENT *Program Budgeting 1983–1984* Victorian Government Printer, Melbourne:1984

Program Evaluation and Review Technique (PERT)

PERT is a form of CRITICAL PATH ANALYSIS which introduced some useful features to the more traditional GANTT schedule. It comprises a timeline diagram of a network of activities and events that must occur before an end objective is reached. It is kind of like a map between points A (Start) and B (Finish), which can be used so everyone knows who is to do what and when. This saves delays and confusions as people say 'I was waiting for you to . . .' It is credited with shortening the US Polaris missile program by two years!—so any of you designing the implementation of programs on this scale should find it particularly useful. Difficulties are in predicting, in advance, the time needed for each task, and also in ensuring flexibility if it turns out that some other tasks can safely be done before others, while it turns out others will have to be contingent on activities not previously thought to be so. A PERT chart might look like that illustrated below (from the *Destination: Decisions* book cited in the references).

References:

EDUCATION DEPARTMENT OF VICTORIA 'Critical Path' in *Destination: Decisions* Curriculum Branch, Chapter 7, pp. 43–46:1985

Program Evaluation and Review Technique (PERT)

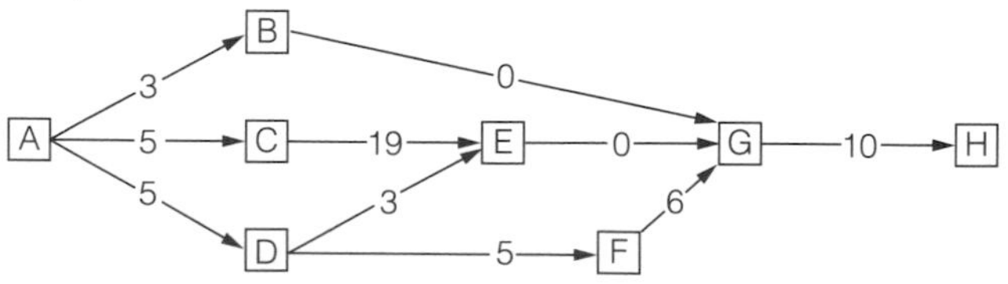
A
B
C
D
E
F
G
H
3
5
5
0
19
3
0
6
5
10

Critical path charts are presented according to the following simple rules:

- Work items or tasks are placed in boxes.
- Arrows show which tasks follow on from others.
- Numbers show how long each task is expected to take. Actual dates for beginning and completing a task can also be written in.

In the example given, task H cannot begin until task G is finished. Task G is expected to take ten days. Task G cannot begin until tasks B, E and F are completed, and so on. The longest path in terms of days is the A–C–E–G–H path which will take 34 days. This is the **critical** path. No delays can be permitted if the project is to be completed on time. On the other hand, path A–B–G–H totals only 13 days. Task B could begin as late as 21 days after work on task C has begun and still feed into task G on time.

THEMES OF QUALITATIVE INQUIRY

1. Naturalistic inquiry—Studying real world situations as they unfold naturally; non-manipulative, unobtrusive, and non-controlling; openness to whatever emerges—lack of predetermined constraints on outcomes.
2. Inductive analysis—Immersion in the details and specifics of the data to discover important categories, dimensions and interrelationships; begin by exploring genuinely open questions rather than testing theoretically derived (deductive) hypotheses.
3. Holistic perspective—The whole phenomenon under study is understood as a complex system that is more than the sum of its parts; focus on complex interdependencies not meaningfully reduced to a few discrete variables and linear, cause-effect relationships.
4. Qualitative data—Detailed, thick description; inquiry in-depth; direct quotations capturing people's personal perspectives and experiences.
5. Personal contact and insight—The researcher has direct contact with and gets close to the people, situation and phenomenon under study; researcher's personal experiences and insights are an important part of the inquiry and critical to understanding the phenomenon.
6. Dynamic system—Attention to process; assumes change is constant and ongoing whether the focus is on an individual or an entire culture.
7. Unique case orientation—Assumes each case is special and unique; the first level of inquiry is being true to, respecting and capturing the details of the individual cases being studied; cross case analysis follows from and depends on the quality of the individual case studies.
8. Context sensitivity—Places findings in a social historical and temporal context; dubioous of the possibility or meaningfulness of generalisations across time and space.
9. Empathetic neutrality—Complete objectivity is impossible; pure subjectivity undermines credibility. The researcher's passion is understanding the world in all its complexity—not proving something; not advocating; not advancing personal agendas; but understanding. The researcher includes personal experience and empathetic insight as part of the relevant data, while taking a neutral stance towards whatever the specific findings are which may emerge.
10. Design flexibility—Open to adapting inquiry as understanding deepens and/or situations change; avoids getting locked into rigid designs that eliminate responsiveness; pursues new paths of discovery as they emerge.

Qualitative Evaluation (Patton, Michael Quinn: 1989, 1990)

HOFFER, Joe R., 'PERT: A Tool for Managers of Human Service Programs' in F. COX et al. *Tactics and Techniques of Community Practice* F.E. Peacock, Itasca, pp. 287–298:1977

Qualitative evaluation

This term has come to be applied to various streams of evaluation which might otherwise variously be called INTERPRETIVE, PHENOMENOLOGICAL, NATURALISTIC, HERMENEUTIC, grounded, anthropological, inductive, experiential, symbolic interactionist, emergent, field-based or responsive! The naming of all these methods as 'qualitative' has much more to do with a reaction to dominance of QUANTITATIVE EVALUATION than with its reliance on numerical data and mathematical and statistical manipulation. The primary flaw in calling some material or evaluation 'qualitative' (*or* quantitative) is that the unhelpful split between words and numbers is perpetuated. Some research and evaluation reports are actually being written up under the headings of 'quantitative' and 'qualitative', rather than headings that relate to the questions, content or purposes of the study. In practice, all verbal matters *could* be counted and all numbers *could* be 'unpacked' to show how they are comprised of a lot of words. It is more important to ask, 'What are the right questions?'. 'How many' or 'How much' type questions will need numbers as an answer. 'Who', 'which', 'what', 'when', 'why' and 'how' type questions may need words. Features of 'qualitative' methodology include those in the table above (Patton, 1990).

Reference:

PATTON, Michael Quinn 'Qualitative Methods in Health Care Evaluation' in *Health Care Evaluation* Public Health Association of Australia Inc., Canberra:1989

Quality assurance/quality control/quality improvement

Quality control is a process widely used in manufacturing industry and typically involves periodic checking of a product to ensure it conforms to a pre-existing standard. It involves the idea of information feedback—typically from supervisor to the production worker. *Quality assurance* is a kind of genteel version for professional and human services where instead of bosses or inspectors inspecting and correcting workers' outputs, the professionals examine each others' work (more often just the processes), to check it is up to standard—either via PEER REVIEW or by specially designated peer Quality Assurance officers, the use of small-scale surveys and benchmarking, etc. STANDARDS PROGRAMS are a closely related mechanism. *Quality improvement* has taken up where quality assurance has reached its basic targets. It focuses on continuous improvement.

Quality circles

As a contribution to ORGANISATIONAL DEVELOPMENT, Japanese companies have established groups of management and workers who COLLABORATE in ongoing research and the contribution of ideas to assist production, product quality and output and innovation. This approach recognises that shop floor workers have practical experience and problem-solving capacities if given a rewarding environment for contributing them. While the end purpose of quality circles in industry is to increase profits, everyday evaluators could use quality circles to increase the meeting of human needs. The monthly meetings described in Chapter 4 of this book have elements in common with this idea.

Quality of life indicators (QUALYS)

These are conversions from apparently uncertain real life value judgements to apparently more reassuring quantified ones, which allows—given finite economic resources and infinite medical capacity to prolong life—a judgement regarding whose life is worth saving or prolonging and whose isn't. They attempt to answer the question, 'To whom can we do the most good per unit of resource used'. Efforts to date have been conceptualised in terms of length of life and quality of life—with these two concepts being united in the measure called QUALYS (Quality Adjusted Life Years). At its simplest formulation, this involves saying that if we can do something which gives a person an extra year of healthy life expectancy, that is one QUALY. If we can only offer an extra year of disabled or distressed life, it would be rated as less than one. From then on, the researchers in this area construct classifications of multiple levels of cross tabulated distress or disability, calculate statistics for each, argue over who it is who should decide which levels apply to which outcomes of any particular medical intervention (patients? citizens? doctors? nurses? managers? politicians?), and whether people's valued states can be standardised and how the benefits can be costed (direct costs—equipment, staff; indirect costs—lost earning power of caring relatives, etc.). Some urge that there should be participative decision-making, as to date the economists have dominated the area. Economists have not been famous for their interpretive sensitivity, but then on the other hand, doctors are rarely trained to consider the human and economic costs of their new technology either.

Reference:

WILLIAMS, Alan '200 Years is Not Enough!' Australian Hospital Association *Monograph*, July:1989

Quantitative evaluation

Quantitative evaluation is really a term that has gained currency as part of a debate about whether numbers or words are better as sources of meaning when attempting to judge the discrepancy between valued or unvalued descriptions of the world. Quantitative material is that assembled to answer questions about 'how many', 'how often' or 'how much' (while so called QUALITATIVE material addresses questions like how? why? when? who? where? which? whose? and what?). It is important to ask the right questions to get the relevant answers. As noted earlier, describing Beethoven's 5th symphony in C Minor as 22 minutes and 19 seconds may be the right description if it is being evaluated as a contribution to a carefully timed radio program but leaves something to be desired if used as a description in response to the question 'What is the value of Beethoven's 5th symphony to the audience?'.

Just as all qualitative material *could* be counted, so all numbers comprise meanings which can be expressed in words. While expressing numbers in words may often increase their meaningfulness, reducing words to numbers seems to reduce complexity and result in more apparent certainty. If we say the service is a seven out of ten, this somehow seems to crystallise matters in a way that makes us more confident of saying, 'Oh, so it *is* O.K. then'. If we say we have determined it is a 7.48 compared to another service which is a 7.2, this gives a refined sense of reassurance. However, when we 'unpack' the wordy rationales, things may seem much more uncertain! Where uncertainty is intolerable then exact measurement may be sought even if the sacrifice of meaning is great.

If there can only be one winner of a race, then it is *this* context that determines that a photo-finish discrepancy can be detected to hundredths of a second! Or, if a local council is near bankruptcy, it may want to count every leaf before declaring it is autumn—and then sub-contracting the street-sweeping service! It is not surprising that the most avid of quantitative evaluation is to be found in central 'command and control' agencies where budgetary considerations and competing claims for funding are a major concern, or in educational agencies where children must be sorted, graded, rated and ranked to determine placegetters in the life stakes, or in health agencies where the capacity to show the precise cost-per-output will ensure funding (regardless of broader value questions about the values of such 'performance').

Nevertheless, everyday evaluators may use quantification in sensible ways to try to 'firm up' some daily impressions. For example, the keeping of simple records about numbers of phone calls, volume of demand, amounts of time spent on tasks, and degree of value placed on activities or services by consumers, have time-honoured value. Such records do not need to be kept continuously. Time series samples may suffice so as not to spend too much time on them. The main thing is to ensure that people agree about their having meaning and value.

Reference:

BRYMAN, Alan *Quantity and Quality in Social Research* Unwin Hyman, London:1988

...WHAT DO YOU THINK OF THIS WEATHER WE'RE HAVING?
...UM, I'D, RECKON IT'S A 5·8 OUT OF 10...
SK

Reflexive evaluation

This is a term which simply means that whether SELF-EVALUATION or GROUP SELF-EVALUATION, the evaluation is intentionally change-orientated. The important meaning of this term is that we are not only being reflective (looking at ourselves in a mirror is a useful metaphor), but also that this effort will assist us to act back on ourselves in ways which *change ourselves* and the things around us—preferably in desirable directions!

References:

FREIRE, Paulo *Cultural Action for Freedom* Penguin, Harmondsworth, Middlesex:1972a

FREIRE, Paulo *Pedagogy of the Oppressed* Penguin, Harmondsworth, Middlesex:1972b

Responsive evaluation

Developed by Robert Stake, this also was a reaction to the dominance of the laboratory science-based experimental approach. He saw it is as based on what people do naturally when they evaluate: they observe and respond. He advocated steps to bolster reliability of observation and opinion-gathering without sacrificing relevance (for example, replicability). His view was that the trade-off of some measurement precision was compensated by the increase in usefulness of the findings. An earlier version of this was called the Countenance Model.

Reference:

STAKE, Robert *Evaluating the Arts in Education: A Responsive Approach* Charles Merrill, Columbus, Ohio:1975

Scenarios

A scenario is a detailed description of an ideal design of a service or a projection into the future. It can be an optimistic, a negative or a most-likely projection, depending on the factors used to generate it. It can be a most helpful way of describing the 'template descriptions in our heads' by allowing them to unfold unencumbered by present realities! Like SEARCH CONFERENCES, BRAINSTORMING and DELPHIS, a scenario can be of use at the point in an evaluation research cycle when creativity and imagination are needed to leap from problem-posing to solution-generating activity.

Reference:

ACKOFF, R. *A Concept of Corporate Planning* Wiley-Interscience, New York:1970

Search conferences

A search conference is future-orientated like a DELPHI, a SCENARIO, BRAINSTORMING or Nominal Group Technique, but, unlike a DELPHI, it is face to face and participative. Developed by Fred and Merrilyn Emery in the late 1960s, it is typically held over two to three days, often in a remote residential setting, and for around 15–20 people. It requires a facilitator skilled in large group processes, and enables the sharing of values and different viewpoints, and the searching for common ground.

References:

EMERY, Fred and Merrilyn EMERY *A Choice of Futures* Martinus-Nijhoff, Leiden:1976

EMERY, Merrilyn *Searching: For New Directions—In New Ways—For New Times* Centre for Continuing Education, ANU, Canberra:1976

Self-evaluation

The whole of this *Everyday Evaluation on the Run* book is essentially about the process of self-evaluation: that process of thinking about what we are doing, why we are doing it, and what is its value—particularly in comparison to things already designated 'of value' or 'not of value'. To call it 'self'-evaluation is to imply that we can start with ourselves as individuals, however, this is not the same as thinking we are individualistic about this. That is, what we are doing, even in the apparent privacy of our own minds, is essentially *social*. All the ways in which we think are derived from language and experiences that are socially constructed, socially learned and socially affirmed or modified. Eventually the self-evaluator needs to 'touch base' in this social sense—whether with friends, peers, fellow workers or critical reference group members, to check that we are on the right track. Self-evaluation is also ideally REFLEXIVE.

Reference:

BRINKERHOFF, Robert O. *Self-evaluation—A Key To Effective Social Programs* Phillip Institute of Technology, Bundoora, Victoria:1983

Service agreements

Service agreements are tools of *audit review* which evaluate against OBJECTIVES. Service agreements state what a funder will fund and what a funded organisation will do, generally for a period of a year, in relation to objectives or goals. Sets of PERFORMANCE INDICATORS are generated so that a detailed contract can be operationally specified in terms of performance targets. An assumption also underpins services agreements that achievement of performance this year will condition funding for the next year. This supplies the crudest outline of an action-planning evaluation cycle. Service agreements make several further important assumptions: that objectives or goals are for desirable states of affairs; that if the activities are carried out then goals will be met; and that the performance indicators, if met, will mean the activities have been carried out. Each of these assumptions can only be checked by moving from an *audit review* approach to an *open inquiry* approach. As there is no provision for this in service agreements, organisations generally find that service agreements lose their critical edge after two or three years. The more they are used for reporting and accountability (to look good) the less risk will be taken in proposing innovative indicators or targets. Some service agreements are becoming more sophisticated and focusing on areas that will *change* (although services need to use an inquiry approach to know what to change and how).

References:

COMMUNITY SERVICES VICTORIA *Framework for Service Agreements—A Co-ordinated Approach* March 1990

HEALTH DEPARTMENT OF VICTORIA: Various sets of guidelines produced, for example, by Regional Offices, or the Office of Psychiatric Services.

Skill review/skill audit

These techniques enable a kind of 'census' to be done, usually by a central authority such as an employer or a trade union, to ascertain the current skills range and levels of skill proficiency in the industry or enterprise. The census may be of a population sample in order to establish a profile of an industry or enterprise, or it may be of individuals in order to establish personal plans. There are two kinds of evaluation associated with skill reviews. Firstly there is the valuation of the different tasks (and skills needed to accomplish the tasks) that go to make up the job positions; and secondly there is the evaluation of industries and workers against this skill profile to ascertain whether change has occurred or the training program has been effective, or whatever. In the first census stage, the process uses more of an *open inquiry* approach; while the second stage uses an *audit review* approach. In skill reviews it is critical *who* decides both what is done and to what extent it is valuable. Two methods which use different techniques for determining both what is done and the relative values of the components, are CODAP (Comprehensive Occupational Data Analysis Programs)—which leaves the vital decisions largely in the hands of the researchers, and DACUM (Design and Curriculum)—which builds in that the decision-making is by those who do the work and who are seen as best understanding the skills they need and use.

References:

BYRNE, Ann 'Skills Reviews' in *Labour Resourcer* No. 6, November, pp. 20–22:1989

KOKKINOS, Anna 'Gender Bias in Job Evaluation Schemes' in *Labour Resourcer* No. 5, April, pp. 11–14:1989

Social impact assessment

Conventionally, this is an attempt at before-the-event prediction of what effects an event or service might have on various groups or populations—just as environmental impact assessments do for natural habitats and flora and fauna populations. They may sometimes be part of an integrated effort which also examines technology, the natural environment, political and economic development as well as social settings. Generally, they try to identify longer term results or effects (rather than immediate outcomes). They might use resident consultation methods, stakeholder scenario groups, or QUALITY OF LIFE indicators. They typically examine alternatives, various future projections, and who will lose and who will gain. They are mostly carried out by external evaluators but can also utilise DEMOCRATIC and PARTICIPATORY approaches.

Reference:

MEIDINGER, E. and A. SCHADIBERG 'Social Impact Assessment as Evaluation Research' in *Evaluation Review* Vol. 4. No. 4. pp. 507–535:1980

Stakeholder evaluation

Stakeholder evaluation draws on similar assumptions to CLIENT-CENTRED, COLLABORATIVE and to some extent PARTICIPATORY and DEMOCRATIC evaluation. It draws on the assumptions that those with an interest in the evaluation, will, if involved, be more likely to contribute to and learn from it, make sure it gets done, make decisions on the basis of it and otherwise act on the results. These assumptions can hold up provided there is enough common ground. The less the common ground, the more risk that the negotiations to keep the process together might get into trouble. Categories of stakeholders are generally described in terms of their relationship to a program rather than their relationship to the evaluation, and the evaluation is more often of a program rather than at the service level (and hence of most interest to managers and policy-makers). Stakeholders may be, for example:

- Policy makers (Parliamentarians, government policy officers, funding bodies, etc.).
- Program managers (for example, National, State or local level).
- Service practitioners (service providers, professionals, non-professional staff).
- Community or consumers (clients, citizen organisations, service users, students, parents, self-help groups, local civic bodies, service clubs, etc.).

As noted before, the greatest strength of attempts like stakeholder evaluation is that they are UTILISATION-FOCUSED. Their deepest potential flaw is if the common ground is inadequate and the separate value-interests lead to it falling apart or glossing over real differences that mean the evaluation is not heeded. From a social justice point of view, the greatest risk of all is if the common ground does not centre on critical reference groups' needs and interests.

Reference:

BRYK, A. (Ed) *Stakeholder-Based Evaluation* Jossey-Bass, San Francisco:1983

Standards programs

Standards programs often develop after years of *open inquiry* have yielded more and more refined understandings about what is of merit or worth. They can be stupendously comprehensive and comprise reams and reams of detailed questions in sections and sub-sections relating to objectives and aims or activities. The answers to the questions indicate that the practices are or are not meeting (pre-valued) standards. Standards programs generally comprise standard manuals, a study by a team that possibly includes some outside peers, a site visit for a few days, and a written report. They are most effective when dealing with services or activities that are relatively unchanging or stable, and where there is enough homogeneity to allow generalised descriptions of What Ought To Be. CHASP in community health, and PASSING in the disability area, are good examples. An additional element may be that services are then accredited (given a formal stamp of approval, as in the Hospital Accreditation Program). They generally do not contain inbuilt mechanisms for changing or improving items—unless an open inquiry approach is added as part of the exercise, or is built into a one, two or three yearly cycle of reviewing the manual. Thus the major problem (besides that inherent in PEER REVIEW evaluations described by Michael Scriven) is that, like all *audit review* approaches, there is the risk of ossification, and the difficulty of altering objectives-based expected practices once they are set in people's minds. Even worse is the situation where the conventions become so established that the rationales are forgotten—and convention for its own sake sets in. Now they *may* be good conventions. But without regular *open inquiry*-type evaluation, we won't know for sure. Their greatest value is, however, to make intentions explicit and identifiable. They often rely on statistical measures, but not necessarily so. Both CHASP and PASSING have non-quantitative questions, and in CHASP'S case, the quantification of ratings is not extensive.

References:

COMMONWEALTH STATE WORKING PARTY ON NURSING HOME STANDARDS *Living in a Nursing Home—Outcome Standards for Australian Nursing Homes* AGPS, Canberra:1987

COMMUNITY SERVICES VICTORIA *Standards for Residential Services* Office of Intellectual Disability Services, Melbourne:1989

DEPARTMENT OF HEALTH *Sexual Assault Services Standards Manual* NSW:1989

FRY, Denise and Lesley KING *A Manual of Standards for Community Health* AGPS, Canberra:1985

SCRIVEN, Michael *The Logic of Evaluation* Edgepress, Inverness, California, pp. 105–113:1981

VICTORIAN ACCIDENT REHABILITATION COUNCIL *Standards for Providers of Occupational Rehabilitation Under Workcare* Melbourne:1989

Summative evaluation

This is Michael Scriven's term to describe evaluation which is done periodically (or at 'ends' of cycles of development of a service program or activity) for management purposes of making decisions about the funding, refunding, completion, continuation, etc. of that service, program or activity. It may focus on 'output'. Scriven gets impatient with people if they point out that, in a continuous cycle, summative purposes are formative in the context of the next stage of that continuous cycle (and that FORMATIVE evaluation might be seen as consisting of lots and lots of little summative evaluations!). Scriven sees summative evaluations as made up of lots of formative ones. Nevertheless, the point may usefully be made that Scriven never intended the interpretation that has been so widely made of his two terms as being *forms* of evaluation. To meet his original purpose for coining the terms, we should not use them as terms describing *kinds* of evaluation but as terms describing two of the possible *purposes* of evaluation, namely, for improvement purposes (formative), and for reporting and decision-making purposes (summative). This book has used the terms *open inquiry* and *audit review* to try to refer to the purposes of evaluation as for improvement (inquiry) and checking (audit), while noting that *both* these kinds of evaluation might be drawn on for reporting and accountability purposes in a way comparable to Scriven's original intentions. That is, *inquiry* and *audit* approaches might *both* be used for *both* formative and summative purposes.

Reference:

SCRIVEN, Michael 'Summative Teacher Evaluation' in J. MILLMAN (Ed) *Handbook of Teacher Evaluation* Sage, Beverly Hills, California:1981

Systems analysis, systems theory

A systems approach to evaluation most typically utilises a linear and machine metaphor drawn from manufacturing industry that may be as illustrated below.

The attraction of this lies in its apparent neatness, and the plausibility of its logic and sequential chronology. It seems like what we should have done! Often it is—particularly with the planning of new projects that have a start and a finish, although even these always have pre-existing histories and will go on to have 'futures'. However for most of the time we are 'in process'—or in a process of perpetual incremental development. 'Starts' and 'finishes' may be imposed arbitrarily, such as according to calendar or financial years, yet *in practice* all the components of the systems model are co-existing. That is, we are more or less constantly assessing needs, constantly forming and re-forming purposes and intentions, constantly deciding on new actions, constantly trying new things, and constantly assessing effects. As suggested throughout this book, these constant feedback loops operate on a very small scale right through to

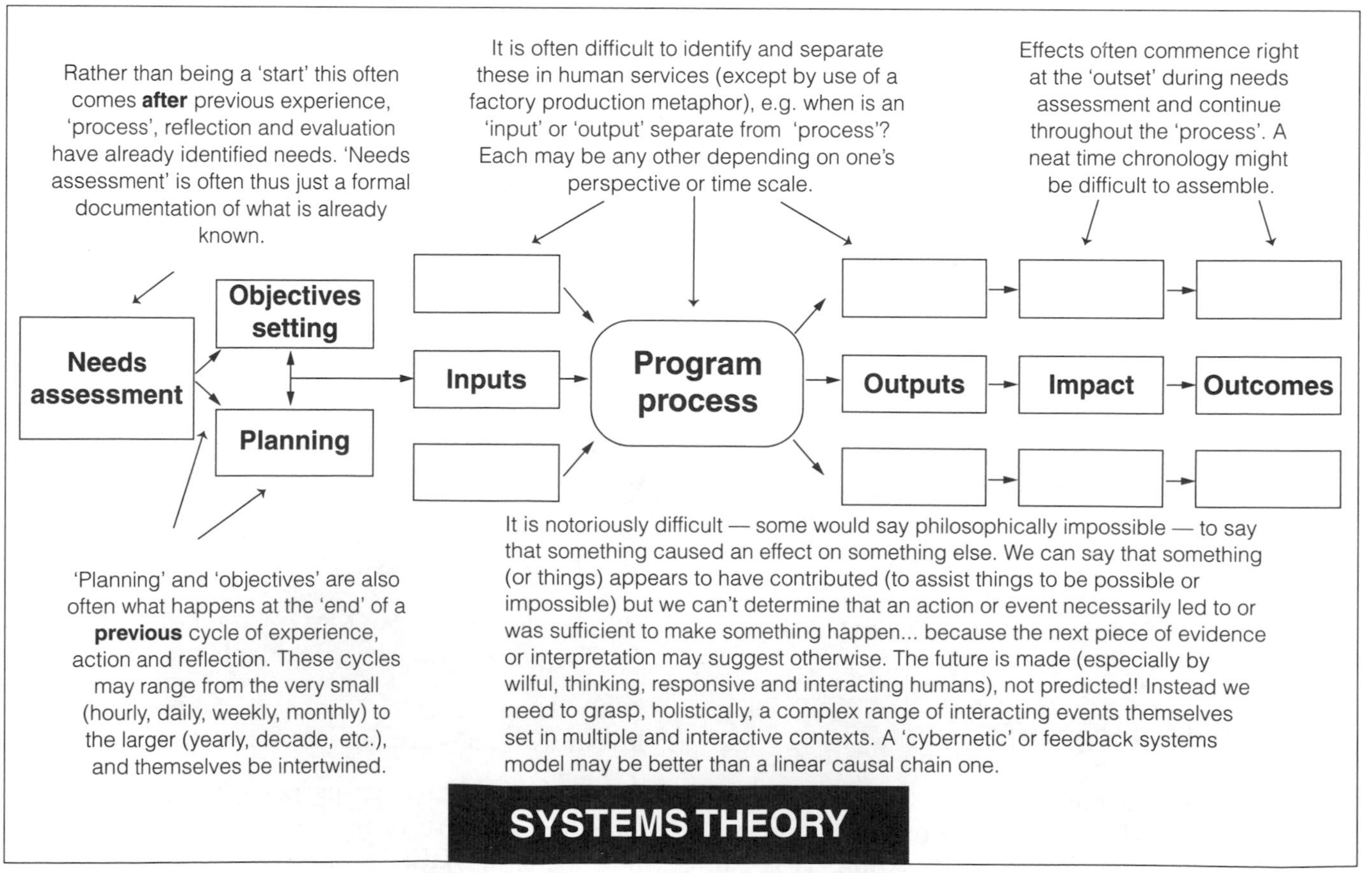
Rather than being a 'start' this often comes **after** previous experience, 'process', reflection and evaluation have already identified needs. 'Needs assessment' is often thus just a formal documentation of what is already known.
It is often difficult to identify and separate these in human services (except by use of a factory production metaphor), e.g. when is an 'input' or 'output' separate from 'process'? Each may be any other depending on one's perspective or time scale.
Effects often commence right at the 'outset' during needs assessment and continue throughout the 'process'. A neat time chronology might be difficult to assemble.
Needs assessment
Objectives setting
Planning
Inputs
Program process
Outputs
Impact
Outcomes
'Planning' and 'objectives' are also often what happens at the 'end' of a **previous** cycle of experience, action and reflection. These cycles may range from the very small (hourly, daily, weekly, monthly) to the larger (yearly, decade, etc.), and themselves be intertwined.
It is notoriously difficult — some would say philosophically impossible — to say that something caused an effect on something else. We can say that something (or things) appears to have contributed (to assist things to be possible or impossible) but we can't determine that an action or event necessarily led to or was sufficient to make something happen... because the next piece of evidence or interpretation may suggest otherwise. The future is made (especially by wilful, thinking, responsive and interacting humans), not predicted! Instead we need to grasp, holistically, a complex range of interacting events themselves set in multiple and interactive contexts. A 'cybernetic' or feedback systems model may be better than a linear causal chain one.
SYSTEMS THEORY

a very large scale, with these small loops 'nesting' within larger ones, which in turn 'nest' within even larger ones.

Perhaps a better metaphor is that of a developing 'living' organism where the interaction with multiple environments and contexts and history means that our activities or services grow (or atrophy) through constant feedback loops. A more dynamic approach, for example, to the evaluation of this book project, would have seen much more scope for change and adjustment to the agreed 'inputs, process, and outputs' in the light of engaging with the context of critical reference groups in the field (for example, to timelines, to extend the project over a longer period of time, to enable reworking of content, more contemplation, feedback, honing of concepts, etc.). Thus where creativity, change, and improvement are characteristic of the service or program, then a systems-based evaluation may feel somewhat mechanistic, constraining and even distorting.

Other and more recent formulations of systems theory and analysis have concentrated more on soft systems, cybernetic or organic metaphors, and the human cognitive construction of these.

References:

HAWE, Penelope, Deirdre DEGELING and Jane HALL *Evaluating Health Promotion—A Health Workers Guide* Maclennan and Petty, Artarmon:1990

ROSSI, P.H., H.E. FREEMAN and J.R. WRIGHT *Evaluation: A Systematic Approach* Sage, Beverly Hills, California:1979

SENGE, Peter *The Fifth Discipline—The Art and Practice of the Learning Organization* Doubleday Currency, New York:1990

Utilisation-focused evaluation

This is a fancy title for saying that this kind of evaluation derives its questions from, and orients its answers towards, those who are going to make use of the evaluation. While all evaluation arguably does this implicitly or covertly (and either well or badly), this approach does so explicitly and overtly and finds it is *more likely* to then do its job well. Michael Patton wrote a whole book on it. Where users of evaluation conflict in values or goals, Patton discusses conflict resolution techniques like MULTI-ATTRIBUTE UTILITY MEASUREMENT, DECISION THEORETIC approaches, FUZZY SET THEORY and GOAL FREE evaluation. Utilisation-focused evaluation, like PARTICIPATORY and DEMOCRATIC evaluation, involves users and decision makers in question-framing (to ensure relevance), methods-selection, design decisions, possibly data-collection, but certainly data-analysis and interpretation. Keeping the whole exercise closely in touch with users' needs keeps it RESPONSIVE. A social justice perspective would add critical reference groups as the most important participants in utilisation.

Reference:

PATTON, Michael Quinn, *Utilization-Focused Evaluation—The New Century Text,* 3rd edn, Sage, Thousand Oaks, California:1997

Well-formed outcome model

This is a goal-setting tool used by the psychotherapeutic communication science called NEURO LINGUISTIC PROGRAMMING. Yet again drawing on the idea that you need to be more aware of where you want to go before you can get there, it assists, for example, nurses to develop plans for patients by asking questions in nine categories and getting patients to state their desired positive outcomes in advance in terms of:

- Positive solutions, rather than dwelling on the problem.
- Identifying images of what the outcome will look like in behavioural terms.
- Working out what effects it will have on the patients' family or group, etc.

Its strength is that it helps make explicit some intentions. Drawbacks are that you may not need to (or be able to) know precisely where you are going before you can set out to get there. That is, life objectives may be more emergent and contingent on other events than the method might allow.

Reference:

MITCHELL, Frank, 'Behind the Painted Smile' in *Nursing Times* Vol. 83, No. 33:1987

Zero-based budgeting (ZBB)

Developed as a sequel to MANAGEMENT BY OBJECTIVES (which was in turn a sequel to PROGRAM BUDGETING), this technique tried to overcome the drawbacks of agencies simply re-submitting the same old budgets each year (plus increments for growth) to funding bodies who just checked the cost amounts were similar to the previous year's and then rubber-stamped them (I'm simplifying!). Instead, agencies were asked every year to start with a clean slate and show every item requiring funding, plus rationale (relating to agency purposes or objectives), and build up a 'new' budget with complete new justifications for each item. Like all rationalistic techniques, the novelty (and value) of 'problematising' everything may wear off unless the technique is used sparingly.

Reference:

Through a Glass Darkly: Evaluation in Australian Health and Welfare Services Vol. 1. AGPS, Canberra, pp. 44–45:1979

SOME READING

FURTHER USEFUL READING

It will have been seen from the last chapter that there are a huge number of written things in the evaluation area (and these aren't anywhere near all there is!). This voluminous literature ranges from heavy-going academic textbooks right through to little guides and manuals produced by government departments, often for particular service programs. Most of it is written more for professional and managerial evaluators and generally lacks an 'every-day' applied perspective. As well, most of the little guides are written with shaky theoretical foundations, and hence often either offer a confusing mix of approaches or opt for one in the mistaken belief that it is the only approach (for example, all the books and guides that start off with the statement 'To do an evaluation you must firstly have clear measurable objectives . . .').

For this bibliography we have chosen the most accessible resources we could find and those which are mainly consistent with the approach of this book. They cover a range of health, education and community services. The small guides may be available through their publishing organisations and the textbooks and journal articles are available in most college and university libraries.

There are now also some excellent journals on evaluation—such as the new *Evaluation* journal produced by Sage Publications out of Tavistock in London, and the *Magazine* of the Australasian Evaluation Society—which is a particularly high quality periodical packed with news, reviews and short technical notes on a range of methods and approaches.

SMALL GUIDES AND ARTICLES

BRENNAN, Marie and Ruth HOADLEY
School Self-evaluation, School Improvement Plan Secretariat, Education Department of Victoria:1984

- This marked a productive phase of activity in the Education Department following the release of the Ministerial Paper on The School Improvement Plan which mandated school self-evaluation. (See also REEVE, Pat et al. *Lessons From Victoria's School Improvement Plan For The Practice of Self Evaluation* SIP Clearinghouse, Education Department:1987.) It is a short and readable booklet describing the practical steps and tasks involved. It makes explicit that education is for the education needs of students, while firmly in the context of a 'school community' comprised of students, teachers, parents, administrators and School Council. Since privatisation of the Education Ministry's Bookshop, this (and other Education Ministry publications cited below) are currently out of print.

DESAI, Uday
'Successful Program Evaluation—Is there an Alternative Framework?' in *International Review of Administrative Sciences*, Sage, Vol. 54, pp. 267–281:1988

- This is a critique of objectives-based evaluation. It presents a partial although mainly academic solution.

EDUCATION DEPARTMENT OF VICTORIA
Destination: Decisions—Decision-making Strategies for School Communities, Curriculum Branch:1985

- Extremely readable collection of techniques and models including action research, advocate teams, brainstorming, commission of inquiry, consensus 1–3–6, content analysis, critical path, Delphi, force-field analysis, goal-free evaluation, interviews, nominal group technique, observation, the possible school, questionnaires, scenario, a second opinion, fishbowl, transactional evaluation, trial by jury. Converts even the most complex into both understandable and useable descriptions. They are applied to school settings but in such a way as to be easy to work out how they would be applicable to other settings. Nice cartoons.

FURLER, Elizabeth
'Against Hegemony in Health Care Service Evaluation' in *Community Health Studies*, Vol. 3, No. 1, pp. 32–41:1979

- This article was an important contribution to the Australian health services evaluation debate as it provided an articulate and critical examination of traditional scientific and laboratory-based approaches when applied to innovative social action program evaluation. It particularly takes issue with a preoccupation with measurement, and with the artificiality of an experimental approach, and also notes the lack of usefulness of these kinds of studies in real-life practice. Not light bedtime reading, but a short article packed with value.

GUTHRIE, Hugh et al.
Making Changes—Evaluation and Validation of TAFE Programs, TAFE National Centre for Research and Development, Adelaide:1985–1986

- This is a set of 21 generally applicable discussion papers including definitions of evaluation, issues and problems, techniques, critical assessment of various evaluation methods, etc. The cartoon below is from one of these papers. The project was a joint one between the RMIT Educational Services Division and the Adelaide National Centre.

HOLMAN, Bob
'Research from the Underside' in *British Journal of Social Work*, Vol. 17, pp. 669–683:1987

- This makes a powerful argument for the investigated doing the investigating and involving the poor in research into the conditions of their own poverty—defining the issues to be researched, deciding on how it is researched, participating in collecting the material, and the interpretation of findings. It uses five case research projects to illustrate. The whole volume of this particular issue of the *British Journal of Social Work* is devoted to evaluation, and contains several good articles (others listed below).

HUNT, Sonja
'Evaluating a Community Development Project—Issues of Acceptability' in *British Journal of Social Work*, Vol. 17, pp. 661–667:1987

- A short readable article touching lightly on several 'social health' community projects (for the elderly, a food and vegetable co-op, etc.), but which raises some fundamental questions about how 'outcomes' are better understood as value-driven decisions and not as matters of 'scientific' judgement. Also touches on the different interests of parties to the evaluation. Concludes that

'Your project's theoretical underpinnings and conceptual framework are intellectually sound and innovative, but your implementational strategies lack focus and reality orientation. Or as we used to say when I was a kid — it's a good idea, but it won't work'

(Guthrie, Hugh et al: 1985-86)

judging an evaluation requires us to ask, 'Whose perspective?' and, 'For whose benefit?'.

KEMMIS, Stephen
'Program Evaluation in Distance Education—Against the Technologisation of Reason', Speech to conference, Townsville:May 1980

- A sophisticated academic argument for critical democratic self-evaluation and against scientistic 'engineering', objectives-based and other related models.

LAWRENCE, John E.S.
'Engaging Recipients in Development Evaluation—the "Stakeholder" approach' in *Evaluation Review*, Vol. 13, No. 3:June 1989

- Usage in Third World development, UN Development Program.

McDERMOTT, Fiona and Priscilla PYETT
The Meaning of Treatment—An Evaluation Handbook for Alcohol and other Drug Treatment Agencies University of Melbourne:1990

- Interpretive social research or explication evaluation approach, that is, concentrates less on identifying the worth/merit, and more on practitioners' understanding their actions in relation to planned activities.

PATTON, Michael Quinn
'Qualitative Methods in Health Care Evaluation' in *Health Care Evaluation*, Public Health Association, Canberra:1989

- This was a paper given to a National Health and Medical Research Council (NHMRC) sponsored workshop in Canberra which was fortunate to be addressed by one of America's leading evaluators. It is an excellent shortish introduction to the rest of his writings (see books below) in which he skilfully explicated ten themes of qualitative inquiry. See entry in Chapter 5 on QUALITATIVE evaluation.

REES, Stuart
'The Culture-Bound State of Evaluation—Implications for Research and Practice' in *British Journal of Social Work*, Vol. 17, pp. 645–659:1987

- Useful observations about the limitations of conventional science, and the practical useability of a more interpretive and value-driven approach.

SAINSBURY, Eric
'Client Studies—Their Contribution and Limitation in Influencing Social Work Practice' in *British Journal of Social Work*, Vol. 17, pp. 635–644:1987

- Mild and reasoned argument for listening to the voice of the consumer.

WILSON, Gai
Self-evaluation Kit, Victorian Association of Citizens Advice Bureaus, Melbourne:1989

- A simple and accessible guidebook with exercise sheets and questions that are specific to CABs. The cartoons below are taken from the Kit.

BOOKS

BRINKERHOFF, Robert O. et al.
Program Evaluation—A Practitioner's Guide for Trainers and Educators, Kluwer-Nijhoff Publishing, Boston:1983

- This is an epic 'package' of several volumes—a sourcebook (guidelines and resources), a casebook (12 real cases of evaluation), and a design manual (directions, worksheets, examples, checklists). It commences with the neatly-phrased 'open-inquiry' directive:

  Evaluation is for making it work.

ANYTHING THAT STOPS THE CAT IS O.K DOKEY
I WAS WONDERING IF WE COULD HAVE MORE HEIGHT...

A VERY TALL VERY LEAFY VERY CAT PROOF PLANT WAS NEEDED..
PLASTIC!

(Wilson, Gai: 1989)

If it works . . .
Notice and nurture.
If it doesn't work . . .
Notice and change. (ibid: i)

The table of contents in the sourcebook comprises a list of questions (for chapters 1–6) which could be used quite effectively to plan evaluation (for example, What will be evaluated? What is the purpose? Who will be affected and involved? etc.). The chapters then contain equally logical lists of sub-questions and present a sometimes bewilderingly comprehensive array of highly detailed specifics. The book says sensible things about techniques and sampling, and the case studies are identified by the questions they address, for example, 'How can I evaluate a workshop?', 'How can we meet a government's information demands?', 'How can we tell if our project is making a difference to pupils?', etc.). It truly is the 'everything you ever wanted to know' in evaluation! Nevertheless, it does assume evaluation can only be done by those with 'extensive competencies in methodology and data analysis', and would best be used by the confident enthusiast who can selectively pick and choose.

BROWN, Lynton
Group Self-Evaluation—Learning for Improvement, School Improvement Plan Secretariat, Ministry of Education, Victoria:1988

- A detailed, sophisticated but readable account of definitions of group self-evaluation, enabling conditions, practicalities, etc. Highly recommended further reading.

BROWN, Lynton
Handbook of Group Self-Evaluation—Learning for Improvement, School Improvement Plan Secretariat, Ministry of Education, Victoria:1990

- A sequel to the first text, comprised of examples of the methodology in use by various Education Department regional offices, interspersed with further commentary. Intended as a sourcebook for consultants who are using the approach with individual schools.

CRAIG, Dorothy P.
Hip Pocket Guide—To Planning and Evaluation Learning Concepts, San Diego, California:1978

- This popular little book is more about planning but the logic and presentation of process is impressive, starting with defining the (real) problem, and using a clever concrete example (a local government constituency which demands reaffirmative action) almost all the way through to illustrate the conceptual points being made. It opts for a more bureaucratic rational, organisational, objectives-based, and quantitative basis for evaluation. Its first page bears some objectives-oriented audit review advice:

  The more you know about where you are going,
  the closer you are to being there. (ibid: 1)

It effectively and usefully illustrates processes of clear thinking, especially regarding clarifying critical reference groups and their interests.

FETTERMAN, D., S. KAFTARIAN and A. WANDERSMAN
Expowerment Evaluation: Knowledge and Tools for Self-Assessment and Accountability, Sage Publications, Thousand Oaks, California:1996

- This is a comprehensive set of case stories and theory pieces for those using more participatory and action-oriented approaches to evaluation—particularly in areas of social justice and disadvantage, such as human services.

FEUERSTEIN, Marie-Therese
Partners in Evaluation—Evaluating Development and Community Programs With Participants, Macmillan, in association with Teaching Aids At Low Cost, London:1986

- This is a massively comprehensive but highly accessible text, which, while oriented to third world development, has a lot to say to Australian audiences. Its Freirean approach is applied to some more conventional survey and quasi-experimental techniques, and makes for a primer on these.

GUBA, Egon G.
Toward a Methodology of Naturalistic Inquiry in Educational Evaluation, Centre for the Study of Evaluation (CSE), University of California, Los Angeles:1978

- Contrasts 'naturalistic inquiry' (NI) with experimental studies. The book presents a genealogy of NI, commencing with a reference to Charles Darwin's field-based naturalists' endeavours—while stressing rigour (structured, disciplined, systematic, revealing of its methods, empirically-grounded). It demonstrates how experimentation is high on manipulation and theory imposition/theory testing, while NI is low on these two counts.

GUBA, Egon G. and Yvonna S. LINCOLN
Fourth Generation Evaluation, Sage, Newbury Park, California:1989

- This was a path-breaking text on new paradigm science as applied to evaluation. Having rejected the term 'naturalistic' as less useful than the term 'constructivist', Guba and Lincoln make a compelling case for replacing old paradigm positivist science with a constructivist methodology. First generation evaluation measured variables. Second generation evaluation was objectives-based. Third generation evaluation was decision and judgement oriented. Fourth generation evaluation is value-driven and collaborative. Dense hard work to read but a significant step forward.

HAMILTON, David et al. (Eds)
Beyond The Numbers Game, Macmillan, London:1977

- This is a textbook of classic readings in educational evaluation arranged around the objectives versus alternative approaches debate. Articles by most of the major thinkers, for example, Tyler, Glaser, Scriven, Stenhouse, Eisner, Stake, Parlett and Hamilton, Barry McDonald and Rob Walker, and Ernest House.

HOUSE, Ernest R.
The Logic of Evaluative Argument, Centre for the Study of Evaluation, University of California, Los Angeles:1977

- Another useful book out of the CSE stable, this one illuminates the view that evaluation consists of the act of persuasion on the basis of arguments about evidence—plausibility and credibility rather than Cartesian certainty. House grounds his logic in the perceptions of the evaluation's 'audience'. Nevertheless, like most other readings on this list, it is not light reading to be squeezed in over a coffee break! It is definitely head-down-in-a-quiet-library stuff.

KEMMIS, Stephen and Robin McTAGGART (Eds)
The Action Research Planner, 3rd Edition, Deakin University:1988

- The 1982 version of this was a more popularised 44 page format, and this is 154 pages of much more detailed text. Pages 22–25 of this version contain an excellent short description of 17 key points of definition. An important piece of reading.

PATTON, Michael Quinn
Utilization-Focused Evaluation, Sage, Beverly Hills, California:1978 (1st edn:1978; 2nd edn:1986; 3rd edn:1997)

- Michael Patton is from Saint Paul, Minnesota and, like residents of nearby Lake Wobegone, he has a creative and metaphoric turn of speech which makes his books a pleasure to read! His books are packed with more advanced material which is mostly consistent with the approach of this *Everyday Evaluation on the Run* book. This was the first of four books around a set of related themes. Please note these comments relate to the second edition as the third edition has only just been published. (Please note also that the third edition is a spectacular new and expanded revision.) It starts with an account of the history of evaluation research as emerging from science offering to come to the rescue of policy-makers and government-funders, particularly when post-war human service expansion collided with late 1970s economic rationalism. It goes on to describe the political process of deciding on focus and content of evaluation by identifying and organising specific relevant decision-makers and information-users around a user focus. Design, techniques, and impact, etc. then flow (Chapters 1–3). He argues also for the value of evolutionary and incremental evaluation (the reduction of uncertainty) which enables increased confidence and a speeding up of change. There is a humorous but important treatment of goals-clarification as a game.

  There are also discussions of Delphi, multi-attribute utility measurement, decision-theoretic approach, fuzzy sets theory, social judgement theory, goal-free evaluation (Chapter 6); goal attainment model, systems model, open systems perspective, active-reactive-adaptive decision-making evaluation, and the construction of goals-objectives distinctions (Chapter 7); outcome evaluation versus implementation, effort, process evaluation (Chapter 8); causation and theory construction (Chapter 9); and science and methodology—quantitative/qualitative, objective/subjective, distance/closeness, induction/deduction, uniformity/diversity, reliability/validity, fixed/dynamic, holistic/componential, traditional science/Verstehen (Chapter 10).

  It describes some now folkloric metaphors (the man looking for the key he lost in the nearby 'dark pasture', under the light pole because that was where the light was; the saying 'when you're up to your ass in alligators, it is difficult to remind yourself that your initial objective was to drain the swamp'). And Nasrudin the Sufi evaluator finds his way through many philosophical thickets!

PATTON, Michael Quinn
Qualitative Evaluation Methods, Sage, Beverly Hills, California:1980 (And expanded 2nd edn, *Qualitative Evaluation and Research Methods*, Sage, Newbury Park, California:1990)

- Second of the four books, this makes the detailed arguments for, and suggestions about how to do, non-standardised, open-ended evaluations (while not being a 'how to', recipe book). Here we have the reappearance of the philosopher Halcolm the Wise (for example, point 4 of Halcolm's Evaluation Laws: 'Evaluation is too serious a matter to be done by someone who has never been a client in a program' [ibid: 15]; or, 'Evaluation results always make clear to people what they had really wanted to know but forgot to ask' [ibid: 90]). The first four chapters of the book present material which demonstrate effectively not only the differences between quantitative data and qualitative information, but also the reason why quantitative data, without qualitative meaningfulness, will, in practice, be unusable or damaging. Incompatible models such as systems analysis and behavioural performance evaluation are contrasted with compatible models such as transaction or responsive and illuminative, goal-free and decision-making models.

  Thereafter, the territory becomes a little more confusing with talk of 'mixed paradigms' (when paradigms, by definition, cannot be mixed), and an approach to the field that, in the absence of an explicit discussion of critical reference groups, occasionally threatens to come close to voyeurism, or what Rob Watts has called 'social ventriloquism'.

However, Patton's 'respect for people' approach generally mitigates this ('To ask is a grave responsibility [it] . . . is to seek entry into another's world. Therefore ask respectfully and with sincerity' [ibid: 254]). However, there is an appearance at times of descriptions of the world being seen as factual or not (rather than that factuality or objectivity being value-guided, relative and mutually subjectively constructed). Nevertheless, Patton does insist on the necessity of entering the field, staying in the field, and engaging with the field—and of making notes that are detailed and meaning-revealing. The material on wording of questions is excellent (pp. 211–243). His chapters 8 and 9 on analysis helpfully identify 'relatively useful perspectives' (albeit accurate, valid, reliable, etc. ones) as the end point rather than positivist 'Truth', and give concrete illustrations of how to conceptualise field material.

PATTON, Michael Quinn
Creative Evaluation (2nd edn), Sage, Beverly Hills, California:1987

- This third volume gives special attention to a range of creative techniques drawing on arts and media professions, metaphor, etc. It describes what Patton calls an 'eolithic' approach (goals emergent) comparable to an iterative open inquiry approach.

PATTON, Michael Quinn
Practical Evaluation, Sage, Beverly Hills, California:1982

- This book is the last of the quadrella.* Chapter 2 is on definitions and models; there are also chapters on utilisation-focused, collaborative, goals-based (he talks of goal-clarification) and goal-free evaluation, thoughtful questionnaires, thoughtful interviews, and management systems methodologies.

REES, Stuart and A. WALLACE
Verdicts on Social Work, Edward Arnold, London:1982

- A well-known study of research on the efficacy of social work. It includes a chapter which reviews research done on clients' evaluations of the services they received and their experiences of these, and some very interesting comparisons of these with social workers' evaluations of their own casework (there are some illuminating examples of clients and social workers evaluating the same encounters!).

SCHÖN, Donald
The Reflective Practitioner, Basic Books, New York:1983

- While this is about how professionals think in practice, its observations apply equally to any everyday evaluator, including the professionals' clients! It talks about tacit knowing and contrasts reflection-in-action (where cumulative knowledge comes from lengthy modifications by trial and error) with technical rationality (where research is separated from practice, and knowing is separated from doing). Amplifies nature of positivism, and talks about problem-setting rather than the pre-determination of means-ends.

WADSWORTH, Yoland
Do It Yourself Social Research (2nd edn), Allen & Unwin, St Leonards:1997

- Beautifully cartooned by Simon Kneebone, this accessible introductory text became a runaway bestseller when first published. This practical guide covers where to start; how to manage a research project; methods, techniques and resources; and interpretation, analysis and communication. It is a companion volume to *Everyday Evaluation on the Run.*

* Australian horse-racing slang meaning one of four (horse races).

By the same author

Do It Yourself Social Research 2nd edition

This introduction to social research methods became a runaway bestseller when it was first published. For fifteen years it has been used by students and professionals in sociology, social work, community development, education, health, welfare, psychology, management, environmental studies, legal studies and many other fields.

Now thoroughly revised and updated, it takes the reader through the basics of research, including:

- Where to start
- How to manage a research project
- Methods, techniques and resources
- Interpretation, analysis and communication
- Examples and resources

Do It Yourself Social Research will continue to be an essential reference for anyone doing research in the social sciences and human services.

'Yoland Wadsworth's *Do It Yourself Social Research* is one of the most remarkable products of Australian social science. Practical in its content, sophisticated in its ideas, the book shows a passion for making social science a tool of democracy. I know of nothing else that is half as good.'
R.W. Connell, Professor of Education, University of Sydney

'. . . incredibly useful . . .'
Elizabeth Reid, United Nations Development Programme, New York

'No jargon, no mystification . . . not patronising. Experienced and new social researchers alike will certainly feel more secure and must do better research as a result of this publication.'
Australian Journal of Social Issues

'One of the most commonly used texts on human service workers' book shelves.'
Lesley Hoatson, community worker and lecturer

'It raised my view of research from "something I have to do" to "something I want to do".'
First year university student

1 86448 415 2